Koi For Dummies

Cheat Sheet

Performing Routine Pond Maintenance

Like anything else that needs maintaining around your house, if you take on a few tasks everyday, the bigger jobs, when they come along, don't seem so impossible. Here are some once a day and once a week-type jobs that will not only decrease your workload, but will also keep you in contact with your pond. When something begins to go wrong, you'll be able to take steps before it becomes a big, fat, expensive problem.

Daily

- Scoop leaves off surface.
- Feed koi when water temps are above 75 degrees.
- When pond is new, check and record water chemistry values daily to track the nitrification of your filter.

Weekly

- Backflush filter.
- Ten percent water change when water temperature is 65 degrees or higher.
- For an established pond, check water chemistry values.
- Vacuum debris on the bottom on the pond.

Buying the Basic Necessities

- Koi bowl (to hold any sick koi for examination)
- Koi meds (see Chapter 12)
  - Ammonia chlorine remover like AmquelPlus
  - Potassium permanganate for combating ich
  - Malachite green for combating ich
  - Dimilin for treating external parasites, such as flukes
- Koi sock net
- Pond thermometer for monitoring water temps
- Skimmer net
- Winter and summer diets (see Chapter 11)
- Water test kit

Consulting Helpful Web Sites

- Associated Koi Clubs of America: www.akca.org
- Koi Club of the Air: www.koiclubof theair.org
- Koi Cymru: www.koi cymru.co.uk
- Koi and Goldfish Health Care: www.koi vet.com
- Koi USA magazine: www.koiusa.com
- Mid-Atlantic Koi Club: www.makc.com

Koi For Dummies®

Handling Seasonal Pond Maintenance

Getting ready for a change of seasons means different things if you live in upstate New York or in southern Florida. Nonetheless, we offer the following lists as general guidelines.

Fall

- Remove all debris in pond as necessary.
- Install leaf net over pond if any trees are nearby.
- Clean skimmer unit and filter.
- Turn off waterfalls and fountains if outside air temperatures will drop below 40 degrees, day or night.
- Change 10 percent of water weekly when water temperatures are above 70 degrees.

Winter

- Install pond cover when nighttime air temperatures drop below 50 degrees.
- Turn on pond heater when night-time air temperatures fall below 55 degrees.
- Clean skimmer and filter monthly.
- Test water monthly.

Spring

- Remove pond cover unless night-time air temperatures drop below 50 degrees.
- Turn off heater when air tempera-ture reaches 70 degrees.
- Salt pond to 5 percent to avoid Aeromonas or Pseudomonas outbreaks.
- Add probiotic to pond at beginning of season.
- Clean filter and skimmer.
- Turn on waterfalls and fountains as long as outside air temperatures remain above 55 degrees, day or night.
- Test water weekly.
- Change 10 percent of pond water weekly.
- Replace UV bulb in UV sterilizer.

Summer

- If you have a pergola, add screen-ing to it for shade.
- Clean filter weekly.
- Change 10 percent of water weekly.
- Check water values every two weeks.

For Dummies: Bestselling Book Series for Beginners

Koi
FOR
DUMMIES®

by R. D. Bartlett and Patricia Bartlett

Wiley Publishing, Inc.

Koi For Dummies®

Published by
Wiley Publishing, Inc.
111 River St.
Hoboken, NJ 07030-5774
www.wiley.com

Copyright © 2007 by Wiley Publishing, Inc., Indianapolis, Indiana

Published simultaneously in Canada

WILEY

About the Authors

R. D. Bartlett began his pet fish-keeping when he netted minnows out of the brooks near Springfield, Massachusetts. He moved to Florida and began working as the general manager for Aquarium Supply, a tropical fish, goldfish, and koi wholesaler, and then opened his own pet shop.

Patricia Bartlett grew up in Albuquerque, New Mexico, and began keeping fish at age 10. She has journeyed to Costa Rica and Peru to net and write about angelfish, discus, and knife fish. She is a recent convert to the wonderful world of koi.

The Bartletts have co-authored numerous pet care books, mostly centering on reptiles and amphibians.

Authors' Acknowledgments

The authors would like to thank the many koi keepers who have shared their knowledge so freely, especially Butch Kuhl of Pond Amour and John Hadley of Superior Koi Heaters. We would also like to express our appreciation to Grace Freedson.

Publisher's Acknowledgments

We're proud of this book; please send us your comments through our Dummies online registration form located at www.dummies.com/register/.

Some of the people who helped bring this book to market include the following:

Acquisitions, Editorial, and Media Development

Project Editors: Kristin DeMint, Christina Guthrie

Acquisitions Editor: Stacy Kennedy

Copy Editor: Pam Ruble

Technical Editor: Toby Goldman, DVM

Senior Editorial Manager: Jennifer Ehrlich

Editorial Assistants: Erin Calligan, Joe Niesen, Leeann Harney

Cover Photos: © Anna Yu/Alamy

Cartoons: Rich Tennant (www.the5thwave.com)

Composition Services

Project Coordinator: Heather Kolter

Layout and Graphics: Claudia Bell, Laura Pence, Barbara Moore, Heather Ryan

Illustrator: Barbara Frake

Anniversary Logo Design: Richard Pacifico

Proofreaders: Cynthia Fields, Melanie Hoffman, Techbooks

Indexer: Techbooks

Special Help: Victoria M. Adang

Publishing and Editorial for Consumer Dummies

Diane Graves Steele, Vice President and Publisher, Consumer Dummies

Joyce Pepple, Acquisitions Director, Consumer Dummies

Kristin A. Cocks, Product Development Director, Consumer Dummies

Michael Spring, Vice President and Publisher, Travel

Kelly Regan, Editorial Director, Travel

Publishing for Technology Dummies

Andy Cummings, Vice President and Publisher, Dummies Technology/General User

Composition Services

Gerry Fahey, Vice President of Production Services

Debbie Stailey, Director of Composition Services

Contents at a Glance

Table of Contents

Introduction

Welcome to *Koi For Dummies,* a book designed for two purposes — to tell you about the beautiful fish known as koi and to make koi-keeping so simple you'll wonder why you didn't pick up this hobby eons ago.

What's so much fun about koi? They're gorgeous fish, and they've been selectively bred for more than a hundred years for color, pattern, size, and harder-to-pin-down qualities like grace in swimming or personality. They're the fish version of lilies of the field, perfect on their own merits. For years they've been called *living jewels,* although we, your authors, find that term a bit on the syrupy side.

Nothing quite compares with koi. Parrots are pretty and can tame down, but they're noisy. Orchids are attractive, we'll grant you that. But after an orchid's bloomed, the pretty stuff's over for a couple of months. And we haven't seen an orchid yet that takes food from our fingers or rolls over to have its belly gently rubbed.

So these are some of the reasons we find koi so much fun. We hope you will, too.

About This Book

We want you to think of this book as a reference you can turn to at any time and find exactly the kind of info you need, so we wrote it in a modular fashion; each chapter and each section within it is self-contained and self-explanatory. You don't need to wade through 12 pages of water stratification theory to find out how to warm up or cool down your pond, and you don't need to know water flow rates to select a filter. Each chapter deals with a different aspect of koi-keeping, even starting with the commitment question: "Do you, Reader, take this koi . . . ?" No, sorry, we meant, "Do you, Reader, want to spend 20 minutes twice a day enjoying your koi and your koi pond?" (Of course you do, and likely you'll want to spend more!)

We hope this book clears up any questions that may have been holding you back, like how to build a pond and how big it should be, what good water quality means and how to achieve it in a pond full of fish, and how to get the best koi for your money (which sometimes doesn't take much money at all).

Although good science is behind this book, we don't bombard you with stuffy abstracts and technical writing that would both panic and bore you to tears. We want you to have fun and keep turning these pages because it's good entertainment and you're discovering some precious nuggets of information. We want you to have fun with koi because we have fun with koi, and everyone we know who keeps koi does so for the fun of it.

Conventions Used in This Book

To help you navigate easily through this book, we set up a few conventions that we use consistently throughout:

- ✔ Anytime we want to highlight new words or terms that we define in the text, we *italicize* them.

- ✔ **Boldfaced** text indicates the action part of numbered steps, the keywords of a bulleted list, or text we suggest you type into a search engine for more information.

- ✔ We use `monofont` for Web sites and e-mail addresses.

When this book was printed, some Web addresses may have needed to break across two lines of text. If you come across these instances, rest assured that we haven't put in any extra characters (such as hyphens) to indicate the break. To use one of these Web addresses, just type in exactly what you see in this book, pretending the line break doesn't exist.

What You're Not to Read

We tried to keep the technical stuff to a minimum because we don't like it either, but sometimes it just snuck in when we weren't looking and we couldn't winkle it out. If you see a paragraph flagged by a *Technical Stuff* icon and you go cross-eyed, skip right past it. Keep in mind, though, that these paragraphs do contain helpful bits of info for koi-keepers who want to go the extra mile or expand their arsenal of koi knowledge.

You also don't have to read sidebar text, which we place in gray boxes. Sidebars contain helpful and often interesting info, but you can be sure all the need-to-know stuff is in the regular text.

Foolish Assumptions

We think we know you — a bit. Maybe we're totally off-kilter, but here's what we assumed about you when writing this book:

- ✔ You like nature, you like bright colors, and you may have had an aquarium in your past. Now you're ready for something a lot larger, but that *something's* got you stymied.

- ✔ You know the basics — koi are fish, fish need water, fish need food. But you're wondering: How do you ramp up to a 1,600-gallon pond? How do you move a fish that's 20 inches long? Are the $200 koi better than the $20 koi?

- ✔ You'd like a fish that's somewhat more responsive than the ones you've seen swimming about in typical aquariums.

- ✔ You like the idea of a fish pet that can live for several decades.

Sit down, you're in the right spot. We're here to eliminate the guesswork.

How This Book Is Organized

This book has four main parts, each dealing with a different aspect of koi-keeping. Each part is divided into several chapters, all relating to that part's topic. We're all about practicality here — just pick your topic, find the part, and voila! You have the right chapters. Here's what the parts cover.

Part I: Koi Basics

This is the starter stuff — how koi developed, the names of the different color varieties, what it takes (time- and money-wise) to keep koi, and a bunch of insider info on getting the best koi deals. You find out how big koi get and get some clues about their growth rates.

Part II: Living with Koi, Inside and Out

So it looks like you've made the right decision — you want to keep koi. But now what? This part is oriented toward materials and pond construction. You find out what supplies you need; how to plan, build, and landscape a pond; and how to maintain a pond when it's up and running. We even have a chapter on setting up a koi pond inside the house. If you like koi, you'll find this chapter very useful. An indoor pond is a good way to occupy the empty bedroom your kids vacated when they went off to college — and it prevents them from moving back home when they graduate.

Part III: Caring for Koi and Keeping Them Healthy

You are what you eat, and koi are no different. This part tells you about koi nutrition and the different components in koi diets. You find out what to feed koi (and even what form to use) at different times of the year. We provide a recipe so you can make some of your own koi food, and yes, you can snack on it as you make it. Puree of collard greens, green peas, and crab meat are quite tasty — before you add the tubifex worms.

This part also covers the more common koi diseases (though you'll never see most of them) as well as the real koi killer — stress — and how to diffuse it.

Part IV: The Big Leagues: Koi Breeding and Showing

Gosh, look at the math: One not-very-fancy koi costs $15; a female lays 50,000 eggs; raise these babies for six months and you have a near-instant fortune in that pond. What a great deal!

Okay, there's a lot more to breeding koi than that, so this part provides some realism to the picture. We talk about breeding koi, raising the young, and the continuous culling that's essential to the process. We also talk about koi shows — why they're so much fun and how you can benefit even if you don't enter the competitions.

Part V: The Part of Tens

Some people like to see how a book turns out, so they start at the back. In this book you won't find out the butler did it, but you will find more useful stuff condensed down to lists. Have you ever idly wondered what on earth you'd do if you lost power for a week, now that your pond's up and running? Chapter 17 has some ideas that may save the day for you and your koi. Need to know whether your koi are getting sick? Run through the list in Chapter 18.

Icons Used in This Book

Throughout this book, we use icons in the margins to focus your attention on certain types of information. Here are the icons you'll see and a short description of each.

This is important stuff, stuff you need to keep in mind. None of it is very difficult.

These are details that a water-soaked koi-keeper thrives on. Skip them if technical stuff makes you sleepy.

These are points or shortcuts that can make life easier for your koi or maybe for you.

Think of this as that sideways look you got from your mom one millisecond before her hand flew out and smacked you on top of your head when you said something out of line. These warnings mean the same thing: Stop right there if you know what's good for you (and your koi).

Where to Go from Here

Like other books in the *For Dummies* series, this is a reference book. Pick a topic and head for the index or table of contents. Both of them give you the page numbers so you can turn to the info you need. If you want to know about koi diets, you don't have to skim a chapter called *Everything about Koi* until you find what you need — instead you just go to the chapter titled *Koi Nutrition 101*. For info on those little white spots on your neighbor's koi, look at Chapter 13 on koi ailments — then take this book to him so he can help his fish get rid of the little buggers!

The watery world of koi lives in front of you. Jump in! Start with the cartoons, read a chapter, or check out the index. It's all here at your fingertips.

Part I
Koi Basics

The 5th Wave — By Rich Tennant

"Ever notice how their eyes just draw you in?"

In this part . . .

*I*f you've never really looked at koi, if you're a new pond owner, or if you're just thinking about setting up a pond and trying some of these great fish, here's your basic database. In this part you find out how these bright jewels sprang out of dirt-colored carp . . . after 50 years of selective breeding. We also explain what it takes — in terms of time, money, and space — to set up a koi pond. This part also gives some insider hints like why you purchase a few inexpensive *canary koi* and how to get some very nice koi for very little money.

Chapter 1

Going "Koi Kichi" — Crazy for Koi

In This Chapter

▶ Discovering koi: More than just a pretty fish

▶ Seeking your own level of koi enjoyment

▶ Grasping the basics of a koi pond

▶ Sneaking a peak at the routine

▶ Taking care: A positive approach to your koi's health

▶ Rallying with a club: All for one, one for all

▶ Introducing activities to grow a koi obsession

*G*etting started with koi may seem to take a lot of effort. So what's to love about them — they're just fish, right? Sure, like a diamond's just a lump of carbon or a Beatles' song is just a collection of musical notes. Koi are the ultimate in fish, combining size, beauty, and grace in one plump package (or rather several plump packages because koi don't like to live alone). Because their ponds are designed to literally complement the fish, the ponds add to the aesthetics of koi ownership. When you watch koi slowly wheel around in their pond, you're observing creatures who occupy another world, one without strife, argument, crowded roads, or any of the other dubious benefits of civilization.

But you didn't pick up this book to figure out our philosophy of koi-keeping, although you'll probably find it sprinkled in here and there. You wanted to know what koi are, what it takes to keep them, and what makes seemingly normal people get crazy about them.

Your questions have you headed in the right direction and you're in the right place. This is the book that tells you how to get started with koi, how to keep them alive and healthy, what to feed them, and how to distinguish the different varieties.

Appreciating the Beauty of Koi: The Underground Fad

Koi can help bring beauty and serenity into your life, and you can enjoy them for those reasons alone. Watching your koi gracefully turn in the seemingly bottomless waters before they come to the surface to nibble food from your fingers can be a calming end to a hectic day.

But koi have another level of appreciation and it's based on their classification. Many koi have been selectively bred to exhibit a particular color or pattern. Depending on the criteria you select, koi come in about 13 varieties. Each color or pattern has a Japanese name, which is where the koi terms you may have heard come into play. With the help of Chapter 2, you'll be able to recognize the basic koi colors.

Koi also have Japanese names for the subcategories of skin type and markings, but, alas, that discussion's beyond the scope of this book. (We wanted you to have something to look forward to on your first trip to Japan, the koi-keeper's Mecca!)

Just like purebred dogs, koi have various levels of quality, with some Kohakus, for example, being better than other Kohakus. You can always read about a good breed, but going to a koi show to watch the judges evaluate the fish is a lot more fun. In Chapter 16 we provide some pointers on what you can expect from these koi shows and reasons why you should go even if you're not entering the competition.

Of course, lots of koi don't fit into specific categories; these mixed strains, whose parents were of two different color- or scale-types, are still gorgeous but don't match the standard classifications. Although you aren't able to show these koi in a competition, they add lots of color and interest to your pond. We include a color-photo section in this book so you can see the myriad colors of koi that just may leave you starry-eyed.

The Three Types of Koi-Keepers

Koi-keeping often becomes quite a social pastime, although not necessarily so. If you do interact with other enthusiasts, it may help to know what you have to look forward to (and where you may be heading as well!).

The koi market has three levels of koi-keepers:

- ✔ **The *koi kichi* (koi crazy) bunch:** These folks buy very expensive koi, so it follows that they know a lot about koi and how to keep them. These individuals feel the best koi are *nishikigoi* (koi from Japan) and they're able to pay the price. Not surprisingly, this is the smallest of the three groups.

- ✔ **The competitive sort who set koi-keeping boundaries:** The second level of koi fanciers are those who enjoy koi, exhibit them in competitions, and form the backbone of koi clubs. They buy good koi no matter where the koi hails from (although all things being equal, they, too, prefer Japanese koi).

- ✔ **The casual hobbyists:** The third group is by far the largest. These hobbyists want good-looking fish that get big and do well in a pond. They want fish with *bling* (which explains why metallic koi are so popular in the United States!). Some of these individuals eventually join the competitive middle group, and some even move into the upper echelon of the koi kichi group. But as casual hobbyists, they furnish most of the money that runs the koi industry, and they're happy with koi from Israel, Hawaii, South America — basically anywhere.

Knowing the Essentials for Any Koi-Keeper

Before we really get started, we want to point out some essentials concerning these fascinating fish and what goes into keeping them.

The winner for "Most Obvious": Koi

Koi do get big (24 inches or more) and they need a good-sized pond, but you can have just as much fun with a $10 koi as one that costs $200. (And yes, koi can run $20,000, but we don't see how anyone can have fun with a fish that costs that much. As you read on, you discover just what makes certain koi so much more desirable to own and why those koi judges are so taken with them.) Please see Chapter 16 for more information on the standards for judging koi.

A transitional home for your koi

In addition to a permanent home for your koi, you need a second, temporary place to quarantine new fish. A quarantine tub allows you to adjust your koi to its new environment gradually. It also allows you to observe them for a time so that those with contagious diseases don't find their way into your main pond and infect your other fish. A transitional tub can also serve as emergency quarters if some calamity strikes your pond and as a hospital area where you can treat sick and injured fish. See Chapter 13 for discussions on this temp housing.

A permanent home for your koi (most likely a pond)

Like making Welch Rarebit ("First start with a rabbit"), if you're going to keep koi, first you have to start with a pond. Pond design and construction have only a few unbreakable rules:

- ✔ Keep the design simple: a rectangle, square, or circle. These shapes are easiest to clean via a filter. If your heart is set on a dumbbell-shaped pond, keep goldfish, not koi.

- ✔ The pond size may surprise you by being smaller than you thought. The minimum size is 6 x 9 feet and 4 feet deep, and it provides plenty of room for a few koi.

  However, little koi grow into big koi (24 inches long or more), and they need room to swim. We feel honor-bound to warn you that koi-keepers tend to build bigger and bigger ponds to accommodate this growing hobby as time goes on.

If you think that koi just may be the fish for you, we guide you through the different styles of ponds and their settings in Chapters 6, 7, and 8 so you know which ones take more work and money and which ones take less.

Pond gadgets: The filter and pump

Status in pond size sets in when the numbers go over five figures, as in a 15,000-gallon pond. But, before you hyperventilate thinking about the work to maintain *gin-clear* (the koi-keepers' term for *clean*) water in a honking-big pond, remember that the pond's filter does most of the work. In Chapter 6 we give you the basics on filter and pump selection. (We group the two together because they go together. The filter only strains the bad stuff out; you need the pump to move the water through the filter.)

Koi eat a lot and produce a great deal of waste, so your pond needs a multifunction filter that can handle mechanical and biological filtration (usually in different parts of the filter), and it needs drains in the bottom of the pond to feed that filter.

Note: Because koi breathe the oxygen dissolved in the water, use a supplementary air pump to add oxygen to the water. The easiest design *bubbles* the air through the top section of the filter drains.

In selecting the right filter and pump, look for a number on the equipment that indicates the gallons-per-hour it can process. The filter and pump must be able to *turn over* (cycle) the water in your pond every two hours. The larger the pond, the larger the filter and pump must be. In case you're wondering about the power consumption, in Chapter 6 we explain how to figure out your per-year costs to operate any pump. (And no, your utility bill doesn't have to be a bad surprise every month.)

The more you hold your utility costs down, the more money you have to spend on koi. Don't you just love saving money?

Understanding the Demands of a Koi Pond

Although the filtration system performs much of the pond maintenance, you still have to maintain the system and the quality of the pond water. These tasks consist of the following:

- ✔ *Backwashing* **(cleaning the filter):** This process has two steps that take little time and effort:

    - • Swishing pond water back through the filter to dislodge all the crud the filter has removed

    - • Opening a valve so the cruddy water empties out of the filter

    Some filters have actual filter mats (a bit like those in your central air conditioner) that you physically remove from the filter, shake or spray off to dislodge the debris, and then replace.

- ✔ **Checking pond chemistry:** You can opt for expensive testing equipment, but a simple $35 kit with test strips is quite adequate. The various colors on the dipped test strips can tell you a lot about the quality of your pond water and whether your filter is doing its job. Chapter 9 gives you goals for your water's ammonia, nitrite, nitrate, and pH, and we explain what to do if any values are out of the safe range.

Keeping Koi Healthy: A Brief How-To

The easiest way to keep your koi healthy is by keeping the water clean, but other factors come into play. Chapter 13 tells you what problems to watch out for and how to handle them if they do show up. The following list is a glimpse of the most important ways you can protect your koi:

✔ **Minimize koi stress.** One factor in koi illness is stress because koi just don't *do* stress well. Moving a koi into a new pond, overcrowding koi, or introducing sudden water temperature changes can all stress koi. Stress drop-kicks the immune system, and then every opportunistic bacteria or parasite takes advantage of the situation. Chapter 12 helps you recognize some of the causes of stress and explains how to head off some of the effects.

✔ **Always quarantine new fish.** You may have thought quarantines went the way of the dodo and the bubonic plague, but for koi, quarantining new fish is the only way to prevent possibly fatal pondwide problems. Setting up a quarantine pond or tub is easy (and you can use the same tub for raising koi babies if you somehow — despite or because of your efforts — end up with koi eggs). We explain the equipment and the process of quarantining in Chapter 5.

✔ **Adjust your koi's environment according to weather.** Wintertime brings prolonged cold temperatures that are hard on creatures that can't produce their own heat to stay warm. When water temps fall, koi literally cannot function; they can't digest food (so you don't feed them for weeks on end), and they have trouble swimming. Watching koi slowly maneuver in a 55-degree pond would be almost comical if it weren't so sad.

In Chapter 9 we offer alternatives to letting your koi overwinter outside. You can avoid some of the cold-water problems by covering your pond and even more of them by covering and heating your pond. In this chapter we also offer some fairly easy pond-covering solutions and talk about heating choices that fit your pond and your pocketbook.

✔ **Pay attention to your fish.** Just like you would for a pet dog or cat, be sure to inspect your koi if you notice strange behavior. Koi are particularly subject to skin ulcers when the water temperature is in the mid-60s, which is typical of an early spring warm-up. In Chapter 13 we show you how to circumvent ulcers and capture your koi so you can treat them.

Koi are subject to external parasites. Your koi's skin may suddenly be peppered with white dots or dangling, hairlike tendrils. (*Oh, yuck,* you say, and we agree.) Maybe their fins develop little, clear dabs of jelly (except these jelly spots have eyes!).

Parasites are a normal part of life for koi, but they're not inevitable. You can get rid of the parasites without having to touch a single one. Chapter 13 gives you the lowdown on these lowlifes.

Joining a Koi Club: What It Can Do for You; What You Can Do for It

Misery may love company, but so does a new hobby. Joining a koi club can help you by giving you immediate access to people who probably know a lot more about koi-keeping than you do (and some are even crazier about koi than you are). When something goes wrong, you have people right there to help you ID the problem and suggest ways to correct it. If your liner springs a leak or you have a radical problem with your pond on a Sunday afternoon, koi club members rally around with their show ponds, extra filters, and aerators to safely house your pets until you can get your big pond operational again. That kind of support means a lot.

At the meetings, you gain all sorts of valuable insight. For example:

- ✔ You can painlessly get the information you need — or soon discover you need — in a convivial atmosphere.

- ✔ You get insider information such as who's upgrading their ponds and selling their old filter systems because they're too small for a 20,000-gallon pond. (How big is that? A bit larger than 25 x 25 feet.) You also get the inside scoop on who's ready and willing to make a koi trade.

- ✔ You can find out when and where the shows are so you can see for yourself that those show koi certainly aren't any prettier than yours.

- ✔ You get a heads-up on breaking news such as a new disease or new legislation, both of which can be destructive.

  When the news first came out about koi herpes virus (KHV), which is both highly communicable and deadly for koi, the clubs were first to spread the word. They also provided ongoing funding for research and set up more effective quarantine protocols.

In addition to helping you and your koi, your club participation can help the hobby as well. Koi clubs are the first line of defense and information for any rule making that may inadvertently include koi (like the invasive-species issue).

Magnifying Your Pleasure: The Many Ways to Enjoy Your Koi

Of course, you can sit beside your pond and enjoy your koi all by yourself, but you can also increase the fun in so many ways. Check out the following suggestions:

✔ **Get creative with the landscape.** What kind of plantings do you have around your pond? Are you content with neatly mowed grass (which you can no longer fertilize due to runoff affecting your pond)? Does the idea of a Japanese landscape, where forms and colors are balanced by placement and mass, intrigue you? Chapter 8 can help you select plantings and accessories for your pond-surround.

✔ **Let your koi multiply.** Do you enjoy your koi so much you'd like more? Breeding koi isn't difficult:

• Hatching the eggs just takes a show pond and an aerator.

• Taking care of the young is a cut and dried process as long as you can handle the every-four-hour feedings and the culling to reduce the numbers to a manageable level.

Chapters 14 and 15 show you what you need to know from start to finish.

✔ **Sign up for a koi show.** After you have a few good-looking koi, you may want to see how they measure up at koi shows. These shows are held every spring and summer, and they're a great way to meet other koi-keepers, buy supplies, and maybe, just maybe, purchase another koi or two. *Note:* You don't *have* to buy koi at a show, but if you start looking at them, you're probably sunk. We tried to warn you.

Chapter 2

Knowing Your Koi

Most people have heard about koi but usually in association with goldfish. In fact, most people think koi are just big goldfish! This chapter gives you plenty of background to understand the start of koi, the different kinds of koi, and their color combinations and body shapes. We also cover the major koi markets, the most popular koi, and how to recognize a winner. Stick with us to raise your understanding of koi to a whole new level.

In the Beginning: A Brief History of Koi

Koi are descendents of *wild* (common) carp that have been selectively bred for color, pattern, size, body shape, scales (or lack thereof), and personality.

Taming of the carp: Koi's grand pappy

The wild carp originated in the freshwaters of the Caspian, Black, and Aral Sea drainages; they moved eastward with human help to

Siberia and China and westward to Europe and the Danube River. Some common characteristics include the following:

- ✔ It gets big, nearing 50 inches.
- ✔ It isn't a picky eater.
- ✔ It's prolific, even under crowded conditions.
- ✔ It tastes good.
- ✔ It's a movable feast.

It was precisely the wild carp's flavor and its ability to adjust to captive conditions that led to the development and breeding of *koi* (the Japanese term for domesticated *carp*). In a country that had minimal access to large domestic animals such as cattle, carp also became a valuable source of protein.

The overall hardiness of the koi suited it perfectly for the process of domestication. Unlike many fish, carp proved to be quite undemanding in terms of water quality, oxygen levels, and diet. As a result, they were able to adjust to a variety of habitats throughout Japan and could breed readily in captive or semicaptive conditions.

Moving from food to art

As the years went by, the koi-keepers in Japan couldn't help but notice any oddball carp. As with any captive breeding program, spontaneous color and body shape aberrations cropped up from time to time. For example, the first unusual color was the red in a Magoi's belly scales or at the bases of the fins. Occasionally a Magoi developed white areas or yellow-brown coloring rather than greenish-black. Koi-keepers started putting these brighter fish aside and breeding them to each other through several generations.

By 1830, the Magoi-keepers were experimenting with the cross of a white carp with a red carp, and the Japanese term *koi* had expanded to *nishikigoi (brocaded* or *colored carp)* to describe the new domestic version. ***Note:*** Today, if you go to Japan or buy fish imported from Japan, you're looking at nishikigoi; when you buy koi raised in other countries, you're simply buying koi. The difference is a little like buying chocolates from Switzerland (nishikigoi) or chocolates from your local grocery store (koi).

The Japanese koi breeders soon realized how lucrative breeding and selling koi destined for the dinner table could be. Some breeders started keeping journals of their nishikigoi, carefully recording the colors and shapes.

But as koi also became valued for their appearance, the koi with especially favored traits commanded a higher price than the koi intended for food. Interest spread among the Japanese people, fueling the desire for ever more beautiful and unique strains of koi.

Launching a hobby

The popularity of koi within Japan flourished after an association of koi breeders held an exhibition of Japanese products in 1914 that included 25 of their prettiest nishikigoi. The concept of a food source that was easy to raise and pretty to boot was irresistible. More koi breeders set up mud ponds.

Nishikigoi went international in the 1960s, when the development of the polyethylene shipping bag for tropical fish meant breeders could ship live fish by air anywhere in the world. For the first time, anyone who really wanted a koi (and had the money) could have one. The poly bag even made it practical for koi fanciers to travel to Japan to pick out their own koi and then ship the koi directly to their homes. As a result, this undertaking that was once unique to Japan has been transformed into a major new hobby with enthusiasts throughout the world.

Assessing the Beauty Marks of a Koi Today

As with any hobbyist, koi-keepers can approach their favorite pastime with varying levels of interest, effort, and expertise. To refine your skills and better prepare you for navigating the world of koi, this section offers you backgrounds on three koi aspects: size, scale type, and body shape (see the following section "The Confusing Part (Made Simple): Koi Varieties" for the rest of the story). With this knowledge under your net, you can easily distinguish a highly prized koi from one that's just so-so.

All terms to describe a koi's color, pattern, or scale type are in Japanese. Although these terms may seem confusing at first, take time to know them so you can hold your own when you talk to other folks who keep, show, and sell koi.

First things first: Understanding the difference between goldfish and koi

Before we can delve into the finer points of koi characteristics, we need to set the record straight on how they differ from their distant cousin, the goldfish.

Goldfish and koi are both members of the minnow family, and they both started out as carp. But they're about as closely related to each other as cattle are to oxen. For starters, although they vaguely resemble goldfish, koi get much larger and have far more demanding housing requirements. Table 2-1 identifies some of their most striking differences.

Table 2-1	Differences between Goldfish and Koi	
Category	*Goldfish*	*Koi*
Breeding history	Began 2,000 years ago in southern/central China	Began in the 1820s in the town of Ojiya in the Nigata Prefecture of northeastern Japan
Historical purpose	A diversion to delight the eye and bring peace to the soul	Abundant, easy, nutritious food source
Size	8 to 12 inches for fancy varieties; 16 inches for single-tailed	Size matters; meter-long (39 inches) are prized
Body and body part shapes	Come in endless permutations of four tail shapes, three body shapes, three eye types, and a wide variety of colors	Vary to a much less degree than goldfish in terms of color and finnage; selective breeding hasn't altered basic body and eye shape from the wild form
Mouth characteristics	No *barbels* (hairlike feelers around the mouth)	Barbels (See Figure 2-1)
Water supply	Require no filtration or aeration unless in a crowded or warm environment	Highly dependent on filtration systems
Activity	Kind to aquatic plants	Ruthless plant shredders

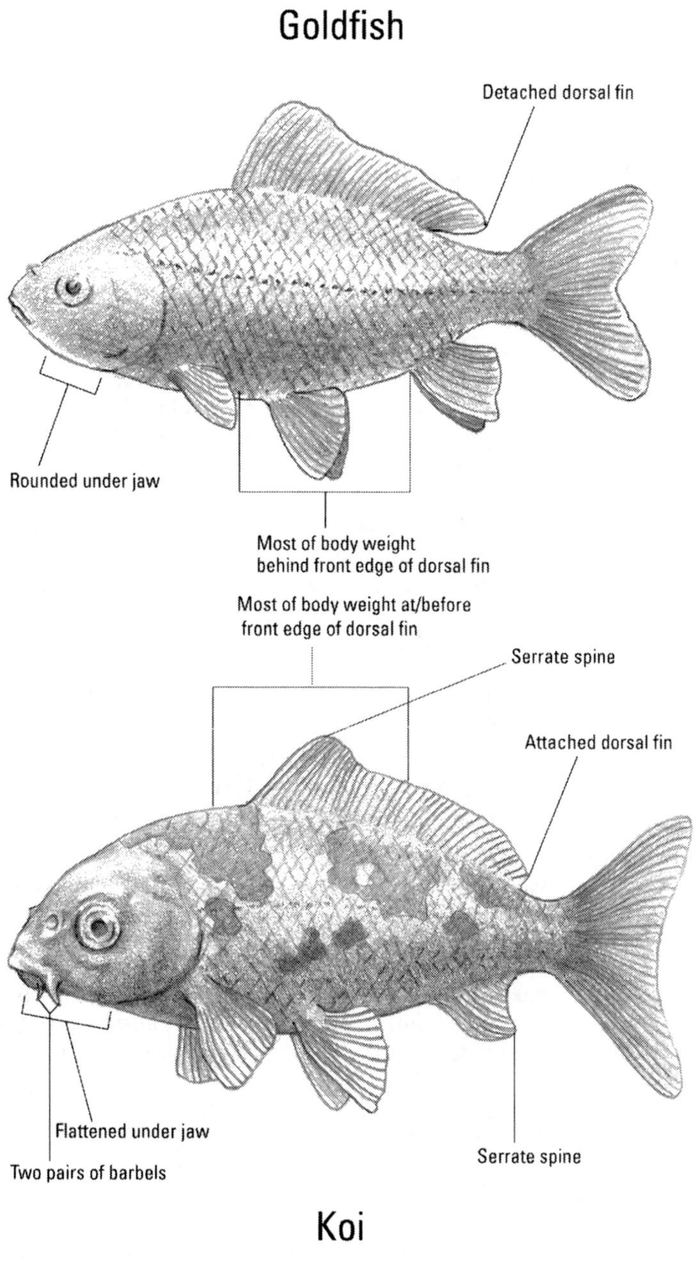

Goldfish

Detached dorsal fin

Rounded under jaw

Most of body weight
behind front edge of dorsal fin

Most of body weight at/before
front edge of dorsal fin

Serrate spine

Attached dorsal fin

Flattened under jaw

Two pairs of barbels

Serrate spine

Koi

Figure 2-1: Physical differences between a goldfish (top) and a koi (bottom).

However, koi and goldfish also have some similarities such as the following:

- A rainbow of colors
- Tail shapes (*Note:* Diehard koi breeders still sneer at the long-finned koi.)

The anatomy of a koi

The koi's body (see Figure 2-2) isn't modified for a specific habitat like many fish are (for example, the flattened, bottom-dwelling flounder). Rather, its shape is probably what you envision as a typical fish shape: tapered and streamlined, but somewhat thick-set to cut water resistance while swimming. Koi also have several other distinguishing features:

- **Three single fins and two paired fins:** The single fins are the *caudal* (tail) fin, the *anal* fin (along the bottom of the body), and the *dorsal* fin (along the top). The *pectoral* fins (at the sides) and the *anal* fins (along the rear of the underside) are the paired fins.
- **Vent:** Eggs, sperm, and waste products exit the body through this combined opening.
- *Operculum* **(gill cover):** The gill cover is a movable flap on each side of the koi's head. Water taken into the mouth passes out of the body at this point, after the gills have absorbed its oxygen.
- **Nostrils:** Koi use their two nostrils for scenting food and predators. The nostrils don't aid in respiration (the gills have that part covered).
- **Barbels:** These two pairs of small, whiskerlike projections near the mouth contain taste buds and help the fish locate food in the muddy waters they often inhabit.

How big are we talking? The size of koi

When it comes to growth, koi harken back to their carp ancestors. You can buy them as small as 4 inches, but 35 inches is pretty much the gold standard when you're talking about big koi. They may need

15 to 20 years to max out (most koi reach about 32 inches), but if you have a big pond — and time — who knows? The only downside to larger fish is that they're hard to show because they're heavier, lose their scales in regular koi nets, and are less able to deal with stress (due to their age).

Note: Koi can grow to 6 inches by the end of their second summer, and that's the size most wholesalers or retailers want to buy them. Koi continue to grow for the first five years, generally reaching 15 to 18 inches; after that, growth slows down.

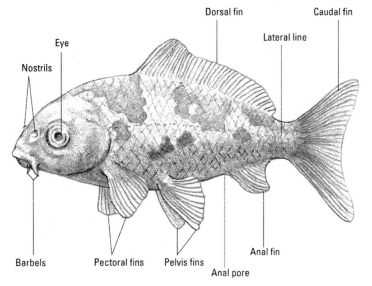

Figure 2-2: The anatomy of a koi.

Recognizing the finer points of koi

A number of characteristics are used to describe koi including scales, fins, and most importantly, color. But the one unwavering standard is the body shape. (Don't worry about remembering all of this — you can turn back to these pages and polish up your skills as many times as you want.)

Starting with shape

More than one hundred years of selective breeding have honed the concept of the perfect koi body (see Figure 2-3 for an eyeful). The following categories break down the essentials for when you're perusing the ponds for a perfect 10:

- **Chub is in.** Koi conformation is a bit of a balance between practicality and aesthetics. The practical matter is that these fish were once bred and designed as food — the rounder, fuller, and more fully packed, the better. Because raising chubby koi required just as much space and food as raising slender ones, chubby won out every time.

  On the other hand, moderation is critical. A fat koi may appear to lack grace and beauty. As a result, a well-formed koi is just like a Barbie doll, neither too fat nor too thin (imagine that!).

- **Fins and body are proportional.** A koi that's too fat has a large body but its fins (which don't change with weight) appear too small. As a result, the fish takes on a cartoon appearance.

- **The sexiest shape is the upside-down pear.** Viewed from above, the body-perfect widens from the pectoral fins to the leading edge of the dorsal fin and then tapers to the base of the tail. The nose is gently pointed, not sharply pointed or foreshortened as if the fish has run into the wall a few times.

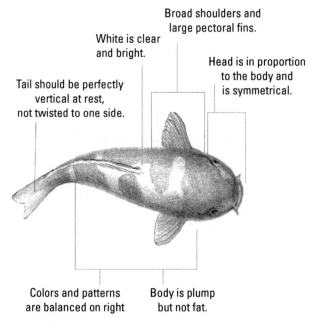

Broad shoulders and large pectoral fins.

White is clear and bright.

Head is in proportion to the body and is symmetrical.

Tail should be perfectly vertical at rest, not twisted to one side.

Colors and patterns are balanced on right

Body is plump but not fat.

Figure 2-3: The ideal koi physique.

Where did those long fins come from?

Butterfly koi got their start through Blue Ridge Fish Hatchery in North Carolina. In the early 90s, the hatchery bought what were called long-finned koi from a fish dealer in New York City. When the fish arrived, it was obvious they weren't koi but only a long-finned carp, and an ugly carp at that.

The long fins were placed in a pond so they could grow up and perhaps get prettier in the process. Their beauty didn't increase but their long fins intrigued their owners. Maybe, they reasoned, those long fins would cross over.

In efforts to breed a long-finned koi, the owners mated the long-finned carp with metallic koi, producing vigorous young that, sadly enough, looked very much like the adult long fins. However, the owners held out hope, knowing that many koi don't develop their true colors until after at least the first year. So they placed the young butterfly koi in their own pond until the end of the growing season. At the end of the season, some of the fish turned out to be quite attractive — Cinderellas in long fins.

Unlike the leather-skinned koi, the arrival of the butterfly koi has been greeted with caution. No butterfly koi has yet won a Champion. But if you like the graceful look of the long fins and you appreciate *hybrid vigor* (the extra vitality that often results from a cross between two closely related varieties or species), you may want to try the butterflies in your pond.

According to tradition, mature females have a more graceful shape than the males, which is why most champions are female. Because champion females are also worth more than champion males (as is common with any pet), owners may inadvertently select their females more than their males to display.

Recognizing scale types

At one time, all koi had the same sort of scales, just like other fish. But as with any other creature that's bred for many generations, oddballs pop up. For koi, there are normal scales and variations:

- **Doitsu:** These are scaleless or partially scaled koi. They can be any color variety. Doitsu koi are divided by their scales (or lack thereof):
  - Leather-skinned (scaleless)
  - Mirror-scaled (rows or groups of distinctly large scales along each side)

You rarely run into Doitsu koi unless you get very serious about koi.

✔ **KinGinRin:** Sometimes normally-scaled koi have *KinGinRin* scales, which are highly reflective, normal-sized scales. The scales look like tiny spotlights running along the sides of the fish and can occur in any color variety. This sparkly quality is becoming more popular in the United States and is now bred into display-quality (inexpensive) koi. The placement of the scales determines their shortened name:

- The KinGinRin scales atop red coloration are *KinRin* (gold).

- The KinGinRin scales atop black or white are *GinRin* (silver).

Scales are usually mentioned only when they're not standard.

Hast thou long finnage?

Butterfly koi are a fairly recent carp development. The term refers to their long pectoral, anal, and tail fins. If butterfly koi grow slowly in a small pond or aquarium, the fins grow very long, almost the length of the body. For example, where the usual pectoral/body-length ratio for koi is 1:5, butterfly koi are 1:3 and occasionally close to 1:1.

In addition, their skin has a metallic hue, and they're very graceful swimmers. The long fins and metallic hue can be passed on to any color variety of koi.

The Confusing Part (Made Simple): Koi Varieties

Koi may seem to be like patchwork quilts, displaying a huge array of colors and color arrangements, but a clear hierarchy of colors exists for describing or showing koi.

In addition to size and shape (see the previous sections), koi judges look at two other characteristics that are a big deal and deserve their own sections:

✔ Color and color patterns

✔ Brilliance

The brilliance factor breaks into two simple categories: metallic and nonmetallic. The metallic and nonmetallic koi are further divided into *varieties,* each named according to their color and color patterns.

Color me koi: The rainbow of many shades

Welcome to the world of naming koi! A white koi with black markings is different — and thus has a different name — from a black koi with white markings (although to the uninitiated the difference can be hard to tell). Along the same vein, a white koi with one black spot is different from a white koi that's peppered with black. (Check out the color section of this book for photos of the various koi varieties.) To add to the confusion (and in an effort to increase their market share), koi breeders continually try to develop new varieties.

Along with head and body shape, the careful placement of color defines a quality koi. *Note:* For serious koi owners, if a koi isn't one of the major varieties, it's just another fish.

Four basic rules help you decide a koi's color:

✔ **Koi are evaluated from the top.** Be sure you're looking down at it, not from the side.

✔ **Any color can have any skin type.** Types include fully scaled, leather-skinned, and mirror-scaled.

✔ **Colors can change.** You can buy a Sanke (a red, black, and white koi), but sometimes the red disappears as the fish gets a little older, leaving you with a black and white fish. So, congratulations — now you own a Bekko. Think of it this way: You're getting two fish for the price of one.

✔ **Markings can spread.** Suppose the blue markings on your Ai Goromo are no longer restricted to the red and begin to spread over the body; your fish is now Goshiki. Again, twice the adventure!

At the other end of the spectrum are *display* or *garden* koi. These koi don't fit any of the named varieties and are far less expensive as a result. Despite their lack of breeding papers, these koi are beautiful and just as charming as the more expensive show-quality koi.

Simply brilliant! The divisions of metallic and nonmetallic koi

Metallic and nonmetallic are show-quality koi, and the closer a particular koi comes to its variety's standard, the more expensive it is. *Note:* The *nonmetallic* designation is accurate, but the term isn't commonly used; the *metallic* designation is frequently used.

In competition, metallic koi divide into three groups (see the subsection "The metallic koi" a little later in this section).

The nonmetallic koi are grouped according to their base color, and we break down the 13-or-so varieties so you have all the info you need before heading for the fish farm.

In all honesty, the classification system is a bit wacko — some koi enthusiasts include KinGinRin (see the previous section) as a variety, so theoretically any shapeless koi of any color with KinGinRin scales can compete against any other KinGinRin. The classification is more of a guideline than a concrete system.

The nonmetallic koi

The standard nonmetallic koi types have no special glow to their scales, just a sheen or luster that doesn't distract from the color or pattern. The fish in this group tend to be reds and blacks because these colors show up better without metallic scales. Check out Table 2-2 for a brief rundown of the nonmetallic koi varieties.

Table 2-2		Nonmetallic Koi Varieties and Their Features		
Variety	*Body Color*	*Accent Color(s)*	*Special Features*	*Other Info*
Asagi	Blue back; red belly	Pale lines show between the scales; fins are pale and accented with red; nose and head are pale, but face may have red cheeks	Back has a diamondlike grid pattern	N/A
Bekko	Solid-colored red, white, or yellow	Black blotches	Name means *tortoise shell*, a reference to the pattern	A good one can cost four figures
Kawarimono	A catchall class	Includes the black *(crow)* koi that have white markings and the brown Chagoi	N/A	The name means *unusual ones*
Kohaku	White	Red markings	Tail base is completely white, but fish is judged on overall appearance; ratio of red to white should be pleasing; red that runs in a lightening-bolt-like pattern from eyes to tail base is very good	This classic koi is Japan's most popular
Koromo	White	Red and white with another color	N/A	This is a Kohaku with one more color over the red only; some markings are cloaked or masked by blue or black markings

(continued)

Table 2-2 (continued)

Variety	Body Color	Accent Color(s)	Special Features	Other Info
Sanke	White	Black and red markings; black is the accent color that appears only above the lateral line	Black coloring is ephemeral; may not appear on younger koi or may appear, vanish, and even re-appear	N/A
Showa	Black	Red and white blotches	Patterns change with age and may not settle until the fish is 2 years old (a variability that people find most alluring); dark markings wrap around from top to belly but don't cover or exceed the red; black areas on the pectoral are in balance	This is a cross between the classic red and white Kohaku and the Kit Utsuri
Tancho	White	One red marking on top of the head	The best head spots are circular, oval, or triangular	Red marking is reminiscent of the sand hill crane, for which the fish is named
Utsuri Mono	Most are black, but a white form exists	Yellow, white, or red patterns overlay the black coloring	N/A	N/A

The metallic koi

These koi are characterized by a reflective layer in the scales that makes the fish seem to glow in bright lighting. They're spectacular in a pond with black or dark green walls. Although metallic koi boast fewer varieties than the nonmetallic, these are popular fish nonetheless.

Because the reflective quality of metallic scales reduces the reds and blacks that are so admired in the nonmetallic koi, a whole different set of colors are prized in the metallic category (see the previous section for the best nonmetallic colors).

Metallic koi, also called *Hikari koi,* are separated into three groups as follows:

✓ **Hikarimuji (or Hikari Muji):** Koi with one metallic color (Because nothing is ever simple in koi-keeping, this group also includes Matsuba koi, which are patterned).

- **Matsuba:** Metallic one-color koi that have a black marking in the center of each scale which gives them a pine-cone-like pattern. They may be gold, gray, silver, or orange.

- **Ogon:** Single-colored koi that may be gold, silver (or platinum), orange, or red and white. This last color mix is basically a metallic Kohaku. A highly reflective head is a desirable quality in the Ogons.

✓ **Hikariutsuri (or Hikari Utsuri):** These are Utsuri or Showa that have gone metallic; in other words, they're metallic red, black, and white koi.

Because the metallic quality of the scales tends to overwhelm the red and black, outstanding examples are hard to find. Put them in a blue show bowl and they look really ugly; put them back in a black pond and they look pretty good. Showing these fish is a study in frustration.

✓ **Hikarimoyo (or Hikari Moyo):** These are multicolored metallic koi, with platinum and red or platinum and yellow.

The Popularity Contest: Which Varieties Take the Trophy?

Some koi varieties are more popular than others. And surprisingly, the most popular koi are quite ordinary, decorative-type koi with no special markings or distinguishing characteristics. This seeming contradiction is good news for people who think that serious koi-keeping requires very expensive koi.

To illustrate this contradiction, consider the following facts:

- ✔ The red and white Koromo is a more popular variety than the Showa (a red, white, and black koi).
- ✔ If your Utsuri Mono is competing against a Koromo, don't be surprised when the judges select the more popular — but obviously plainer — Koromo.
- ✔ The Tancho (an all-white koi with a red rosette on the top of the head) is possibly the most popular koi of all despite its rather plain color scheme.

Different koi are popular in different countries. For example, Japanese koi-keepers favor the traditional, normal-scaled koi in some combination of white, red, and black colors. But in the United States, the brightly reflective KinGinRin koi are popular. Japanese breeders may also prefer the older koi varieties with normal scales, but breeders in other countries enjoy the leather-skinned, mirror-scaled GinRins and long-finned varieties more.

Long fins haven't gained the acceptance level of other koi characteristics in competition, so they're usually in a separate class. Nonetheless, the long-finned morphs are very popular with hobbyists and with companies who supply display-quality koi for public ponds.

The Karate Kids of Koi: Tategoi and Their Potential

Tategoi means *keepkoi,* a koi that is worthy of keeping. These are koi with potential, koi that by dint of breeding or appearance have the potential to get better, become prize winners. Tategoi are usually young fish, but they can also be mature fish whose potential is just being realized.

The term is also widely misused for marketing, much like the term *investment dressing,* where a $2,500 dress suit is supposed to make the wearer look great and stay stylish for years. A crafty koi breeder can label any koi *Tategoi*— and how is a newbie going to know any better?

The hallmark of a real Tategoi is its skin — not the color or texture, but the quality. The markings are intense and well placed. In addition, the head is unblemished, the body is solid but not fat, and the fins are in proportion to the body.

Who decides whether a koi is Tategoi? Ay, there's the rub. Anyone can decide that his fish, one or all, have the potential to be champions. But it makes a lot more sense to depend on the breeder's reputation, how long the firm's been in business, and your relationship with that breeder.

Points to keep in mind when looking for a Tategoi:

✔ Ask a fish dealer that you respect to serve as your agent. Tell her

- How much you want to spend

- What kind of koi you want

- What size fish you want

Be specific. If you're going to spend the money to buy a Tategoi, buy one you're going to enjoy. The fish dealer makes the trip to Japan, but she's shopping for you and your needs, not just for a Tategoi. Consider these other purchasing options:

✔ Some koi dealers bring in a group of high-quality, young koi as a weekend special event. You look over the fish and buy the one you like best. Maybe it's a Tategoi, but maybe it's a pretty koi that simply delights you every time you feed it.

✔ When your local pond store gets a new shipment of koi from Japan, be among the first to check it out.

Chapter 3

Making Sure Koi Are Right for You

In This Chapter
▶ Measuring your koi space
▶ Calculating your time commitment
▶ Figuring the costs
▶ Pricing out pond construction
▶ Weathering the elements

For most people (probably you, too), the idea of koi-keeping is one that evolves from a couple of inexpensive goldfish in a small backyard pond with a filtering system and a bunch of plastic cattails. At some point, as you sit on a lawn chair at the edge of the pond, watching your goldfish, you may wonder, "Could there be more to pond keeping than this?" And the quest begins: You surf the Web under *koi,* borrow koi books from the public library, and check with a local pet store to find a local goldfish and koi club. You go to a meeting, go on a pond tour, and go to a koi show, where members talk about ponds of 6,000 gallons and filtering systems that seem large enough to clean up Lake Erie.

Suddenly your goldfish just don't have what it takes. You want serious fish, fish that swim into your palm to eat, gorgeous fish that are bigger and bolder. . . .

What you want are koi.

But are koi for you? That's the question. And the answer is in this chapter, which tells you how much you have to commit (space-, time-, and money-wise) if you want a koi pond. This chapter isn't designed to discourage but to enable you to plan more effectively and sensibly if you choose to purchase koi.

Do You Have the Space It Takes?

You have two basic considerations to bear in mind when deciding how much space you'll allot to your koi. The first and most obvious point is the actual size of the fish and the swimming room that they need. The second point is less apparent but just as important. Koi have hearty appetites and produce huge amounts of nitrogenous wastes. An appropriately large volume of water dilutes ammonia and other toxic substances so they're less harmful to the fish and less burdensome on your filtration system.

Calculating a koi's fin-flippin' space

Several long-tested formulas can help you figure out how many koi fit in your pond or aquarium, and they all work off the simple concept that bigger fish need more space than smaller fish. The formulas give different answers, so for the sake of not driving you crazy, take the middle road. As if you haven't noticed, koi-keeping isn't an exact science; it's science mixed with art.

Crowded koi have less margin of safety than uncrowded koi. Figure 1 ½ inches of fish per square foot of surface area. To avoid crowding your fish and allow for growth, stock your pond well below the upper limits of the formula. For example, in a 6-x-9-foot pond, the formula allows 81 inches of koi or ten 8-inch koi. See Table 3-1 for calculations of koi that fit in the most common pond sizes.

Table 3-1	Number of Koi for Common Pond Sizes			
Size of Pond	Inches of Koi (at 1.5" per sq. ft. of pond surface area)	8-Inch Koi	10-Inch Koi	12-Inch Koi
6 x 9 feet	81	10	8	7
8 x 12 feet	144	18	14	12
10 x 14 feet	210	27	21	17

Plan ahead for the possibility that your fish will outgrow their accommodations. In some cases, a stronger filter may increase your pond's capacity a bit, but eventually you may need to install a larger pond or find a new home for some of your fish. Although parting with a favorite pet may be difficult, remember that overcrowding (either by size or number of fish) sooner or later causes the death of all of them.

Estimating the space your koi's habitat requires

Keeping koi can take up your entire yard, part of your yard, or just a corner of your living room — depending on your time, interest, and finances. Keeping only a few small fish that you'll give away as they outgrow their accommodations is obviously a different prospect than maintaining a dozen adult koi in a large garden pond.

The space for your koi pond is more than just the hole that contains the water. In this section, you discover some less obvious factors to consider. But deciding on the pond's size is perhaps the most important decision that faces the new koi owner, so please think carefully about your choice.

How much outdoor space do you need for a pond?

When figuring the space that your pond and surrounding areas will need, consider two components:

- ✔ Size of the pond

- ✔ Access area to the pond, including space for the filter

 The smallest pond you can build for koi is 6 x 9 feet across and 4 feet deep, or just over 1,500 gallons. This is way big enough to afford swimming space (and years of growing space) for ten 8-inch koi or six to seven 12-inch koi, or roughly 81 inches of koi (if physicists can have light-years, we can have koi-inches, right?). A pond must be deep enough and large enough to allow the fish to move vertically and horizontally without feeling cramped. The depth of a pond (4 to 8 feet) also gives the koi a chance to swim down and out of a predator's reach (such as herons and raccoons and, in one case, the family cocker spaniel, who nabbed his fish directly from poolside).

Here are the other size considerations you need to keep in mind:

- ✔ **A pond of any size needs an access area of at least 5 feet along one long side and space for your filter along a short side.** The access area allows you to feed and closely observe your fish and is the main place from which you manage routine chores, such as removing leaves and netting sick fish.

- ✔ **You need a clear area of 2 to 3 feet around the filter.** This space allows you to perform such tasks as backwashing, winterizing, and replacing the hose. You may as well provide this space along the entire side that your filter's on so you can get to it easily.

✔ **You need some access around the rest of your pond.** Pond leaks, for example, can crop up anywhere, and you've got to get near the leak in order to fix it.

Adding in the access strip and the filter strip along two sides of a 6-x-9-foot pond gives you a pond footprint of 9 x 14 feet. Use a garden hose to loop out a rectangle of that size in your yard. So you don't have to measure each area, place a strip of masking tape on the hose at 46 feet — 9 + 9 + 14 + 14 — from the end.

Of course, you can go larger if you have the space, but the *absolute maximum* you want for a koi pond is 9 x 14 x 4 feet deep. The reasons for this limitation are pretty simple:

✔ When you need to medicate the entire pond (as you occasionally must), the bigger the pond, the higher your med costs.

✔ If you need to catch a particular fish, the bigger your pond, the harder it is to net the fish (and the more stressed your fish can get from being chased).

Can they stay inside? Indoor space requirements

You can keep koi inside your home in a large aquarium; you just can't keep them very long. Well-fed koi grow quickly, and they'll soon be too big for all but the very largest aquariums.

Aquarium housing for koi only works if the koi are 6 inches max. When fish are longer than that, they're too big for an aquarium indoors and need a larger pond to flip around in, which typically fit only outside (unless you have an enormous house, that is). Newly hatched koi generally reach a length of 6 inches by age 2, so even if you start with small fish, you need to have an outside pond or a foster home rather quickly.

Is Time on Your Side?

Keeping koi should be a thoroughly enjoyable prospect. However, along with the pleasure comes the responsibility of providing your new pets with proper care. By having some idea of the time you'll need to invest, you can more easily understand how koi ownership will affect the rest of your schedule.

Keeping up a koi pond

The time involved in the care of koi and upkeep of their pond varies with the season and, in some cases, with the geographic location of the pond. You'll face busy times and quiet times, each with their own necessary tasks and unique rewards. In this section, we examine how seasonal changes affect both your fish's behavior and the degree of care that you need to provide.

- ✔ **Summer:** During the summer, you need an hour each week to clean the filter, do a partial water change, and check water quality. Your koi need feeding once or twice a day (maybe 5 minutes in the morning and 20 minutes in the evening — long enough to sit and enjoy your fish). Total time each week: about 2 ¾ hours.

- ✔ **Winter:** Wintertime routines for ponds in northern climes are much more relaxed. You need to cover your pond to keep the water temperatures at least 52 degrees F, and you may need to heat your pond as well. A variety of commercial pool covers (see Chapter 9) and submersible heaters are commercially available. Check the water temperature daily and the water chemistry every two weeks. Time needed? Less than half an hour a week.

  For ponds in the southern Sunbelt, where nighttime air temperatures rarely dip below 60 degrees, continue feeding your fish daily, checking your water chemistry weekly, and cleaning your filter every other week. The time to complete this work alternates between 45 minutes one week and 90 minutes the next week.

- ✔ **Spring:** When spring approaches, you have some basic pond-housekeeping chores. Begin with vacuuming out any sludge and making a partial water change; then clean and restart the filter. These steps take about 90 minutes, counting the water change time. In a few days, the beneficial bacteria become re-established in the filter.

Being prepared for a lifelong commitment

Koi are hardy little suckers. With good care and attention to the water quality, your koi may outlive you! In Japan, a koi of 100 years isn't unusual.

Although some pond keepers trade up or trade down (depending on the size of their koi, the size of their pond, and their own desire for change), other fin-fans prefer to keep their koi, watching them mature and enjoying them as family pets. For the pond keeper with bad luck or sloppy pond-keeping skills, the average life span of a koi is less than a month.

With luck, you figure out the problem (maybe early enough to save the koi) so you can take steps to change course for this or future attempts. But, if you have bad luck in the beginning, do a reality check before you invest any more time, money, and effort. Ask yourself, "What should I do differently next time?" Of course, when dealing with live animals, you must face the prospect of loss and accept that forces beyond your control may intervene. But a koi owner can take comfort in the fact that the basics are straight forward.

Following a loss, the best course of action is to research the problem thoroughly by reading about koi in general and your own situation in particular. Reread this book, paying particular attention to those areas you may have skimmed over in your excitement to begin. Speak with other hobbyists, koi suppliers, and, if possible, professionals at your local public aquarium (many such institutions have staff or volunteers who are happy to address questions from serious hobbyists). Armed with your new knowledge and resources, start over slowly and carefully. As you gain experience and wisdom, your successes will increase.

Do You Have the Bread to Buy, House, and Care for Koi?

In the excitement of starting a new hobby, it's very easy to underestimate the expenses involved. Some, such as the price of the fish, may be obvious, but less evident costs abound as well. This section alerts you to all the monetary considerations in the keeping of koi. After reading it, you'll be able to make an informed decision as to how much your interests will cost to pursue. By starting on a scale that's appropriate for your budget, you avoid future disappointments.

The cost of the fish alone

The cost of koi has a vast range: They start at about $10 for koi 3 ½ to 4 inches long and go to $20,000 or higher for just one adult! The younger koi usually sell in groups of six or more. However, in larger cities with many retail outlets, you can purchase young koi individually.

The smallest and least expensive koi are sold in bulk from breeders at the end of a summer, when the fish that hatched that spring are about 4 inches long. Usually these koi go to other breeders or to wholesalers. These people may resell the 4-inchers directly, or they may *size up* the fish over the winter.

The equipment that gives your koi a home

To take care of koi, you need certain basic equipment. Table 3-2 contains the most essential items.

Table 3-2   Equipment Costs for Keeping Koi Outside

Item	Range	Median
Filter system	$500–$1,200	$650
Fish net	$45–$75	$60
Heater	$500–$1,200	$900
Medication basics	$50–$350	$200
Protein skimmer	$50–$150	$100
Pumps (you need two)	$380–$450 ea.	$400 ea.
UV sterilizer	$225–$400	$325

If you plan on keeping koi indoors, your expenses will be considerably less, as you won't need a heater or UV sterilizer. The least expensive option is a traditional aquarium of 55 to 100 gallons (of course, in this case, you're limited to keeping koi of approximately 6 inches or less in size). Indoor pools and quarantine tubs vary enormously in cost because of the wide variety of sizes and materials. In general, the prices for the enclosures and the life support equipment are a good deal higher than for traditional aquariums but less than for outdoor ponds.

See Table 3-3 for a general rundown of the equipment expenses for keeping koi inside in an aquarium.

Table 3-3   Equipment Costs for Keeping Koi in an Aquarium

Item	Range	Median	Other Info
Aquarium (standard shape)	$50–$500	$350	Designer tanks are significantly more costly.
Air pump	$25–$50	$35	Buy a battery-operated air pump for power outages; cost is about the same.

(continued)

Table 3-3 (continued)

Filter and motor (as one unit)	$75–$250	$175	Large, heavily stocked tanks require stronger, more expensive models.
Protein skimmer	$50–$100	$70	

The necessary funds for koi maintenance

Although your main cash outlay will be in the startup phase of your hobby, be aware that koi cost money to maintain. Certain expenses, like food, arise on a regular and predictable basis. Others, like medications, are less easy to foresee. Your most common ongoing expenses are shown in Table 3-4.

Table 3-4   Common Ongoing Expenses for Keeping Koi

Item	Cost
Food	Less than $5/month
Electricity	Easily $200/month for the water pump, aerator, and UV sterilizer; much more if you heat your pond with electricity.*
Filtration medium	$20/month
Water-testing kits	New kits every four months at about $50, or $12/month

Note: Natural gas heating may be less expensive, but even it isn't cheap.

Life-support system parts need replacement eventually, as pumps burn out, hoses leak, and filter parts break down. Stock all the basic medications when you first purchase your fish, but be aware that you may need to purchase additional drugs as unforeseen medical problems arise.

Other unpredictable expenses include emergency situations — a power outage or disease outbreak that causes the loss of many fish, for example. Or, perhaps a predator such as a raccoon takes up residence nearby and you need to hire a trapper to remove the animal. Situations like these are impossible to predict, but you need to budget for general emergencies when figuring out your future expenses.

Building a Pond? Construction Costs to Consider

Ponds are holes in your garden that you line with one of the following items:

- A rigid, preformed plastic shape
- A pond liner (a thick but pliable plastic sheet)
- Cement (in effect, a swimming pool for fish)

Each type of pond construction has its advantages and constraints, but two elements are consistent regardless of the construction type: permits and the inevitable hole in the ground. In this section we cover those factors first and then go into each type of construction and its estimated costs.

Securing the necessary permits

Pond construction also has permit issues, so don't be surprised if you need one permit to dig a pond and more permits for the plumbing and electrical work. Keep in mind that many municipalities require ponds to be fenced to ensure the safety of other people; the construction of this fence is subject to strict guidelines and may require a permit as well.

It's impossible to estimate permit costs because they vary greatly and are often tied to the size of a project and to local property values. Consider this matter carefully, however, because the cost of permits and legal advice, if necessary, can be quite high. Property owners who fail to proceed legally can be subjected to heavy fines and significant construction delays. Of course, the tragedy that can result from an improperly fenced pool in an area with small children speaks for itself.

Digging the hole

The first part of actual pond construction is digging the hole. You can

- Hire this labor out to an operator who has a backhoe. In our area, it's $80 per hour. (If you get it this cheap, add a tip, okay?)
- Rent a backhoe and perform the labor yourself if you're experienced or you think it sounds like fun. Renting a backhoe is by the day or half-day, at $150 per half-day or $275 per day.

> ✔ Hire laborers to dig the hole. Laborers and cement finishers are $15 per hour in our area.
>
> ✔ Dig it yourself with the help of some willing friends (and a whole lot of refreshment incentives).

Obviously, backhoe rental, cement, and labor expenses vary by location and the size of the job. Backhoes with operators rent by the half-day, and, because the rental fee includes travel time, plan to budget at least a half-day.

You may think scooping out a hole in the ground is a fairly simple operation. Two words of advice: Never assume! And never underestimate the number of shovels of dirt a 9-x-6-x-4 hole can hold. (Okay, that was more than two words.)

Buying a preformed pond

The average preformed plastic pond is too shallow and too small to house koi. However, outlets dealing specifically in outdoor ponds and fish are well worth searching for. They stock a variety of preformed ponds in many sizes, some of which are quite large and have shelved areas along the edges, where you can place aquatic plants. You can buy a preformed fiberglass swimming pool that a truck delivers to your site and lowers by crane, but these pools often have a pale turquoise color, not the dark coloring that a koi pond needs to be. (See Chapter 6 for more of these pond specifications and explanations.)

Installing a pond liner

Pond liners are simple to use and not expensive. They're not a forever-type pond (like cement), but their do-it-yourself qualities and low replacement cost make these the pond of choice for most hobbyists. Plan to install plumbing for the filter and pond skimmer before you place the liner. Then, after you've laid down the liner, you can cut through it to fit the filter and skimmer *bulkheads* (the fittings around pipes that penetrate the liner and make the opening watertight). The 45-*mil.* (thousandths-of-an-inch) liner comes by the square foot, which makes it easy for you to determine basic costs.

To determine the size of liner, use the following formulas:

Length: Length + 4 feet + (2 x depth)

Width: Width + 4 feet + (2 x depth)

For a 6-x-9-x-4-foot pond, you calculate as follows:

Length: 9 + 4 + (2×4) = 21 feet

Width: 6 + 4 + (2×4) = 18 feet

So, you need a liner that is 21 feet x 18 feet. For pricing purposes, that's 378 square feet.

Buy a patch kit that's marketed for the liner size that you've chosen because sooner or later all pool liners leak. (Check out Chapter 9 for more about upkeep.)

Pouring a cement pond

Cement ponds are every koi owner's dream. They're permanent, leak-proof, essentially maintenance-free, and elegant. But they're also expensive — and, again, size and shape do matter. The cost from start to finish for a basic 9-x-6-x-4-foot pond with all the essential elements (permits, filter, drains, lights, and so on) in Florida is approximately $5,500.

Don't attempt to construct your own cement pond unless it's your profession. (*Note:* Being handy doesn't in any way qualify you to install a cement pond!) A very specific set of skills, along with experience, is necessary if the pool is to look good and function properly. Contrary to popular opinion, cement work like pond construction requires far more than a strong back. And working with a professional in planning your pond is a very rewarding experience.

Cement ponds have one very appealing feature: After you agree on a design with a pond construction company, your work is done (except for handing over the payment, of course). However, working with a construction company has a few caveats. Make certain your contract spells out details like

- ✔ The slope of the bottom of the pond (it should center around the bottom drains).

- ✔ The number of underwater lights, their size, and placement.

- ✔ The number and placement of drains and outlets for filters and pond skimmers (see Chapter 7 for more information on building a pond).

Accounting for Your Climate

Geographical locations — and their climatic pluses and minuses — greatly affect the pond and koi in your yard.

- ✔ **In the South:** Koi-keepers in the South probably never need to heat their koi ponds; ponds stay warm enough in colder weather with a simple cover. However, during the summer, these same koi-keepers may need to add a waterfall or fountain feature to cool the pond water.

- ✔ **In the desert:** Koi-keepers in arid areas like southern Arizona need to top off their ponds with fresh water to replace water lost through evaporation. They also need a protein skimmer to filter off that scummy layer of pollen that settles after the summer monsoons.

- ✔ **In the North:** Koi-keepers in the North bear the brunt of expenses (like heating costs during the winter). Most koi-keepers elect to cover their pond when water temperatures dip below 52 degrees F, the point at which koi become relatively inactive (see Chapter 9 for the specifics on these covers). The cover can be Pliofilm stapled to a 2-x-4-foot frame just a few feet above the water. *Note:* When covering places and plants to avoid frost damage, the covering must be in contact with the earth or the pond's cement apron all the way around the pond in order to hold in the latent warmth of the earth.

For northern Koi-keepers, the big difference in cost is electricity and natural gas costs during the winter. One koi-keeper we know spent $600 a month to warm his pond, but he had a big pond, not the modest postage-stamp-sized pond we propose here.

Heating a pond in the north is not a DIY project because too much is at stake. Talk to other koi owners about how they handle heating their ponds, call a couple of commercial koi heating-system contractors, and check with your local utility to see whether their engineers/conservation staff suggest using propane over electricity. You may even consider building a structure over the pond (like a greenhouse or conservatory) that's attached to the house so you can enjoy your heated pond in midwinter. Even if it costs you the proverbial arm and a leg, at least you'll be able to see and interact with your koi while the weather outside isn't fit for man or beast.

Chapter 4

A Koi Buyer's Guide

In This Chapter

▶ Finding the right source for your koi

▶ Becoming a discerning koi shopper

▶ Arranging for shipped koi

*A*t last. Finally you can drag out all those colorful koi books you've been stocking up on, unearth the price lists, sit back in the deck glider, survey your koi domain, and get ready to make some choices. The task now is to truly define your wants, successfully acquire the fish of your dreams, and safely establish them in your pond. In this chapter, we help you determine the best places to look for those dream koi and make sure you're getting affordable, healthy koi.

The good part of this decision making is that your initial choices need not be your final choices. You can start out on the inexpensive side of cost and upgrade when you truly feel the need. The fun part of koi-keeping, though, is that many people stay with their original koi — they find the fish so much fun to keep and so personable that they don't want to part from them.

Oh Where, Oh Where to Buy My Koi?

Unless you make the trek to Niigata, Japan, the only way you can actually see the fish you're buying is generally through a local purchase. If you're willing to take a leap of faith — until you see how well the system works — you can try the Internet and the classified ads in koi magazines. This section introduces you to the three major markets in koi breeding and then offers more specific advice about koi shopping in the United States.

Recognizing the major markets: Japan, Israel, and the United States

Where you buy your koi, it turns out, is not nearly as important as *what* you buy. Ultimately, you want koi that match your personal taste, whether that means they're inexpensive, expensive, or somewhere in between.

A hop, skip, and a jump overseas: Japan

Japanese koi are the ultimate koi — koi-keepers want them, dream about them, and want to travel to Japan to buy them. These koi are the result of over 100 years of captive breeding and very careful *culling* (selecting); they're raised by individuals who may be third-generation koi breeders.

In Japan, the cool, mountainous, prefecture of Niigata is the locus for prize-winning koi. This is where the colors and patterns that koi-keepers covet were developed, described, and perpetuated. Enthusiasts wishing to see the Holy Grail of koidom travel halfway around the world (at considerable expense) to see the koi facilities and buy koi, and they're never disappointed. Even if you're not planning to show your koi in competition, your Japanese koi are of better quality than most keepers see in 30 years of koi-keeping.

The trip itself is a great adventure and a delightful opportunity to experience the Japanese culture. Purchasing koi in Japan is something of a courtly ritual that involves polite interactions between yourself, the other buyers, and the seller; it will, no doubt, be the highlight of your journey.

A quick jaunt over the Pacific: Israel

The koi market is so robust that other countries are following Japan's lead. Kibbutzim (collective farms) in Israel that have raised food fish for years now have koi-breeding operations.

At first the members of the kibbutzim raised koi for the middle market, the many pond owners who discovered they enjoyed the hobby. Through careful cultivation techniques, the members became extremely successful in raising quantities of koi. But, as their market expanded to new countries, the kibbutzim farmers realized there was a market for higher-quality koi. The quality of the Israeli koi began to edge up.

Today, Israeli production is very high (breeding a lot more and culling a lot less than the breeders in Japan). Nevertheless, Israeli koi maintain a reputation for being great substitutes for Japanese koi, especially for people who can't afford to buy from Japan.

Most of the Israeli production goes to England because air travel distances are shorter than the Israeli–U.S. connection or even the Japan–England connection. Koi from Israel generally aren't available in the U.S.

Koi on American soil (in waters, rather)

American koi range in quality from just-imported *nishikigoi* (the preferred Japanese term for *koi*) at *please inquire* prices to domestic, decorative koi in unclassified colors and patterns. Most American breeders are in the northeastern states or California, but an increasing number are springing up in the southern tier of states, where land costs are lower and the number of pond heating days is lower.

American breeders work on three levels, supplying very high quality koi to the upper range of the market, very good koi to the middle market, and handsome but undistinguishable mutts to the pond-keepers market. Today the demand for koi, pond construction, and other pond services is so large that many breeders do well without participating in the upper end of the market.

Comparing the three great koi locales

The competing koi-breeding operations in Israel and the United States have a few points going for them:

✔ Their locations provide a longer growing season than Niigata, Japan, where growth is limited to approximately five months each year. In Israel and parts of California and the southern United States, the mild climate allows the koi to grow throughout the year, or nearly so. The season is shorter in the northeastern United States but still approaches six months in length.

✔ Due to the warmer weather, they're able to stagger their breeding dates to provide varied sizes of fish.

✔ They're closer to major markets, such as England (and the United States, of course), than Japan is.

✔ They produce more fish. Israeli breeders focus more on production than on superb conformation to take advantage of the perception that Japanese koi are expensive. For example, 27 percent of Israeli hatched fry are raised to 5-inch lengths. Japanese koi breeders, on the other hand, routinely dispose of more than 99 percent of a hatch before the young are 1½ inches long.

Does this mean every koi from Japan is better than an Israeli koi? Not at all. A good koi is only as good as its genes. You can get excellent koi from Israel, and you can get not-so-good koi in Japan. However, Japan does have a much longer koi-breeding history, and its multigenerational breeders have genetically true lines — they produce young that look very much like the parents.

So, although Japan is hands down the best place to buy the world's sexiest koi, it comes down to you. If you're not absolutely mad about koi, you can find beautiful ones to fill your pond from American or Israeli farms.

Until recently, Israel had one problem that Japan did not — koi herpes virus (KHV). Israel's first outbreak was confirmed in 1999, but then Japan also had an outbreak in 2006. According to the press, the KHV was confined to one breeder and traced to imported stock. After several months of concerted effort by the Japanese breeders and absolute quarantines and extirpations, Japan's outbreak was considered eradicated by the end of summer 2006. Now Israeli fish breeders grow Koi in entirely isolated and enclosed environments and also vaccinate to immunize fish, controlling the spread of KHV.

Visiting your local garden store (or pet store or aquarium shop)

Finding the perfect koi (or at least the near-perfect koi) may be as easy as visiting the pond section of your local garden store, pet store, or aquarium shop between April and September. This is possible in many areas of the United States as well as in other parts of the world where the hobby is enjoyed (if you live in Japan, you're about as lucky as you can get when it comes to obtaining terrific koi). In addition to the basic, generic koi that local emporiums stock, store owners are usually very nice about ordering up for a customer who's interested in a bit-out-of-the-ordinary koi. Most often these fish are ordered from local breeders, but stores that specialize in koi may be able to obtain them from abroad as well.

Shops usually group koi by size and price, and 6-inch koi run about $18 each. The larger the koi, the higher the price. Keep in mind, though, that garden shops and pond stores may not be your best place to shop for championship or championship-potential koi. For that specialty, plan to make friends with a koi dealer or breeder.

Heading straight for the source: Local breeders

Purchasing locally is the easiest and least complicated way of acquiring your koi for two reasons:

- ✔ It allows you to choose the patterns and colors that you like the best from a multitude of koi.
- ✔ It precludes the necessity of shipping the fish and the stress they undergo as a result.

With any luck, you have three options for buying your koi locally:

- ✔ **From a fellow koi-keeper:** Most koi-keepers try to breed fish at some point, or they find that the fish have taken matters into their own fins, as it were — and baby koi have invaded the koi pond. Whether by luck or by artifice, the young koi survive and, like all other koi, they grow. As a result, local keepers often have small koi for sale at a very good price.

- ✔ **From a local breeder:** Pull out your local phone book and check the yellow pages under *ponds*. A few phone calls can help you discover whether koi are available locally in a number of varieties.

- ✔ **From a local commercial breeder:** Although a local vendor may say his firm is wholesale only, you may be able to order from him if you meet the quantities requirements. *Note:* Wholesalers often contribute koi to local koi auctions, another way for you to get a really good koi or two for not much money.

 As you select your favorite koi, many (if not most) of them undergo *ontogenetic* (age-related) color or pattern changes, especially in color intensity. Your carefully chosen, hand-picked fish may develop into a creature with an entirely different appearance from the one you selected.

Going once, going twice, sold at a local koi auction

Most koi clubs have annual or semiannual auctions or raffles to raise funds for the local club. In most cases, members simply bring in their excess fish or net some bargains by purchasing another member's extra fish.

Club auctions: The best prices in town

Recently we attended a neighborhood koi auction hosted by our local koi club. The auction/cookout was held in the backyard of one of the local club officers, who also served as chief cook and auctioneer. Along the edge of the yard were a dozen show tubs holding dozens of koi segregated by size (4 inches to 18 inches or more). About 50 koi-folks were there, some who had traveled more than 100 miles. Everyone was friendly, polite, and eagerly awaiting the main event.

Compared to other auctions, the sales pitches were tame — almost sedate. The auctioneer allowed potential purchasers to determine which koi they wished to have auctioned first. Those fish were gently netted and bowled for everyone to see, and as they were bowled, the auction took place. Of course, the largest and most colorful fish went first, and they were remarkably cheap. In fact, most fish sold for $20 to $50 although a few fetched $100 to $300. At the end of the sale, the more generic, smaller selections sold for about $25 for a bag of six or more.

After a fish sold, a club member carefully edged it into a plastic bag (some fish were so large that they were pushing the capacity of the bag!) with enough water to cover the fish. Each bag was topped off with pure oxygen to assure the fish breathed comfortably until it reached its new home.

The actual sale lasted for just over an hour, but the presale jabber and cookout allowed folks of like interests to get together for a friendly pow-wow about their hobby. And members who left with a bagged fish in hand also left with an unmistakable I-got-a-deal smile on their faces!

Prices for these koi are extremely reasonable. For example, a breeder at a recent auction reportedly bought a $500 koi for $40. At that same auction, 6-inch koi sold for $10. If you're really lucky, you may hit the jackpot: A club member may want to sell her Japanese-bred and -hatched koi that have gotten too big for her pond.

The extra advantage of buying at a club auction is being able to talk to the previous owner to find out what he's fed his fish, which ones seem particularly shy, or even how its color developed. For example, a particular Showa Sanshoku — black koi with white and red markings — is slow to develop its red coloration.

 To find out about clubs and upcoming events in your area, check one of the popular koi hobbyist magazines or surf the Internet (search by using your local area and the keywords *koi auctions, koi clubs,* and so on).

In addition to the hard cash, these events promote a good amount of camaraderie. Check out the nearby sidebar "Club auctions: The best prices in town" for a recent example.

Surfing (online) for koi

You can spend a lot of money on koi, and with the help of online purchases and auctions, you can spend that cash very quickly. The good news is that young koi (from 4 to 8 inches in length) that you purchase online aren't expensive.

Actually, we like Internet purchases a bit better than those in the classified sections of magazines because you can request pictures of the koi you're interested in. (Classified ads may also provide a Web site where you can see the fish, but that seems to be an additional step for the same results.) Basically, you can purchase koi online two ways:

- ✔ **Private koi dealers:** These dealers vary greatly in the quality of their operations and the fish they offer. Because you're cutting out one step of the usual purchase process, you should expect to pay less than you would at a store.

  You can find online dealers by searching under *koi sales* and similar keywords. You may want to narrow your search to local areas in order to cut shipping costs.

  We urge you to find out all you can about a seller's reliability and integrity before placing and paying for your order. Most shippers require advance payment for the fish, its packing, and the air freight, so the cost can be significant. Ascertain the honesty of the shipper *before* the money leaves your account.

- ✔ **Web site auctions:** On an open-bid site, koi owners and sellers list their fish, post a picture, and mention a monetary reserve amount (below which the fish will not be sold). Then it's up to you, the bidder, to post your bid. And how high can these bids go? On the AquaBid site (info for this site is in the following paragraph), you'll see many ads for very inexpensive koi. Then again, you may come across an absolutely spectacular koi. (The one we found most appealing was a 32-inch, 25-pound Aka Matsuba Ginrin with a modest reserve price of $3,500.)

  To get in on the fun of an online auction, click on *koi* under *freshwater fish* at www.aquabid.com.

  Just as with online sales, research the koi seller's reputation and shipping policies before bidding online.

Going "away" for your koi

If you want to make a trip overseas for your koi, try to join a sales trip (usually in late October) hosted by a stateside koi importer. The best way to locate them is through personal connections such as members of your koi club or association. If you don't have these connections, talk with importers who advertise in koi magazines or on the Internet.

By going with an importer who's dealt with Japanese breeders, you stand a much better chance of meeting the breeders whose stock you really want to see. And because your trip leader already knows the protocol of buying from the Japanese, the prices will be better. For the inside scoop on buying koi in Japan, check out the sidebar, "The protocol of viewing and purchasing koi in Japan."

The protocol of viewing and purchasing koi in Japan

The concept of *acceptable* behavior by customers who are shopping for koi varies from one culture to another. For example, the Japanese prefer great decorum and restraint, but the American and European sales events show less restraint.

In today's hurried and often bellicose times, the Japanese protocol for viewing and purchasing koi may seem to be in a time warp because they're based on respect and politeness — not only for the fish but also for your fellow koi enthusiasts and the dealer. (Definitely not Wall Street mentality!)

Remember that, just as all koi aren't created equal, neither are all koi customers (in the dealers' eyes). As a result, Japanese koi breeders tend to give familiar and repeat customers preferential prices.

The following tips may make that first Japanese koi purchase a little easier:

✔ **In most cases the posted price may *seem* non-negotiable, but if you feel comfortable enough to try, never attempt to negotiate in public.**

✔ **Always ask the dealer questions about the fish (including price) in private.** Because the dealer may use a sliding scale of pricing (known customers getting somewhat better prices), asking in public is considered impolite. However, a dealer may choose to announce the price to the entire crowd.

✔ **If you're interested in a particular koi, ask the dealer to bowl or tub the fish.** This, of course, allows you a better look at the koi.

✔ **If someone else requests a dealer to bowl a fish for closer viewing, that person has first choice.** In other words, refrain from selecting one of the bowled koi until the prospective customer releases the koi back into the pond.

✔ **Keep quiet.** If you're a prospective buyer, don't talk with that customer until the selection process is completed.

✔ **Hold your horses.** Don't ask the price of the bowled fish until the potential buyer has declined it by turning it loose in the pond.

Determining What You See and What You Get

What kind of koi do you want? Do you want pretty fish for your pond, or do you want to try your hand at a high-quality koi? (After all, a show-quality koi doesn't cost any more to feed than a garden-variety koi.)

Your first priority is to buy healthy koi that'll settle down in your pond and flourish. But knowing whether a koi is unhealthy or likely to become ill after you get them home can be difficult. Fortunately, koi have certain fairly simple hallmarks that you can look for to help you choose both the most pleasing and the healthiest ones out of the gate. We cover both beauty and health in this section to help you make the best selections.

Choosing colors and patterns to suit your style

If your koi is simply for your viewing pleasure, then the colors and patterns should simply please you. However, if you have even an inkling that you'll want to show your fish some day, you have other considerations.

For all your koi choices, the colors should be as crisp and clean as possible. The differences between the show koi and those that are almost-but-not-quite-for-show koi aren't obvious to the casual observer — maybe the red spot on the head isn't centered, or the fish has red on the tail fin, or the color blotches may not have distinct edges. For many koi-keepers, these koi are beautiful enough.

These non-show-quality koi can be divided into two camps: koi that are a clearly definable variety with a flaw or two, and just pretty koi.

But if you're considering showing your fish, familiarize yourself with the colors and patterns that are most eagerly sought and rigorously defended by the show judges. The fact is, even though you think your koi's specking of black in the orange or white fields is charming, a show judge will consider it a disqualifying feature. (See Chapter 2 for a brief overview of these ideals.)

Younger koi swim into two categories:

✔ **Tategoi:** These are young koi with potential, the offspring of show-quality koi that promise to develop into show-quality koi. (Sure, you can get Tategoi from average koi, but that possibility is as likely as getting a show cocker spaniel out of two neighborhood cockers.)

How do you know whether you're really looking at Tategoi other than the price? Unless you know koi, you don't. Anyone can claim they're selling Tategoi, so you have to be able to trust your seller.

For example, in 2006 the owners of Happy Koi, a koi-breeding and -selling business in South Africa, estimated the cost of their koi-with-promise that they selected from "the best of the best young koi" during a buying trip to Japan, at $134 each. They buy these fish for what they *expect* the fish to become: "a great deal more — we can't promise you but these look very good."

✔ **Non-show-quality young koi:** These young koi are far less expensive than their Tategoi counterparts, particularly if they come from local breeders. Expect to pay $15 to $20 for a 4- to 6-inch local non-show koi. Be sure to consider shipping costs for one that will travel some distance to reach your pond.

Admittedly, you can't be certain what an adult koi will look like. Color and pattern are likely to change in some varieties until your fish reaches adulthood. In fact, juvenile koi are big-headed, angular little creatures that show very little of the overall grace of a well-conformed adult.

By the time a koi is 6 or 7 inches long, you usually have some hint of its conformation. By then it's out of the angular stage, and its back, sides, and belly are beginning to curve gracefully. The belly shouldn't be distended or bloated. If a koi looks nice at this 6- to 7-inch-long stage, it's likely to continue improving.

Considering size: What's right for you?

The right size of koi depends entirely on your wants and your budget. You can start off with any size koi you like, but be warned: Like diamonds, big fish always cost more. You can start with adults, or you can start with smaller koi and watch them grow up. In a nutshell, there's no perfect size of koi other than the size that most appeals to you. (For additional information on starting your pond, see this chapter's later section "Best bets for the indecisive: Advice from yours truly.")

For the new koi-keeper who wants to start out simply, buy fairly inexpensive young koi — those 8 inches or less — in groups. It's one purchase, one set of negotiations and arrangements, and instant pond population.

Buying a group of young koi may seem like an easy way to jump-start your pond — and it is. But those koi are going to grow. If your pond is already near capacity with koi, adding several new koi is a bad idea.

You can purchase some brightly colored 6-inch koi for your pond from a local pond store or an online vendor without busting your budget. Prices for what's politely called *display-quality*, 6-inch koi run $45 to $75.

If you buy a 10-inch fish directly from the breeder, keep the following in mind:

- ✔ The fish is probably special if a breeder is willing to maintain it for three years. Maybe its conformation or color distinguished it from its littermates.

- ✔ The price for a good-quality (but not show-quality), 10-inch koi in the United States ranges from $85 to $140.

When you're ready to add some pizzazz to the pond, ramp up your expenditures. Look for good-looking koi, maybe even some named varieties, and be selective. Buy what pleases you.

If you ultimately want big fish, consider starting with adults of 18 inches or larger. Koi can live in excess of 30 years, so even if you buy adults, you'll still have plenty of time together. You can buy an adult-size fish from a fish dealer or a fellow koi-keeper; you can look for show quality or not-show quality. Only your preferences and budget set the limits.

Selecting healthy koi

Although seeking a fish in A-1 health should be foremost in your mind (even ahead of color and pattern), this requirement becomes especially important if the fish must be shipped by air or ride in a vehicle for several hours. Such handling, even at its best, can quickly stress out a healthy koi for several days. If the fish is below par to begin with, the trip can be fatal. Of course, even generic koi should be free of malformations.

Before you pick out a particular koi from a group in a quarantine tub or a dealer's show tank, look at them as a whole. Consider the following characteristics about the group:

- **Are they oriented vertically in the water?** Fish that are ill may *list* (tilt) from front to back or side to side. Unless they're feeding, the head shouldn't be oriented toward the bottom of the tank.

- **Do they seem to move easily through the water with no jerkiness?** Skeletal malformations, swim bladder problems, and a host of other conditions can disrupt normal swimming patterns. (See Chapter 13 for more about uncoordinated swimming; sometimes this can be treated, and sometimes it can't.)

- **Are the fish rubbing themselves on the bottom of the tank or against objects within the tank?** If so, they may be trying to dislodge parasites.

- **Are the koi swimming about in a frenzied fashion, or do they seem unusually listless?** Both behaviors can indicate water quality problems or disease.

- **Are the koi gasping or gulping air at the surface of the water?** This behavior can indicate low oxygen levels (which eventually stress the fish) or water quality problems.

If the answers to the preceding questions raise any concerns, ask to see another batch. Better yet, resist your impulsive urge and find another source. However, if the koi pass the group test with flying colors, you're ready to take a closer look.

Ask to have the fish you like bowled, and then look at it for a few minutes in the bowl. Before you fall in love with its color or its pattern, get steely-eyed about its health. Expensive or not, buying an unhealthy fish makes no sense. As you give the koi a good inspection, ask yourself the following questions. If you answer "Yes" to any of them, move on to another fish, tank, or supplier.

- **Does the fish have any rough spots? Do its scales seem to puff out away from the body?**

  Koi whose scales stand out from their body like a bas-relief may be exhibiting *pinecone scale,* a symptom of an overall internal infection, or *enteritis,* which causes such pressure from within that the fish actually bloats, pushing the scales out. This symptom is a very bad sign. (See Chapter 13 for more on this problem, but first, go wash your hands.)

✔ Is it missing part of a fin or part of its tail?

✔ Looking at the overall proportions of the fish, do you notice any stubby parts?

✔ Is its mouth asymmetrical or its snout sharply pointed?

✔ As the fish swims past you, is one side of the body wider or more curved than the other, rendering the fish asymmetrical in appearance? Does the tail curve up or wiggle to one side only?

✔ Are the eyes cloudy or protrude abnormally?

You can also ask the dealer to bag the fish. When it's in the bag, you can examine the koi's mouth, underside, and tail. Signs of infection, such as fuzzy, grayish, or white patches, may appear on the lower aspects of the koi and aren't otherwise easy to see. (See Chapter 13 to find out more about koi illnesses.)

Fish that look healthy may still carry external parasite eggs that won't hatch until conditions are right. Be aware that transferring the fish to a new pond may give these eggs the opening they need to proliferate, particularly if the fish has been in a cool pond and is moved to your warmer pond. This problem doesn't mean you bought an unhealthy fish or that the vendor's a crook. No treatment kills external parasite eggs. For the treatment of parasites and other koi problems, check out the details in Chapter 13.

Best bets for the indecisive: Advice from yours truly

If you're just starting your koi-keeping hobby, start with a small group of inexpensive, brightly colored koi, the kind you can readily find at garden shops, online, or from a breeder. (Not every fish from a breeder is a champion or even show quality. Breeders are happy to sell these average-Joe fish.)

Even after you're well versed in the hobby, these *canary* koi (so called because they test your knowledge and the survival conditions in your pond) may be all you need to keep you happy. Certainly they place far less strain on your pocketbook than even the cheapest named varieties. And those little generic koi need a place to live, grow, and age as much as their more expensive brethren do. *Note:* The good news — or bad news — is that generic koi usually don't reach the jumbo sizes of the more exotic, line-bred, Japanese koi.

If and when you decide to buy some of the identifiable varieties of koi (see Chapter 2 for these), we recommend that you start with these three:

- ✔ **Kohaku (red and white):** This variety is the most popular koi, particularly in Japan.

- ✔ **Sanke (white with a red and black pattern):** This is the second most popular variety.

- ✔ **Showa (looks like the Sanke, but it's black with a red and white pattern):** The Showa is the surprise koi, the one whose pattern can change as it gets older. People tend to like it because of its unpredictability.

Showa is also most prone to mouth deformities and a bad head shape.

Buying Koi "To Go"

When you buy koi from a distant breeder or vendor, the fish are shipped to you on an agreed-upon date. If you're actually visiting the vendor and want to take the fish home with you, you and the vendor decide the best time for you to return for your bagged fish. Part of the discussion also includes the kind of payment the breeder or vendor desires. Expect to use a credit card or cash, particularly if you're dealing with a vendor who's out of state or in another country.

In the koi world, delay between the purchase and acquisition of your fish is standard operating procedure. The buying of koi is supposed to be a pleasant event for both the buyer and the seller, not just an exchange of money for a fish. Part of the process is a discussion with the breeder or seller about:

- ✔ The koi's present diet

- ✔ How many days the fish will fast before shipment (so their digestive systems are clear and don't gunk up the water in their shipping bag)

- ✔ What happens if the fish get sick before they're shipped

Although these topics sound touchy, they're common topics in the koi-selling business.

Part II
Living with Koi, Inside and Out

The 5th Wave   By Rich Tennant

"Naturally we need to adjust the chemicals, but it seems to be the only thing that relaxes him after work."

In this part . . .

So you've decided koi are for you. What a great decision! This is the part to read before you go out *just to look* at koi. (Are you kidding? That's like *just looking* at the flavors in an ice cream shop!)

The first requirement is a pond, and the info is all here — from selecting a size and shape to choosing the materials and building the pond. Ponds can fit every size budget, yard, and house (yes, you can build your pond inside, and we'll tell you how to do it). This part also has the nitty-gritty on what supplies and pond accessories to check out, how to transport koi, and why quarantining new koi is a fact of life.

Chapter 5

Preparing for Your Koi's Homecoming

. . . .

In This Chapter

▶ Location, location, location: Your koi's new home

▶ Safety first: Quarantine those newbies

▶ Stock up: Readying the nest

▶ Point A to point B: Transporting koi from near or far

▶ The first month: Handling your koi with care

. . . .

Getting ready for your first koi is like waiting for the holidays. You can't wait for the date, but you have so much to do first! This chapter is a step-by-step guide that helps you prepare your koi's first home, lists the supplies you need on Day One, explains how to get little Gill from point A to point B, and then swims you through the release of your new fish into its new digs. Later in the chapter we explain the differences between buying koi from Japan and buying them locally (trust us, you're going to need this info someday) and the details of setting up a quarantine tub (trust us again, you're going to want one of these).

Deciding Where Your Koi Will Live (Temporarily or For Always)

You have a number of options for housing your koi, each with advantages and disadvantages. Following is a brief overview of the most common types of dwelling places; details of establishing the habitats come later in the chapter.

✔ **Aquarium:** An aquarium gives you good visibility of small koi, particularly if the tank is on a waist-high stand. One reason some koi-keepers like to keep their young butterfly koi in a tank is because these koi are such graceful swimmers.

If you go the aquarium route, look for a breeding tank rather than a show tank. Breeding tanks are lower and longer and give your koi a greater swim range. Show tanks are more verti- cally oriented.

Koi can jump (even the little ones) especially when they enter unfamiliar surroundings, so add a cover for the tank. The limited size of an aquarium means it can't be a long-term choice.

✔ **Inside pond:** Indoor ponds offer a better home for your koi than an aquarium tank by providing enough room for your koi to swim. Usually located near a home's entryway or den area, these ponds are attractive accessories in their own right.

Most of these ponds are less than 2 feet deep and include bottom drains, a concealed water spigot, stone seating around the edge (for you, not the fish!), and a small fountain or water- fall for sound.

Even though your indoor pond is shallow, be sure yours is inaccessible to unsupervised children.

✔ **Outside pond:** This pond is the ultimate koi home, offering design options not available to aquariums or most indoor ponds. When properly designed, an outside pond allows you to watch your koi grow to their full size.

Taking Necessary Precautions: Preparing the Quarantine Tub

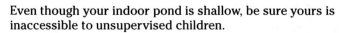

When you buy koi from another koi-keeper or at a local auction, you're tempting fate if you don't quarantine them first. Plan to quarantine the koi before they enter their permanent home (no matter what type of aquarium or pond you have) for these important reasons:

✔ The new koi's immune system can be affected by

- The stress of bagging and transporting.

- Exposure to higher or lower water temperatures.

- Exposure to different pH levels.

✔ Pathogens that normally wouldn't affect your new fish sud- denly proliferate.

Quarantining involves isolating your new fish in their own tub for up to 21 days. During this time you observe them, feed them lightly, and provide a little preventive treatment, even when dis- ease is not apparent. If you live in the north and buy koi in the dead of winter, your new koi spend at least a month in the quarantine pond until your outdoor pond warms up.

Later in this chapter we give you all the details of the process, but in this section we first show you how to prepare the quarantine tub.

You can avoid quarantining if you get your fish from a local dealer who routinely quarantines his fish before he offers them for sale. Just ask the dealer before you buy. You still need to adjust the fish gradually to your pond to avoid temperature and pH shock, but at least you can be reasonably sure that they're healthy.

What you need for the job

The quarantine tub has to be separate from your pond — no shared air hoses, pumps, filters, or nets.

The basic tub can be

- A show tank (a self-standing vinyl tank with a PVC framework about 6 feet wide and 30 inches deep)
- A small, above-ground, vinyl swimming pool
- A big polyethylene stock tank

Deciding what size of tub to use is a juggling act. A large tub is good for large koi and for maintaining relatively stable water chemistry and temperatures. A smaller tub, however, is better for closely observing your koi and medicating an entire tub. Your koi dealer or members of a local koi club can advise you on where to purchase various types of tubs.

Your tub needs the following equipment and materials, most of which you can get from your local pet or pond store:

- Air system consisting of
  - Air pump
  - Airline tubing
  - Airstone (a big one, 12 inches long)
- A bottom drain
- Blue insulation foam (the kind you buy in 4-x-8-foot sheets from home improvement stores)

  You need one piece large enough to fit directly under the tub and enough other sheets to form an insulating jacket around the sides of the tub.

- Dechlorinator/dechloraminator (at least one gallon)

- ✔ Filter

- ✔ Heater

- ✔ Netting (the kind you use to keep birds away from fruit trees)

  The netting keeps the koi from hopping out of the tub.

- ✔ Salt (a couple of pounds non-iodized)

  Kosher salt (available at most supermarkets) makes the best tonic for your koi, helping them deal with minor skin issues and external parasites.

- ✔ Support equipment such as nets, siphons, and buckets

- ✔ Tape (masking and packing or duct tape)

- ✔ Tub thermometer

- ✔ Water pump with a capacity of 240 to 400 gallons per hour

- ✔ Water test kit for ammonia, nitrates, and salt

Along with the necessary equipment, consider spending extra money for the following items to make the maintenance easier for you and the quarantine period easier on your fish:

- ✔ **Add-on bottom drains:** These drains install with a 2-inch PVC pipe over the tub edge. No need to empty the tub one bucket at a time or siphon the good old-fashioned way.

- ✔ **Bead filter:** This filter provides mechanical and biofiltration in one small footprint; cleaning and back flushing are fast and easy.

- ✔ **Salt meter:** This meter eliminates the guesswork in keeping the water at 3 percent salt.

- ✔ **Shop lights:** If the tub is indoors in a windowless area, install shop lights with paired full-spectrum UVA and UVB fluorescent bulbs over the tub. The lights help you see what you're doing, and they help minimize the fading of your koi's colors.

Your usual supplier of pond products has (or can order) the bead filter and salt meter and possibly the other items. If necessary, you can purchase the lights and PVC pipes at most home improvement stores.

Rub-a-dub-dub, setting up the tub

Plan to set up your quarantine tub a few weeks before your new fish arrive. You need this time to install the mechanical parts (air pump, heater [particularly if the pond is outside], water pump, and filter). The new filtration media also need a week or so to acquire the beneficial nitrifying bacteria.

But — before you can do anything — you have to decide where to put the darn tub. If you can protect it from the elements, you may want it beside your house, or you can place it in a basement. Remember to consider these factors:

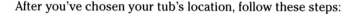

- ✔ You want to be able to work easily with the tub and your fish.

- ✔ The tub needs to be near a source of fresh water because you'll be changing out 20 to 30 percent of the water each day.

- ✔ The discarded water needs to go into your sewer or septic system (It's 3 percent salt, which isn't good for lawns or streams.)

After you've chosen your tub's location, follow these steps:

1. **Put a layer of the blue insulation foam directly on the ground or flooring.**

2. **Put the tub on top of the blue foam and add more sections of the foam to form a jacket around the tub. Trim the excess with a serrated knife and use masking tape to temporarily hold the jacket together; use packing tape or duct tape to permanently hold the sections together.**

   The base and jacket help control the tub's water temperature.

3. **Add the bottom drain over the edge and hook the filter up to the drain pipes.**

4. **Add the water pump inline after the filter and place its outflow pipe over the edge of the tub (opposite the drain pipe if possible).**

5. **Fill the tub with water to 6 inches from the upper edge.**

   Use water from your pond for at least part of this fill in order to populate the filter with friendly bacteria (this takes a week or so). Dechlorinate any water that comes from your municipal water supply.

6. **Turn on the pump and make sure all joints are tight.**

7. **Add salt if you're using it.**

8. **Check to make sure the shop light is the right height.**

   The light needs to be low enough to give good light but high enough so you don't crown yourself every time you lean over to look at your koi.

9. **If you're using a heater, turn it on a day or so before you add your koi. Check water temps after three hours of operation and make certain they're within acceptable levels (75–80 degrees).**

Shopping for Initial Supplies

Before you bring your new love(s) to their watery home, be sure you have all the necessary supplies. The following is a quick list to get you started:

- ✔ **Koi food:** Because feeding your fish is so important, we devote a whole chapter (Chapter 11) to navigating the nutrition aisle at your local pet store. Needless to say, you need the chow before your fish makes it out of the bag.

- ✔ **Non-iodized salt:** Keep a couple of pounds of this stuff on hand in addition to the amount for setting up the quarantine tub. (Kosher salt is best.) It's your koi's best tonic in dealing with minor skin issues and external parasites.

- ✔ **A water-testing kit:** You need a kit separate from the one for your quarantine tub so you can check the pond's water levels regularly for nitrites, nitrates, salt, pH, and chlorine. (Yes, you can tote your pond kit back and forth, but we suggest you avoid the hassle.)

- ✔ **Floating koi bowl:** In case you need to examine a koi closely without taking it out of the water, a floating koi bowl allows you to scoop up the fish and confine it within the pond or tank for a short time.

- ✔ **Round koi net:** This net helps you guide koi into the floating bowl.

- ✔ **Sock net:** This narrow net has mesh at each end and a solid portion in the middle. The end of the net is open.

  Helpful for transporting koi when the trip from the bag to the pond is more than a lift and a swing, the net supports the fish's weight during transfers and can immobilize the fish in the water while you examine its face, gill plates, and tail through the mesh. To release the fish, just lower the net, take your hand off the open end, and let your fish swim through.

- ✔ **A gallon of dechlorinator/dechloraminator:** Keep a gallon on hand in addition to the amount for the tub and pond setup.

Just as people prepare for their own emergencies, you want to be prepared for your koi's most common illnesses and mishaps. Grab a box of your choosing, label it *Koi's First-Aid Kit,* and fill it with the following:

- ✔ **Ammonia remover** to reduce high levels of this toxic waste product

- ✔ **Cotton swabs** to dab medicine onto cuts or fungus

- ✔ **Dechlorinator** to render tap water safe for the koi

- ✔ **Dimilin or Program** (yes, the same product you use on your dog for fleas) for fish lice and anchor worms

- ✔ **Eugenol** to use as a fish anesthetic

- ✔ **Fluke Tabs** or **potassium permanganate** to get rid of flukes on the koi's gills or body

    Fluke Tabs cost more but they're easier to use.

- ✔ **Hydrogen peroxide** to clean wounds and disable potassium permanganate (see previous reference) in the pond if you accidentally use too much

    It's also useful as a temporary aerator if your pond's power goes out.

- ✔ **Microscope with slides and slide covers** to inspect the cells of a sick fish

    Very serviceable microscopes cost less than $250. Look for one with 40x, 100x, and 400x magnification, a built-in light source, and a mechanical stage adaptor that scans the entire smear.

- ✔ **Kosher salt** to treat minor skin injuries

- ✔ **Tweezers** to remove large external parasites

- ✔ **Water test kits** for pH, salinity, ammonia, alkalinity, nitrites, and dissolved oxygen levels

You can find most of these items at your local pet or pond supply store. The fish-related items are also readily available online. Buy microscopes through biological supply houses or online (sometimes you can find a used microscope that'll do the job).

You may already have some of these items from setting up your pond (the salt, dechlorinator, and water test kit, for example). If so, consider yourself ahead of the game. (Pass *Go!* Collect $200.)

Getting Your Koi Home

Of course you'll be anxious to get your first koi home in a hurry. However, the process is quite important and requires some forethought on your part to help your fish arrive safely.

Bringing home local koi

When you buy from your local garden shop or breeder, you get instant gratification — simply pick out the koi you like and take them home.

No matter where you buy the fish, the process is the same:

1. **Small koi (less than 6 inches long) are netted out directly and bagged. Larger koi are urged into a show bowl with a koi net; the bowl and contents are then poured into a large plastic bag at the surface of the pond or bin.**

   The dealer adds enough water to fully cover the body of the fish.

2. **Usually the dealer tops off the bag with compressed oxygen and closes it with a rubber band.**

3. **He places the plastic bag(s) in paper bags to provide at least partial darkness.**

   This darkness helps reduce the stress that the koi experience during transport. The dealer may provide a box to prevent the bags from rolling about during transport, but bring your own just to be safe (a Styrofoam cooler works well). You can also pack newspaper around the bags to cushion the fish and help prevent excess movement.

Keep the bags cool on your way home because the small amount of water in the bags can heat up quickly. The best way to keep the bags cool is to pack them in a Styrofoam or plastic cooler. Ice isn't necessary, but do include a container of cold water if you're using public transportation during particularly hot weather.

Shipping your koi

If you purchase koi from a source that's not local (whether it's Japan — lucky you! — or another state), you may need to have the fish shipped.

Booking the flight

Be forewarned: Expect to pay at least $100 in air freight/cargo charges (domestic flights). These charges are based on volume or weight (which ever is greater), and koi-plus-water can be heavy. Also keep the following warnings in mind when booking your fish's flight home:

- ✔ **Oversea fish must enter the United States at a port of entry.** These are in major transport hubs such as Los Angeles, Miami, and Chicago.

- ✔ **Be mindful of the flight time.** When you or another person books the flight, make sure the fish are on the shortest, most direct flight possible.

The on-ground time is actually the most stressful. As the cargo bin doors open, the outside temperature rushes in. Shipments with a connecting flight must spend transfer time on the tarmac, where they're exposed to local temperatures.

✔ **Avoid dangerous weather scenarios.** Check the weather forecast at the originating site, at the final destination, and at any intermediate sites for the flight.

Don't plan to ship when snow storms are expected or when temperatures may be over 90 degrees. Even if the airline accepts your shipment, you're still subjecting your koi to temperature extremes that are beyond unhealthy. Do your own weather research.

Transporting the fish

The good news is that breeders and koi sellers know how to ship koi by air, so you don't have to worry about them goofing up. They also know how to keep track of orders; you don't get a Tancho when you ordered a Bekko.

1. **The seller takes digital photos of each fish before she readies the fish for shipping.**

   The high-end nature of the nishikigoi business generally assures extreme care in shipping details, but mistakes in identification of specific fish do occur (some Kohaku tend to look very much alike). In that case, the breeder has the responsibility of getting the correct fish to the correct buyer (hence the digital photos as a sort of verifying measure). If a mistake is made, the breeder must make arrangements for selling the koi to a dealer or individual in the United States.

2. **The seller isolates the fish in large show tanks and then places them in large plastic bags.** These bags are like the ones for tropical fish except they're 3 millimeters rather than ¼ millimeter thick.

3. **The seller places the koi-in-a-bag in a cardboard box lined with pieces of Styrofoam and then closes the box flaps.**

4. **At the airport, the breeder or the representative takes care of the paperwork and the koi are loaded into the cargo bin of the jet.**

5. **When the koi arrive at a port of entry in the United States, they're inspected by United States Customs and Fish and Wildlife Service to make certain the shipment and the paperwork match.**

Imported fish also incur the expense of a customshouse broker who makes certain all the paperwork is in order. Check with the local United States Fish and Wildlife Service (800-344-9453) ahead of time about arranging for a broker; practices vary from place to place.

6. **The new owner compares the fish to the digital photos sent by the agent to make sure they're the same fish.**

After You Get Home-Sweet-Home

The process of transporting your fish to your home is one of the most stressful events in a koi's life. But settling into a new home with different water quality and surroundings is another hurdle that the fish faces. Proceed slowly and carefully at this point so you don't add to your koi's stress.

Easing your fish from bag to quarantine tub

When your fish arrive at your nearby airport, either you pick them up from the cargo area or a delivery service (like Delta DASH) brings them to your door. Now that your koi are finally inside your home, you can start to enjoy the rest of the process.

Open the box carefully and lift the bags out. Follow these steps to help your new pal adjust to his temporary abode:

1. **Float the plastic bag(s) on the quarantine tub's surface for 15 minutes while you wait for temperatures to equalize.**

   This time period is reasonably safe, but if you're unsure, do a quick check with a thermometer.

   If the fish are gasping at the top of the bag when you first open the box, open the bags and hold the bags open as they float in the quarantine tub. If the fish stop gasping, you can re-tie the bags. If the water in the bag is very warm, however, you may need to hold the bags open until the temperatures equalize.

   The only reasons for the gasping behavior under these conditions are a pre-existing illness, a lack of oxygen, or over-heating during transport.

   If the fish are lethargic and floating on their sides in the bag, open the bags at once and add some tub water to the plastic bag. Hold the opened plastic bag upright in the

quarantine tub for five minutes for temperature adjustment. Then lift your fish out and release them into the tub.

2. **After 15 minutes, open the bags and check the pH of both
   containers with your water test kit.**

   If the difference between the two waters is greater than 0.2
   (6.9 and 7.3, for instance), add some of the water from the
   quarantine tub to the plastic bags and retest. (You may
   want to enlist someone to help out in this process because
   you need more than two hands to hold the bags open at
   the water's surface as you test and make the necessary
   adjustments.)

3. **At the end of 20 minutes, reach down into the bag, place
   your hands under the fish, gently lift it from the bag, and
   release it into the tub.**

   Your hands must be wet and close to the side of the tub so
   the koi perceive the bulk of the tub as part of the blockade.
   Keep the lift low so the fish lands in the water if it wiggles
   free. Figure 5-1 shows how to correctly hold koi during
   the move.

A fish's slimey coat protects it from infection and attack by
micro-organisms. Never pick up a fish with a towel or use
anything rough on its skin.

Figure 5-1: How to hold koi.

Don't empty the water from the bag into your quarantine tub. A bit of incidental spillage probably won't cause any problems, but the tub has clean water, and the bag doesn't.

4. **Cover the tub with netting, turn out the lights, and give the fish a couple of hours to adjust.**

Let the quarantine begin!

The majority of koi-keepers who use quarantine feel it's a time for the fish to get used to the new home, a new diet, a new owner, and slightly different but well-controlled water chemistry. To help fish acclimate to the new surroundings, follow this quarantining process:

1. **For the next three weeks, observe the koi.**

   Be sure each fish is feeding (this may take a day or two because the fish are undoubtedly nervous in their new surroundings) and swimming about normally. Be particularly alert for signs of stress, disease, or parasitic infestation (gasping at the surface or rubbing along the sides of the tub). See Chapter 13 for a more complete discussion of koi ailments and treatments.

2. **Make the daily water changes (20 to 30 percent) while keeping the water temperature about 72 degrees; add dechlor after every water change.**

   Koi immune systems are at their peak at a water temperature of 72 degrees, but some pathogens can't function outside of 40 to 60 degrees. Because your new koi's immune system will be stressed by the adjustment to its new home, keep the quarantine temperature at approximately 72 degrees so these pathogens don't take hold.

If disease symptoms appear, you need to do some diagnostics (see Chapter 13) and call on your koi friends or your veterinarian. *Note:* We mention veterinarians second because only a few veterinarians are trained and experienced in koi medicine. When you're feeling your way through a new process, it's reassuring to have someone with experience peer over the edge of your tub and say with delight, "Ah, anchor worms!" At least then you know where to begin your research for treatment.

Having top-notch water conditions in the quarantine tub is crucial for reducing the stress on the fish and providing optimal healing conditions.

Don't switch between your koi pond and your quarantine tub without washing your hands or using Roccal (an inexpensive, noncorrosive, colorless antiseptic for aquaria worldwide). Fish that are already in your pond may carry micro-organisms that, although harmless to healthy, well-adjusted koi, can wreak havoc on stressed koi. Even if you don't have fish in your pond yet, you do have a host of bacteria and other pathogens there, and they can cause illness in koi with compromised immune systems.

Some koi-keepers deliberately stress fish under quarantine by

1. **Gradually decreasing the water temperature to 60 degrees for three days.**
2. **Gradually increasing the water temperature to 75 to 80 degrees.**
3. **Holding the water at that temperature for three days.**

If pathogens are present, they almost certainly become active during one of the temperature fluctuations, and the koi-keeper can then treat the disease. Salting is usually enough of a treatment.

Other koi-keepers routinely add MelaFix to the tub per the manufacturer's recommended dosage and skip any temperature manipulation. (MelaFix is an antibacterial extract that you can purchase at most pet or pond supply stores.)

Transferring koi into the aquarium or pond

Your pond is in. You've manicured the setting and prepared the water. (We're assuming you skipped ahead to read Chapters 6 through 8 before bringing home your koi!) You've also spent considerable time sitting on the deck overlooking your koi-palace-to-be. You're ready.

When you're confident that your new koi are healthy at the end of their three-week quarantine, you can finally introduce your royal swimmers to their aquatic castle.

Koi can go directly from quarantine tub to pond if the pH values and temperatures are close (0.2 range for pH, 5 degrees for temperature).

If you're using an outside pond, keep in mind that the water must be 70 degrees or higher. Adding a new fish to a too-cold pond shuts down the fish's immune system exactly when he needs it the most. If the water isn't warm enough, leave your koi in its quarantine tub until warmer weather arrives.

The pond temperature is likely to be different from your quarantine tub's temperature. Take a few precautions to avoid stressing your fish:

1. **Turn off the heater in the quarantine tub and let the tub reach room temperature overnight.**

   You want less than a 10-degree difference between pond and tub temperatures so your fish aren't shocked.

2. **The next morning, if the tub and pond temperatures are more than 5 degrees apart, you need to bag and float your koi in the pond.**

   • Use your koi net to bowl your koi (take the handle extension off your net if you're inside).

   • Pour the bowl into a waiting and partially submerged poly bag or lift your koi into the bag. You want just enough water in the bag to cover the fish so the bag isn't too heavy. Rubber-band the bag closed and lift the bag out of the tub.

3. **Carry the bag to your aquarium or pond, ease it into the water, and let it float for 20 minutes to equalize the temperatures.**

   Keep an eye on the bag(s). Don't let them heat up in the sun.

4. **Open the bag, lift out your koi, and release it.**

Oh, happy day!

Chapter 6

Planning Your Koi Pond

. . . .

In This Chapter

▶ Thinking through pond problems and options upfront

▶ Choosing your pool materials and shape

▶ Settling on the perfect location for your pond

▶ Filtering out your choices

. . . .

Koi fanciers joke that there are three certainties in life; an outdoor koi pond is one of them. A garden pond adds a whole new dimension to koi-keeping. Only small fish can stay indoors, and as they outgrow their tank, you have to find something to do with them. A pond offers the option of keeping koi long term so you can watch them grow and begin to understand their individual ways. In short, it allows you to make real pets of these fascinating fish. If you're serious about koi and want to give them an enriching environment, then a pond is really the only way to go.

This chapter helps you decide whether a pond is the logical next step for you and, if so, how to plan for one. We discuss the planning process, including where to locate your pond and what options you have for size, style, and materials. (We cover the supplies to run the pond in Chapter 3.) To give you an accurate picture, we also examine the legalities of pool construction as well as the potential problems you may encounter.

Considerations to Toss Around Before You Dig

In making a major decision, it's a good idea to check out all the angles and consider the consequences of that decision. But a koi pond? That's easy enough. It's a simple structure with a simple purpose. How complicated can this choice be?

This section helps you answer that important question by highlighting three potential problems that may affect your choice.

Then we take a look at your existing pond or pool so you can decide whether you can adapt it for your koi.

Avoiding potential problems

Adding a koi pond is much more detailed than simply digging a hole in the ground, putting in water, and allowing the koi to swim to their hearts' content. When you're contemplating a pond, consider two potential problem sources — small children's safety and your neighbors' concerns — before you even start digging.

Safety is key: Small children and small animals

Koi ponds are irresistible to adults *and* children. Who doesn't love those big, friendly fish that come right up to the water's edge at feeding time? Unfortunately, unfenced koi ponds and small children just don't mix. Each year children drown in water as shallow as a few inches, so a pond of any size is a major hazard.

The area around the pond and any protruding rocks can be wet and slick due to algae; both adults and children can easily slip and fall. If the fall results in the person becoming unconscious, a drowning can easily result.

Also consider the dangers for the mentally challenged or physically infirm persons who may gain access to the pond. Although pet dogs and cats are usually sensible around water, tortoises and guinea fowl have been known to drown even in shallow outdoor ponds.

Whether the safety issues are yours or a neighbor's, don't quibble. Add a fence, even if it isn't required, and tell your neighbors why you're doing it. That way you all know you've done what you can to prevent the unmentionable.

Considering your neighbors' concerns

Next-door neighbors have a vested interest in your yard, or they think they do. This attitude is especially true if they have safety concerns (see the previous section). Your neighbor may also be worried that the pond can become a breeding ground for mosquitoes (consider the media attention given to the West Nile Virus).

Occasionally ponds draw raccoons, ducks, or other animals that may annoy neighbors — even loud frog choruses have been a source of complaints. When you tell your neighbors you're thinking about building a koi pond in your yard, you can remind them that the pond will be behind a fence. If the circumstances were reversed, you'd appreciate the heads-up.

Cutting your way through the red tape

If you're seriously considering a koi pond, get ready to jump through some hoops at your city or county municipal building. Before you can break ground, you have to obtain the appropriate permits from your local municipality.

How to acquire the right permits

To ensure that you cover all your bases and don't have any problems with your city or county, you first have to make an important choice:

- ✔ **Hire a contractor to build the pond for you.** One of this person's responsibilities is to obtain all the necessary permits. (Check out Chapter 7 for more info on hiring a contractor.)

- ✔ **Do it yourself.** If you build the pond, you need to acquire all the necessary permits and file the appropriate paperwork.

When going it alone, keep these important steps in mind for acquiring the permits:

1. **Call or e-mail your municipal planning and zoning department and the building department.**

   In some areas, these departments go under different names or their functions are combined. Usually a zoning department is a good place to start. If your city or county has a general help line (for example, 311 in New York City), you can check there for specifics on how to proceed.

   Ask whether your city or county has code restrictions on ponds in general, on their size or depth, and on their placement. (For example, does it need to be set back from property lines? Can it be in the front yard or backyard?) If you need permits, ask what kind and what their costs are.

2. **Keep a log of whom you talk to, the date you talk to that person, and what he says.**

   Keeping track of which department needs which permit can be confusing; when you're talking about a $5,000+ project, you're talking about *real* money.

Dealing with city or county regulations isn't too expensive. Permits are generally based on the estimated cost of the construction, usually $65 to $125 each. Your only real expense is your time, but it's time well spent if you can avoid *cease and desist* orders (*C and Ds*

that your municipality issues in response to projects without permits), expensive fines, and liens. Municipalities can and do play hardball on construction regulations.

Why the permits are important

Getting the appropriate permits (and the ensuing inspections) protects you in three ways:

✔ If someone in your neighborhood decides that she doesn't like the idea of a pond — in your yard or anywhere in the free world — having the necessary permits in your hand saves you a lot of trouble.

✔ The inspections that are part of the process assure everyone that you're building to code. In addition, this built-in safety factor can pretty much guarantee that you won't get electrocuted by your wiring system.

✔ If you decide to sell your house, any construction without a permit (even on something as elegant as a koi pond) can be cause to void a sales contract. It'll also make you look (and feel) like a cheap schmuck.

Your local city or county municipality rep can tell you which permits are required. Typically, you need an electrical permit for your pump and filters and a plumbing permit for water and gas lines. You may or may not need a fencing permit, but a fence is generally a very good idea.

 Some cities suggest that you include a site plan with the permit applications so the issuing officer has a better understanding of the construction. You can sketch this plan out yourself, or you can use a software program (very reasonably priced). The program lets you enter your yard shape and dimension, your pond shape and dimensions, and various design elements. You end up with a printout of your pond and its location in your yard. Very cool.

What if you already have a pond (or pool)?

If you're seriously considering a koi pond for your yard and already have a shallow goldfish pond (or a cement hot tub), you may be in luck. You can probably adapt the goldfish pond to a koi pond by digging it deeper or by adding a larger and deeper pond next to it and knocking out the intervening wall.

Even if your existing pool isn't as large as recommended for koi (6 x 9 feet), you can make a small pool deeper to house at least a few fish.

The real advantage of making a pre-existing shallow pool much deeper (a minimum of 4 feet is recommended) is to keep koi in a relatively small space. Plan to add plumbing for the bottom drain(s) and a raised lip (if the pond doesn't already have a ledge). See Chapter 7 for an illustration of a raised lip.

Can you turn a swimming pool into a koi pond? In a word, yes, but you need to make a few changes. You need to

- Remove the ladder(s) and fill the holes left by the screws
- Give away the container of chlorine
- Round the corners of the pool

(Check out Chapter 7 for instructions on converting a pool into a koi pond.)

Deciding to take it indoors: Knowing what you're taking on

If you're seriously considering an indoor home for your koi, the location of your koi's indoor home is an important but often over-looked consideration. It needs to meet several criteria:

- **The floor below the pond or aquarium must be suitably sturdy.** Even the smallest possible aquarium, 50 gallons, weighs in excess of 600 pounds when filled with water and gravel.

- **If you use an aquarium stand, it must be level and topped by a sheet of cork or foam.** Even minor pressure points can cause a crack to develop.

- **A source of electricity should be close by.** Ideally, the outlet is off to one side so accidental spills can't touch it.

- **You must allow space for your filter.** Otherwise, you're in big trouble.

- **Your koi's home should be in a quiet location away from windows.**

  Fish may react to water-borne vibrations from televisions and slamming doors. Consider also whether the noise from the filter may disturb your home's residents; plan accordingly.

  Sunlight through windows can foster the growth of algae and raise water temperatures in a nearby aquarium or pond.

- **You may need flood insurance.** Considering the damage that the water from a 200-gallon tank can cause, flood insurance may be a wise choice.

Planning for weather changes with an outdoor pond

A pond heater and cover can keep your koi at least marginally active during cold weather. You can buy the parts separately and install them yourself, or you can purchase self-contained units that hold the gas boiler, circulator, expansion tank, temperature control, and temperature sensor all in one. You may want to retrofit one of these units into your current filtration system, but consider adding a single custom-built unit to take care of UV sterilization, filtration, and heat. It may be well worth your time and money.

In the heat of summer, you can cool a pond with water movement, a waterfall, a water fountain, or trickling water down a flume (add bog plants to a flume to take up nitrates). As the water moves and is exposed to air, evaporative cooling takes place.

Looking at Your Pond Options

When planning your koi pond, you have many options. However, the three most common types of designs are concrete-block wall ponds, liner-alone ponds, and concrete-block walls with liner. This section looks more closely at these three types to help you decide which one is right for you and your koi. After you decide, check out Chapter 7 for the building specifics on these ponds.

Choosing your material

Koi ponds have come a long way since the first mud ponds in Japan, and you need to decide from the beginning whether you want a concrete pond or a liner pond.

Concrete ponds

Concrete ponds are a serious investment, but many koi-keepers feel that the advantages more than offset the extra cost. Consider the following pluses:

- Largely a one-time expense
- Instantly beautiful; small additions (such as a marble, tile, slate, or brick pond edge) make them even more visually appealing
- Durable (can't be punctured by the weight of the water pushing against stones or buried sticks); cracks can be patched

Because concrete ponds are rigid systems, they have to be strong enough to deal with frost heaves and mobile soils (like sugar sand or clay). You can't scrimp with a concrete pond, so you'll want to budget for the raw materials (the concrete and rebar) from the start. In cold climates, the concrete needs to be at least 6 inches thick and reinforced with wire mesh and rods.

Taking a long-range view, you can transform your concrete pond into a swimming pool by simply changing the color of the interior coating and switching to a different filtration system. This is a practical alternative if you ever move or decide that you no longer want to take care of koi.

Liner ponds

Liners are made from flexible polyvinyl chloride (PVC). Although the liners are available in several thicknesses, the minimum for pond construction is 20 millimeter, single ply. Be sure that the liner is rated *fish grade* because there are several types of flexible PVC and some are toxic to fish or plants.

In regard to durability, 20 millimeter PVC has a lifetime of approximately 10 years, but 32 millimeter PVC can last 15 to 20 years.

Butyl rubber liners aren't very common in the United States, but they're well worth searching for. Long popular in Europe, butyl rubber liners are 30 millimeters thick, are unaffected by sunlight, and can last 50 years or more. However, butyl rubber can cost up to twice as much as PVC and is more difficult to repair.

Liner ponds are by far the most economical of all pond types because you essentially have no assembly work. Consider these other advantages:

- ✔ Placing a liner takes a bit of work, but it's still faster (and easier!) than building a concrete pond.

- ✔ Liners are usually one piece (which lessens the chance of a leak), but you need to install them carefully to minimize folds and areas of stagnant water, which create *anaerobic pockets*. Fresh, oxygenated water can't circulate to these pockets, so harmful anaerobic bacteria (those that can't live in the presence of oxygen) take hold, causing foul odors and decreasing the water quality.

- ✔ Although sunlight hastens the breakdown of a liner, the liner membrane isn't typically exposed to sunlight.

- ✔ If the liner springs a leak, you may be able to patch it or drain it and lay a new liner atop the old one.

Liners do have a downside: Over time, the surrounding ground tends to shift, causing the liner to shift as well. Those neat vertical sides become a bit less vertical. Although this sagging isn't obvious to non-koi people, it can drive koi purists nuts. For the second go-round, many owners install liners over rigid concrete walls. These second ponds are almost always bigger and (sigh) better.

Concrete ponds with a liner

Concrete ponds with liners have concrete block walls. The walls and the pond's bottom (which isn't concrete) are covered by a liner. These ponds combine the beneficial features of both liner ponds and concrete ponds and fall somewhere in between in terms of expense and difficulty of installation.

A good design now makes a difference down the road

As with most endeavors, building a koi pond properly from the start is easier than fixing problems later on, so consider your options carefully before beginning. Lay out several shapes with a garden hose, and view them from all possible angles (including your home's windows) that may face the area.

Consider also the depth of your interests — if you know you're a fish fanatic, then you may as well build the largest pond within your means. If you tend to lose interest in hobbies rapidly, then a simple pond may be your best bet.

Before buying materials, consider such points as your soil and your yard's slope. Will rocks or roots limit your pond's depth? Does the slope favor one shape over another?

Why pond depth is important

Koi are big fish. They need to swim not only forward but also up and down in varying depths of water. A pond that's at least 4 feet deep provides the vertical range of motion they need. The depth also helps stymie potential predators, such as long-necked blue herons and grabby raccoons.

A deeper pond also has a more stable temperature. It stays cooler in summer and warmer in winter (this is important if you're in the northern latitudes and plan on heating your pond). A 6- to 8-foot depth is the maximum that you — and your koi — will ever need.

Selecting the appropriate size

The wider the koi pond, the more koi you can put in it. However, you need to consider practical upper and lower limits before you decide on the size of your pond.

The smallest pond with enough space for growing koi (and they all grow from 3 to 6 inches a year) is about 6 feet wide, 9 feet long, and 4 feet deep. A pond this size holds just over 1,600 gallons, which just happens to be your target gallon figure. *Note:* Although you can say your pond holds 1,600 gallons in discussions with other people, koi-keepers modestly round the size of their ponds to the nearest 500 gallons. So in conversations with other koi-keepers, your pond holds 1,500 gallons.

How do you know how many gallons fit into any given pond? Follow these calculations:

1. **Determine the rough dimensions of your pond.**

2. **Multiply the length times the width times the depth.**

3. **Multiply that total number times 7.48 (the number of gallons in a cubic foot of water).**

For example, a pond with a water area of 8 feet x 7 feet x 4 feet is 224 cubic feet. When you multiply 224 by 7.48, you know the pond can hold 1,675 gallons.

Be sure you fill the pond to the actual depth that you figured. Most ponds have about 6 inches of *freeboard* (the distance between the water's surface and the top edge of the pond), so a 4-foot-deep pond may only have 3½ feet of water.

The shape of the pond affects the formula you use to figure the number of gallons the pond holds. For example, a circular pond uses the area of a circle ($\pi \times$ radius, squared) multiplied by the depth, multiplied by 7.48. So, for a 4-foot-deep circular pond with a 10-foot diameter, the formula is

$$\text{Gallons} = (3.14 \times 5)^2 \times 4 \times 7.48$$
$$= 246.49 \times 4 \times 7.48$$
$$= 7,374$$

Opting for a simple shape

Carefully consider the shape of your new pond. The KISS principle (Keep It Simple, Sweetie) can help — not because of your pond's feng shui but because of the water movement. The more convoluted, dumbbell-like the shape, the less efficient the water circulation and your filter will be. On a day to day basis, you can more easily determine whether your pond is chemically balanced when it has a simple design.

For filtration efficiency, the simplest and most efficient pond shape is round with a funnel-like bottom leading to the filter drain. However, this isn't very attractive. After your friends realize that the pond resembles a simple funnel, you'll never hear the end of the jokes. Nevertheless, you can build a gorgeous, efficient koi pond and still incorporate the design elements that make a round pool so workable.

If you're happy with plain-Jane aesthetics and ease of care, another good shape is a simple rectangular or oblong pond. This shape is easy to keep clean because

✔ It's big enough to locate two filter drains along the midline.

✔ You can angle the water returns to nudge crud such as fish waste and dead leaves to the center of the pond.

✔ The pond has no dead areas (poor water circulation) because nothing stops the water from flowing.

Where to Dig Your Pond — Location, Location, Location

If you decide to build a pond, place it where you can enjoy it the most. Most people prefer a tranquil place in their backyard so they can easily view it from a window or back porch. Other people take pond visibility to heart and place their pond both indoors and outdoors (see Chapter 10 for more info on this variation).

Keep in mind the following potential locations when determining the perfect place for your pond:

✔ **In the full sun:** A pond in full sun is heaven for algae, so you need to pay attention to the filtration system and the UV sterilizer. Your pond design should incorporate some rocky overhangs or other shaded spots for the koi because they need shade, too. A cloth- or vine-covered pergola over one end can provide a respite for koi and koi watchers.

✔ **Under a tree:** A pond beneath a tree is going to have pH and leaf or pine-needle challenges. The leaves fall into the pond and start to rot, causing the pH to become acidic. A good pond skimmer that has a pump and filter media can catch some of the leaves, but you still need to net leaves daily.

✔ **Next to trees:** Trees next to a pond present another problem. Tree roots can tilt sidewalks, pierce pond liners, and crack a cement pool. (Yes, you can patch liners and seal cracks in a cement pond yourself; see Chapter 9.)

✔ **Next to a house or garage:** A pond that's under the edge of the roof overhang (where rain can fall into the pond) has a dramatic spike in pH after a rainfall. You need to monitor the pH. (You can buy an easy kit for this, or you can buy a pH pen. See Chapter 9 for more on this tool.) Count on changing 10 percent of the water after a heavy rainstorm to keep the pH where koi like it (about 6.8 to 7.7).

✔ **Near your neighbor's yard:** If your neighbor raises prize-winning roses and frequently uses spray insecticides and fertilizers, you may want to rethink placing your pond next to her yard. Place your pond at least 4 feet from a property line so it's beyond the range of any incidental fertilizer or insecticide spraying. You can also check the direction of the prevailing wind (if there is one) and then locate your pond so your neighbor is normally downwind.

Finding the Right Filtration System

Unless you have a natural stream flowing through your yard, you need a good filtration system to keep koi alive and healthy. Filtration isn't just an aesthetic consideration — it's also a necessity for maintaining the water quality your fish need. The movement of water returning to the pond from the filter also disturbs the water's surface, causing its oxygen content to rise. Fish in poorly oxygenated waters rapidly become stressed and die.

Koi are large, active fish that produce copious amounts of waste and use up lots of oxygen. Ideally your pump and filter need to process the total volume of the pond at least once every two hours. *Natural* systems (ones that rely on plants for oxygen and snails to recycle waste products) are doomed to failure unless you maintain very small fish in very large ponds.

This section looks more closely at the importance of a filtration system in your koi pond and points out the critical elements of a good system.

How a filtration system works

A filtration system for koi is mechanical (straining out the solid and semisolid matter from the water) and biological (removing the dissolved ammonia and other chemicals that fish excrete). The system works in tandem with the pond skimmer, which removes leaves and pond scum. As the filtration system pulls water from the bottom of the pond, the skimmer pulls water from the pond's surface.

Pond filters are either above-ground units or gravity-fed units below the surface of the pond.

- **Above-ground filters:** These filters (about the size of a garbage can) are single or multiple units that sit directly on the ground, adjacent to the pond. They're fed by a water pump that pulls water from the pond via a flexible rubber or PVC pipe. (You'll need to dig a trench from the pond's external drain pipes to the filter and construct a brick or stone-lined pit in that trench for the water pump.)

  Although the pumps for the above-ground filters are submersible and you can conceivably place them in the pond, you don't really want to do that. A pump outside of the pond is infinitely easier to service or replace if a problem occurs.

- **Gravity-fed filters:** These pond filters must be lower than the surface of the pond. Usually these filters are three separate chambers in a brick- or concrete-block-lined pit that's adjacent to the pond. The water pump is located between the last chamber and the pond, taking the clean water from the filter and pushing it back into the pond. These pumps use less power than pumps for the above-ground filters, so they're also more popular with koi owners.

Regardless of which filtration system you use, you can decide where and how the water re-enters the pond. Some people direct the water through a waterfall, through a shallow plant bog with watercress or other plants that consume the nitrates, or through directionalized outlets. (Bonus on the outlets: Some koi like swimming against the currents that the outlets set up.)

The next two sections introduce the two basic types of filtration systems.

Standard filter system

This traditional filter system (see Figure 6-1) divides the mechanical and biological filtration components. The filter may have either two mechanical and two biological components, or three mechanical and one biological component. The mechanical component consists of two chambers:

✔ The settlement chamber pulls in pond water so solids and semisolids can settle to the bottom.

✔ The second chamber pulls the first-stage clean water from the top of the settlement chamber and strains smaller solid pieces of waste via interlocked brushes or a series of fiber mats.

In the third or fourth unit (a biological filter), convoluted plastic balls or PVC turnings provide surface area for *aerobic* (friendly) bacteria. These bacteria require an oxygen-rich environment, which the movement of water over the plastic or PVC material provides. (Aerobic bacteria are a critical part of the filtration process because they consume ammonia and nitrites in the water and convert them to less toxic nitrates.)

The clean water that emerges from the biological filter goes through the water pump and back into the pond.

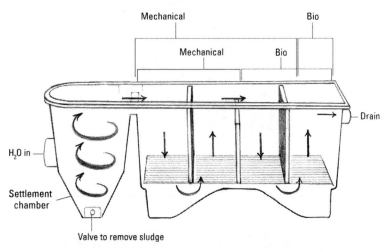

Figure 6-1: A standard pond filter, with mechanical and biological filtration components.

The bead filter

The bead filter combines both mechanical and biological functions in a single, undivided unit (see Figure 6-2). This filter pulls water into a chamber that's half-filled with floating plastic media bits (or beads) that provide surface area for the growth of friendly bacteria. As the water travels through the beads, the solid and semisolid materials are filtered out. At the same time, the bacteria convert the ammonia and nitrite to nitrate. The clean water is then channeled to the pump for return to the pond.

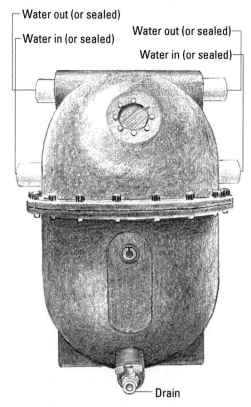

Water out (or sealed)

Water in (or sealed)

Water out (or sealed)

Water in (or sealed)

Drain

Figure 6-2: A bead filter.

Choosing the right features for your system

Your filter subsystem needs to be large enough to circulate and clean the pond water at least once every two hours. A 1,500-gallon pond needs a filter with a 750-gallon-per-hour (gph) capacity, but you won't be sorry if you buy one with a 1,500 gph capacity. The more often the water is circulated through the filter, the cleaner it is — both mechanically (more debris removed from the water) and biologically (more chances for the beneficial bacteria to break down nitrogenous wastes).

Larger filters are, of necessity, powered by stronger pumps, which in turn cause greater turbulence as the water is returned to the pool, allowing more oxygen to mix in with the water. This feature is an important consideration for large, active fish — most especially during the summer when the warm water holds less oxygen than cold water does. Plan to install an appropriately large filtration system when you set up your pond, even if the koi are small. If all goes well, they'll grow and may soon over-tax a small system.

When you're comparing filters, check out the surface area of the *biofilter,* the section that acts as home to the aerobic bacteria. Because this component needs a lot of surface area to make the water clean, you'll find the better filters generally have more surface area.

You can also purchase some add-ons to a basic filter system, all of which make your koi more comfortable and ease your work and worry load. Some extras include the following:

- ✔ **UV sterilizer:** This add-on between the filter/water pump and the outflow pipes is a self-contained unit that uses UV light to kill single-celled organisms like algae and protozoans in the water. (The filter can't get these because they're too small.) Eliminating these plant forms avoids the pea-soup syndrome.

- ✔ **Pond heater:** For ponds in northern climes, consider adding a pond heater. Koi can overwinter in northern areas like Detroit, but their survival factor goes way down if your pond isn't deep enough or if the weather warms and then takes another nose dive. Unless you heat your pond, expect to lose a few koi at the end of every cold season. A gas- or electricity-powered heater is plumbed between the filter and the pond.

Don't spend your money on an all-in-one pump and filter that sits on the floor of the pond and plugs into a nearby electrical outlet. These units may be okay for a garden pond, but they're awful for koi because

- ✔ They don't have much cleaning capacity.

- ✔ The filter material quickly clogs.

- ✔ You have to remove them from the pond and disassemble them in order to clean them.

- ✔ Hoisting the water-and-sludge-filled filter out of the pond and then hosing off the components is a wet and messy chore.

- ✔ A submerged electrical pump is a short waiting to happen.

The cost factor: What does a pump cost to run?

When figuring out which filtration system to purchase, you also want to consider the cost of running the system. And because the pump needs to run all year, your costs also run 24/7/365.

To figure the cost to run a pump, follow these steps:

1. **Note the number of watts the pump uses.**

   For example, a pump can use 350 watts per hour.

2. **Divide the watts by 1,000 to determine the kilowatts.**

   For this example, divide 350 by 1,000 to get 0.35 kilowatts per hour.

3. **Take the number of hours in a year (365 days times 24 hours) to figure out how many kilowatts your pump uses in a year.**

   For this example, $0.35 \times 8,760$ hours = 3,066 kilowatt hours.

4. **Take what you pay for a kilowatt.**

   Check on your energy bill. If you can't find the info, call your electric or gas company. In 2005, the national average was 9.44 cents per kilowatt per hour.

5. **Multiply the cost of kilowatts per hour by the number of kilowatt hours your pump uses per year to find the true cost to run your pump.**

   For this example, you pay 9.5 cents $\times$ 3,066 or $291.27 per year to run the pump.

Chapter 7

Building Your Pond

*I*f you want to build a koi pond in your yard, you have many decisions to make. The first and foremost decision: Are you going to build this pond yourself or hire a professional to do it for you? If you're considering hiring a contractor to do the dirty work, you want to make sure you find one who knows his stuff (more on that later in this chapter).

After you decide on the builder, you need to figure out which type of pond you want to build because the type of pond greatly affects the types of building materials you choose. But where to start? (If you haven't read Chapter 6, you may want to check it out now to get the big picture on planning.)

Don't worry. Take your time and try to enjoy the process. This chapter reviews some of the more common construction methods and gives you the good and bad points of each type. We also walk you through the three different types of pond constructions: with a liner, with a liner and concrete-block walls, or simply with concrete blocks.

This chapter also tells you how to complete the pond with a filter system, lighting, skimmers, and other components. Finally, we help you avoid problems as your new pond settles in.

Who Will Dig (And Build) Your Pond?

Building a pond isn't a decision to be taken lightly. Your first major step is to make the all-important decision of whether to build the pond yourself or hire a professional contractor.

If this is your first koi pond, discuss your plans with other koi fanciers before you turn a single shovelful of dirt or call a single contractor. This move will save you a lot of grief. Other koi keepers are very willing to share their *been there, done that* experiences.

This section covers the pros and cons of building the pond yourself compared to hiring a professional. If you do decide to hire a professional, this section helps you ask the right questions.

Doing it yourself

If you have the skills, you can certainly dig and build your own pond. You may need a few friends to help because it's definitely hard work.

Knowing what you're getting yourself into

Digging and building your own pond is physically hard work. You have to deal with many issues and situations, including:

✔ **Lifting the (heavy) dirt:** One of the first problems is how to lift the dirt out of the future pond area without crushing one of the dirt sides. If you do decide to go this route, you can create a ledge to help keep the sides from crushing — see Figure 7-1.

✔ **Removing the dirt:** After you dig the dirt from the pond, what are you going to do with it? You'll have way too much to scatter into your lawn or dump into *raised* flower beds; you'd have the only 7-foot chrysanthemum bed in town!

You may be able to run a classified ad offering free dirt and find someone who can use it. As a last resort, you can haul off the dirt and dump it in a landfill — for a fee.

✔ **Digging trenches for the filter pipes and (maybe) a site for the filter:** You'll need to dig trenches for the filter pipes, and a pit for the pump (for an above-ground filtration system) or a larger pit to contain the filter and pump (for a gravity-fed system). All of the pits will need to be brick or cement block lined, to avoid cave-ins and for access.

✔ **Walling in the pond:** You can use a liner, or go for the more solid approach of concrete blocks.

> ✔ **Finishing the pond edge:** You'll be adding capstones or a raised lip at the edge of the pond.
>
> ✔ **Installing and hooking up the filter system:** This is where the rubber will meet the road for the success of your pond.

At this point we can understand if the idea of building your own pond is beginning to sound less like fun and more like work.

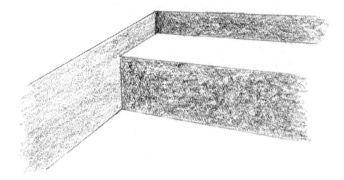

Figure 7-1: Creating a step while digging to avoid crushing the pond's sides.

Hiring workers to help with the dirty work

Hiring out the digging may help. You can hire someone with a backhoe and include dirt disposal as part of the deal. That part of the task is then done, quite likely in less time than it would have taken you and three of your best friends — or ex-best friends.

Even if you do take on the actual construction of your pond, you may want to hire out parts of the job. This includes a fiberglass installer or a pump service that gets your ready-mix concrete into your backyard, or a masseur who makes house calls.

Hiring a professional for the entire project

You may decide to hire a koi pond construction firm to handle the entire project. With this arrangement, you're involved in the site selection and pond design. The contractor does the rest. The cost of your pond increases with the more experts you bring onboard. But money well spent at this point can save you dollars and huge headaches down the road. Remember, you only have to do it right once . . . until you want a larger pond.

Finding a reputable contractor

If you decide to hire out the construction of the entire pond, make sure you find a reputable contractor. Ask the following people for advice:

- ✔ **Your koi friends:** Ask them about contractors they can recommend and about construction issues that have come up in their own pond projects.

- ✔ **Folks you find in the phone book or online:** Set up your own query system. Look in the yellow pages of your phone book. Go online and type in **pond contractors** and your zip code. Ask your friends and neighbors if they know of any pond contractors, or if they know of someone who might know of a contractor.

Asking the right questions

To find out whether a contractor is the right one, start with the right questions. You can discover a lot about the prospective contractors with these questions:

- ✔ **How many koi ponds have you built?** Ask specifically about past projects. Individuals who build garden ponds or swimming pools may not know how a koi pond is different, and you need to find this out. A koi pond requires a different drainage system, filtration system, and pump than a garden pond or a swimming pool (check out Chapter 6 for more information on these essentials). A builder who assures you that "3 feet is plenty deep enough" is not going to be the builder of your dreams.

- ✔ **How many years have you been building koi ponds?** If he hesitates and does that sideways-shift-of-the-eyes thing, brace yourself. This guy knows koi ponds like you know early Sanskrit.

- ✔ **Are you comfortable telling me about problems you've had in building koi ponds?** An honest construction person, one who is comfortable with his (or her) own abilities may start to laugh at this question, and then proceed to tell you about the huge rocks in the excavation site, the early snowfall/ enormous rainstorm, or the middle-of-the-project design changes. Understand that unavoidable/unforeseen problems will increase the cost of a pond, so keep some money available for these problems.

- ✔ **Can you provide references from previous koi pond projects?** Make sure you check these references! Talk to people whose ponds were built by each contractor and go look at the ponds. Ask about problems with pea soup syndrome or other water-quality issues (see Chapter 9 for more on these questions).

Closing the deal

After you've chosen one particular contractor, make sure you finalize all the details before you sign the contract. Yes, these are points that the builder and potential pond owner need to agree will be factored into the design.

They include:

- ✔ **The koi pond must have at least one bottom drain for every 16 square feet of bottom area, and the floor of the pond must be tilted down toward the drains.** The tilt ensures detritus that falls to the floor of the pond will be channeled towards the drains and into the filtration system.

- ✔ **The pond must not have a gravel, rock, or sand flooring.** It must have solid, smooth flooring, so there's no spaces for anaerobic bacteria to hide, and so the suction from the filter can pull waste into the drains.

- ✔ **The pond must have vertical walls** with a minimum depth of 4 feet, so the koi can escape predators and for better water temperature control.

- ✔ **An external pump is the only sane choice.** Pumps stop working, and no one relishes the idea of jumping into a koi pond, grabbing a nonworking pump, and lifting it out of the pond (you did turn off the electricity before you jumped in, didn't you?). Pumps last maybe three years, and the financial side of replacing them is painful enough.

You may want to add a clause that holds back the final 10 percent until the pond is operating according to mutually agreed-upon guidelines.

Converting a Swimming Pool into a Koi Pond

If you already own a swimming pool and find you aren't using it much these days, you may be glad to know you can easily revamp it, for not a whole lot of money, into a terrific koi pond. This is the route lots of koi-keepers tend to take.

In order to convert your swimming pool into a koi pond, you need to take the following steps, more or less in the order given:

1. **Drain the pool and remove the ladders.**

   Use waterproof patching putty to fill the holes left by the screws.

2. Round all corners in the pool.

Doing so prevents dead areas of no water circulation and prevents detritus from lining the bottom perimeter of the pond. To round the corners:

- **Add a baffle at a 45-degree angle at each vertical corner.**

    You can use bricks, stacking them on top of each other (see Figure 7-2a). You can also use 1-x-12 boards laid upright against the corners and secured in place with those big blue cement screws (see Figure 7-2b). Waterproof the boards with a thin layer of cement.

- **Add a smaller 45-degree baffle (made from cement) between the bottom perimeter of the pool and the sides.**

3. Change the filtration system and install larger drainpipes.

A swimming-pool filter is a *high head* (meaning high pressure and strong pump), low volume system. A swimming-pool filter can take eight hours to circulate the entire pool, which tells you something about the water quality in the average swimming pool. A good koi-pond filter should circulate the pond capacity every two hours.

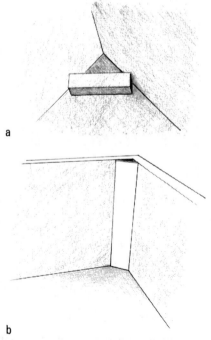

a

b

Figure 7-2: Rounding the corners of a pool.

4. **Change out the drainpipes for 4-inch-diameter pipes.**
   You'll also want to change out the drain units for domed
   drains that can incorporate aeration.

   Changing the drainpipes means literally chipping in a new
   trench for each drain, through the bottom of the pond, in a
   line from the filter to the drain. There's no sense in removing the old drainpipes — they may be sealed in place by
   cement. Place the new PVC pipes into the new trenches.
   Dig a trench on the outside of the pond, next to the wall, so
   you can connect the plumbing to the filter on the far end.

5. **Add a raised lip to the edge of the pool** to avoid ground-
   water intrusion. This includes any kind of runoff water., no
   matter what the source. (See Figure 7-3 for an illustration of
   the components of a raised lip.)

6. **Paint the pool a dark color with an epoxy-like pool liner.**

   You want to paint your empty pool for two reasons: You want
   people to notice your new koi pond and not say, "Oh, you've
   put fish (pause) in your swimming pool (with lowered
   eyebrows and a sideways glance from narrowed eyes)."
   Also, you need to seal the cement (and umpteen years of
   chemicals) away from your fish.

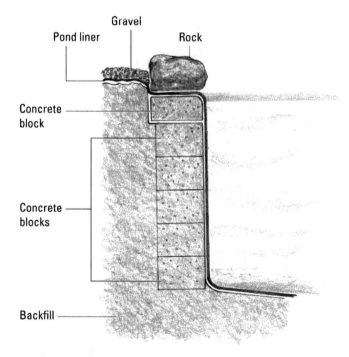

Figure 7-3: A raised lip.

Buy a paint-on or spray-on epoxy paint that's made just for this purpose. You want a product that seals off the cement and has a bit of flexibility so it can serve as a liner, preventing tiny tile and cement cracks from becoming a problem. This is pretty much a specialized product, meaning you will not find it at a paint store or at a home improvement store. Go online and type **epoxy pond liner and sealer** — one brand is called Pond Armor.

Selecting the Building Materials for Your Spanking New Pond

A basic koi pond must be at least 4 feet deep and about 6 feet wide x 9 feet long to afford the minimum swimming area for your growing koi. This size pond holds just over 1,500 gallons (and this is considered a small pond!). Experienced koi experts say a 3,000-gallon pond is as easy to keep as a 1,500-gallon one, but a smaller pond is a lot less intimidating for a beginner. It's also less expensive to build.

Whether you're building a liner-alone pond, a concrete pond, or a concrete and liner pond (check out Chapter 6 for more general info on these three types of ponds), ensure that it's appropriate for your new koi by choosing the right building materials.

First, keep in mind the following general points regarding materials, no matter what type of pond you choose:

✔ The materials used for the pond must be watertight and non-toxic to fish.

✔ The materials must be long lasting; liners are guaranteed for 20 years, and concrete ponds, like diamonds, are forever.

✔ The surface of the pond needs to be even and smooth, so detritus and bacteria can't find a refuge.

To get started, noted that all three pond types need the following general materials:

✔ Large-enough diameter drains and PVC pipes, which bring the water from the pond into the filter.

✔ A filter outflow, which takes the filtered water back into the pond.

✔ A filter and pump, connected inline to the drainpipes and the filter outflow in the pond (depending on the type of filter, the pump is between the filter and the pond or between the filter and the outflow).

The following supplies are specific to a liner-alone pond:

- ✔ You'll need a liner, one large enough to line the entire pond with at least an 18-inch overlap at ground level.

- ✔ The pond dimensions will stay more constant if the liner is, in effect, suspended from a concrete collar or ring at ground level. The collar will take concrete and rebar.

- ✔ You'll need bulkheads for each drain, light, and skimmer that goes through the liner. These bulkheads seal the openings, so no water can ooze through the openings. Water under pressure can be pretty sneaky, working its way into areas you thought would be no problem at all, so a bulkhead is a must for any opening.

You need the following materials for a concrete/cement block pond:

- ✔ Enough concrete for the floor, and enough concrete or concrete and cement blocks for the walls

- ✔ Rebar for the flooring and walls, to strengthen the concrete

The following supplies are specific to a concrete and liner pond:

- ✔ Concrete and rebar for the collar, walls, and floor

- ✔ A liner large enough to line the pond and for an 18-inch rim once the liner is in place

Going with a Liner-Alone Pond

Several types of liners are available in the marketplace, and even the best liners are inexpensive. Look for a liner that is 45 or 60 mils thick. For a small 9-x-6-x-4-foot koi pond, a 45-mil liner costs about $170; a 60-mil liner costs about $285 ("mil," in this case, means thousandths of an inch).

Liners alone work for small ponds 4 feet deep x 6 feet x 9 feet (which is our suggested minimum). The deeper the pond excavation, the greater the chance that the sides will collapse inwards of their own volition as the pond is dug or as the pond fills with water.

Starting with a pond wall ring

You can reduce the chance of a wall collapse and still use a liner for a bigger pond by installing a pond wall ring — also called a pond collar — before you begin digging the pond itself. The pond wall ring is a solid concrete footer (a concrete base that will support a larger heavier structure above it or hanging from it) at the top edge of the pond. The liner is suspended from this ring.

To put in a pond wall ring, take the following steps:

1. **Stake out the shape and dimensions of your pond.**

2. **Dig a trench about a foot wide and 10 inches deep at the outside edge of your soon-to-be pond, all the way around your pond.**

   The actual dimensions of the ring depend on the type of soil you have. (Sand and heavy clay soils require a wider and deeper ring, up to 15 inches wide and 10 inches deep, with rebar added.) This trench becomes your pond wall ring.

3. **Line the pond-side of the trench with 1 x 8s or with 8-inch-wide strips of oiled plywood.**

   Take care to stake the wood so the interior edge of the ring will stay vertical when you pour concrete into the trench.

4. **Add wire braces and rebar to the pond ring trench, with at least two (and preferably three) lengths of rebar throughout the trench.**

   The rebar sits atop the wire braces and ends up in the center of the poured concrete.

5. **Pour or pump the concrete into the pond ring to a depth of 6 inches (10 inches for clay soils, which are notoriously slippery).**

   Figuring out how much concrete you need isn't difficult. A yard of concrete contains 9 cubic feet. Each linear foot of your 12-inch-wide, 6-inch-deep trench takes ½ cubic foot (6 x 12 x 12 inches), so 18 feet of trench requires 1 cubic yard of concrete.

6. **Wait about half an hour and use a *float* (a rectangular trowel, used as a smoothing device) to smooth the top surface.**

   Use an edging tool to round the pond-side edge of the concrete so the edge won't cut or pierce the liner when you install it and pull it up over the edge of the pond ring.

7. **Tamp the poured concrete to collapse any air pockets. Let it set up for 24 to 36 hours before removing the wood.**

   Let the concrete cure for another 36 hours.

At this point, the pond wall ring is about 4 inches below ground surface. Later you'll secure the liner's top edge to this ring and then mortar bricks or concrete blocks on top to create the pond edge.

Excavating and adding the drains

After the pond ring has hardened, you can begin the real fun — digging. You can dig by hand or with a small backhoe.

Drains may seem like a pain to install, but they are a vital part of the system of keeping your pond clean. A good drainage system, coupled with a good filter, means your pond will stay clean with comparatively little work on your part.

Digging trenches for the drainpipes and the drains themselves only has to be done once, if you do it right — when else can you get such a payoff?

After you remove the dirt from the pond drain trenches, take the following steps:

1. **Use a round-tipped shovel to round all corners in the pond (at the sides and at the bottom).**

   Use the rounded tip of the shovel to scrape the corners round and remove the scrapings. Rounding the corners makes it easier for the filter returns to set up a circular current in the pond. This helps keep the pond clean., and it also provides a current for the fish to swim against, a bit like those narrow swimming pools that have a strong current to make swimming more work.

2. **Build a wooden bridge across the width of the pond and extend it about 3 feet beyond the edge of the pond at both ends.**

   This bridge becomes your safe access to the pond, enabling you to place the drains and the filter return — and remove any extra dirt — without clambering in and out over the edge.

3. **Place the bottom drains.**

   Center the drain(s) along the long measurement of your pond, each with a 4-foot radius. The filter system in a koi pond is designed to pull detritus in from a 4-foot circle around each drain. That's why you locate the drains at 8-foot intervals.

4. **Once the filters and drains, are in place, add dirt to the floor, starting at the perimeter and working towards the drains.**

   Your goal is to slant the bottom of the pond towards the drains 2 to 6 inches per foot.

5. **Add the *filter outflow*, the pipes that will take clean water from the filter back into the pond.**

Filter outflows can be positioned in several ways. You can send all or part of it through a bog pond next to the koi pond and let it drip from the bog pond into the koi pond. You'll need a big bog pond to effectively treat 750 gallons an hour, or whatever your hourly pump flow might be. To send only part of the filter outflow through a bog pond, use a Y-shaped PVC joint in the filter outflow, and send half to the bog and the other half directly into the pond or into a waterfall that feeds the pond.

To use the full force of the filter outflow to create current in your koi pond, dig carefully under the pond collar and bring the filter outflow into the pond in a corner, right through the 45-degree baffle you put in place (you'll seal around the pipe with Silastic, or you can buy one-piece out-flow pipes that are cast with the mounting plate in place). You can add joints in the PVC piping to create one high and one low outflow.

For a large pond, you can set up two filters, each handling two or more drains and returning the water to the pond via corner outflows as described above, but in opposite cor-ners and directed in opposite directions.

Make sure you dig carefully. With a liner, the fewer bulkheads through the liner, the fewer leaks now and in the future.

Inserting the liner

If you've read the preceeding sections and followed the steps, you've dug your hole, removed most of the dirt, added your drains, and slanted the bottom of your pond. Now you need to insert the liner. Take these steps:

1. **Add a cushion to the bottom of your pond to prevent tree roots from puncturing the liner.**

A liner doesn't have much give when it's held against the earth by 1,500 gallons of water. (That's almost 12,500 pounds!) You need to provident some kind of shield to protect the liner. Install a liner underlayment that's made for this purpose. Cost is about $2.25 a square yard.

2. **Trim the underlayment around the drains.** As you place the underlayment, take care not to step on or trip over the drains. Cut an X over each drain so you can push the under-layment down over the drain; then trim the points off or tuck them under.

3. Unfold the liner and slide it over the pond opening.

Allow the liner to drape down into the pond.

4. Hold the liner so it sags into the pond, but adjust its position so it overlaps the pond on all four sides by about 18 inches.

Let the liner flow down into the pond and keep the edges of the liner out of the pond. You generally need three or four people to help with this step because the liner is big and heavy. You want to stay back from the edge of the pond because you don't want to break the edge of the collar or crumble the side of the pond.

5. After the liner is lowered into the center of the pond, select one person to get into the pond to arrange the liner as it moves down.

This person flattens the folds so the liner lies as flat as possible, while the people above him or her pull and loosen the liner as directed.

6. The person in the pond is the one who will pull the liner taut over the bottom drains and cut the lining for the bulkhead installation over the drains.

Start with a simple "X" in the center of the drain, for positioning of the bulkhead, and then trim off the corners to create a permanent opening in the liner. Screw the bulkhead in place, making certain that the liner is between the two components all the way around the drain. Many people add a rim of sealant such as Silastic before they attach the bulkhead to the drain.

After you've cut and installed the liner around the bottom drains, only minor shifting is now possible. This is where you'll tidy the folds in the corners of the pond, and stretch the liner out over the edge of the pond opening.

7. Once the liner has been linked to the bottom drains, you can begin adding water to the pond, continuing to adjust folds of the liner to create as few deep folds as possible.

Deeper folds become havens for anaerobic bacteria, so go for shallow pleats rather than deep folds.

8. You can install a skimmer at the surface of the water.

Skimmers can be protein skimmers, to take in and filter out surface foam, or they can be surface skimmers, that take in leaves and other solid-surface debris. Either one replaces what you'd do with a long-handled skimmer; the protein skimmer is specifically designed to dispose of surface foam.

Where and how the skimmer is fastened to the pond wall depends on the design of the skimmer. Surface skimmers need to be mounted so the water level hits at the middle of the intake; protein skimmers need to be mounted so the opening is at water level. In either case, with a pond liner, a rigid backing needs to be in place behind the liner so the skimmer can be fastened via a bulkhead to the brace behind the liner.

9. **Pull the liner up over the edge of the pond ring. Using washers and masonry screws, pin the liner in place atop the pond ring.**

10. **Add brick or concrete blocks to the upper edge of the pond, atop the pond ring and liner.**

The top layer of bricks or blocks is called the capstone, and its upper edge should be at least 6 inches above ground level to keep rainwater runoff out of your pond.

Creating a Pond with a Liner and Concrete-Block Walls

For many koi fanciers, the pool of choice has a pond liner that's *propped up* by rigid, concrete-block walls. This version combines some of the economies of the pond liner with the do-it-once-and-forget-it appeal of concrete block. It also permits you to build a sizeable pond for not a lot of money.

Shoveling dirt: Dig time

You begin this pond by digging. Depending on how much work you want to do, you can dig the pond yourself (a lot of work) or with some strong friends (less work, a lot more fun), or you can hire a backhoe operator with a small backhoe. If you want to dig the pond yourself, follow these steps:

1. **Lay out a garden hose on the ground to create your roughly oval or roughly rectangular pond shape or stake out your pond shape and size.**

   You'll build your pond inside these lines.

2. **Start digging.**

   Create a ramp at one end of the pond so you can remove the dirt via a wheelbarrow (you'll need to fill in and tamp down that end of the pond when you finish the excavation), or let the backhoe do the labor.

3. **After the pond has been excavated, the first concrete work will be for a footer that will underlie the walls of the pond.**

   This is much like the pond ring used for the liner-alone pond, but this time, it will be at the bottom of an excavation, not next to it. The footer is poured into a trench around the perimeter down inside the pond. Stakes, string, and a level can help you dig an even trench.

   The footer's depth and width depends on your soil type. The footer must bear the weight of the walls and the pressure of the water. At a minimum, the footer needs to be 12 inches wide and about 8 inches deep. Your concrete supplier can tell you what sort of soil you have in your area and may suggest the dimensions of your footer.

4. **Add wire braces every 2 feet or so along the footer trench.**

5. **Place the rebar atop the wire braces, so when the concrete is poured, the rebar will be in the center of the concrete.**

   Place at least two lengths of rebar and preferably three throughout the trench. The rebar gives extra strength to the footer.

6. **Buy ready-mixed concrete; when the truck delivers it, wheelbarrow it from the street to your pond site.**

   Your cost will be about $100 per cubic yard. You can also mix the concrete yourself, using a small concrete mixer. These rent for about $100 a day.

7. **Pour the concrete into the footer at the bottom of the pond excavation, and move it into the far reaches of the footer with a concrete hoe. Use a float to smooth the concrete and a 2-foot level to make certain the top surface of the footer is essentially level.**

   Having a level footer makes it easier to place level layers of concrete block. After you've troweled or floated the upper surface smooth, you're done — for 24 hours.

8. **Allow the concrete to cure for one day.**

Laying the block walls

Even if you've never laid block before, you can lay your own concrete block (as long as you keep your pond size modest). Just remember two important caveats about using concrete:

✔ **It's hard work.** The blocks weigh 40 pounds each. You may not want to do this by yourself — sharing the workload is a good idea.

✔ **It's not cheap.** The blocks can be expensive. And even though laying your own concrete block is less expensive than hiring a pro, you don't want to make any costly mistakes. If you hire a professional(s) to lay the block and the walls come out wavy, you're not the one who has to fix it. (And yes, knocking apart concrete blocks is harder than concreting them together.)

After you let the footer cure for a day (see the previous section), you're ready to start laying the wall. Stick to these steps:

1. **Use stakes and string to keep your blocks straight.**

2. **Lay the first layer of block on their sides, with the block openings facing into the pond.**

   Your filter intake pipes will thread through these openings without any extra work on your part.

3. **Locate the filter as close as possible to the drain locations.**

   In koi-pond plumbing, the shortest, straightest plumbed path is always the most beautiful.

4. **Use your level to keep the block rows even as you build the walls, tamping the blocks with the heel of your hand or the end of your trowel to settle each into alignment.**

5. **Lock the corners of the pond with alternating blocks from each side, just as you've seen concrete-block houses built.**

6. **Round the corners with bricks or wooden brace (See Figure 7-2).**

7. **To increase the strength of the walls, insert rebar down into the walls as the layers of concrete block build up. Then pump concrete down into the walls to create a solid concrete wall.**

8. **Keep laying the block until the upper edge is about 3 inches above ground level. Stop here; you won't lay more block until the plumbing and liner are in place.**

After the plumbing and the liner are in place, you'll finish the cement work on your pond. For ponds that are almost at ground level, you'll add a layer of capstones — flat cement blocks or cement bricks without openings atop the final level of cement blocks — and pull the liner over this solid layer. You'll use washers and cement screws to hold the liner in place toward the outside edge of this stone layer. Then you'll add another layer of capstone, concealing the liner between the layers.

For ponds that are built up from the ground's surface, perhaps to create a seating edge along the entire perimeter of the pond, or if there are restrictions on how deep a pond can be dug, be certain that your liner will be large enough to reach from the bottom of the pond, up the walls of the pond, to the far edge of the first layer of capstones.

You may need to shore up the walls within the pond pit temporarily with plywood sheets braced with 2 x 4s pounded into the dirt on the floor of the pond for a day or so until the concrete sets.

Aligning the drains

Once the footer and the walls are in place, you're ready to add the bottom drains, but before you begin this phase, you'll be working outside of the pond, installing the plumbing for the filter.

1. **Dig a trench from the pond edge (at the approximate location of each drain) to the filter installation point.**

   Complete this step a day or two after you lay the bricks, just before you remove the wall braces.

2. **Run a length of 3- or 4-inch PVC pipe along each trench.**

   These pipes will pull water from each drain to the filter.

3. **Backfill the walls of the trench with gravel or sand from the excavation, tamping it into place as you add it.**

   You may need to buy gravel or a load of sand if your soil is clay; clay soils can't be used for backfill because they're inherently slippery.

4. **Place the filter drains in the pond floor, equidistant from each other and the sides of the pond and near the external drainpipes you just added.**

   Four- or six-inch drains work well. Because the filter drain units are about a foot high, you'll have to dig down into the dirt floor of the pond to bury the lower 6 inches of the drain unit. Add drain pipes between the drains and the nearest external drainpipe.

5. **As soon as the drainpipes are hooked up, add dirt to the pond bottom until you have a slanted floor, slanting down to the drains at a rate of 2 to 6 inches per foot.**

   When you've completed this step, only the round drain unit top will be exposed.

Adding the liner

Now you're ready to add the liner underlayment, the liner. You'll secure the liner with cement screws and washers and add another layer of capstones . The steps are the same as in a liner-alone pool. Check out "Inserting the liner" earlier in this chapter for the basics about these steps.

The all-concrete-block pond

The all-concrete-block pond uses the same steps as the pond liner with concrete-block walls with two exceptions:

 ✔ The bottom of this pond is poured concrete.

 ✔ The liner is replaced by a paint-on or spray-on coating that seals the block and mortar.

It's possible to build the components of this pond in different orders. The design we describe starts with the hole in the ground and then adds the footer for the walls, the filter outflows, the walls, the bottom drains, and finally the concrete bottom. Other designs will start with a pond excavation, but then will add a poured-concrete bottom then add the walls, install the bottom drains, and finally add a second layer of concrete on the pond bottom.

Base your design in part on

 ✔ Your type of soil

 ✔ The height of your water table

 ✔ How much of your pond will extend above the surface of the ground

Discuss these variables with other individuals who have built koi ponds in your area, a professional pond builder, or even a structural engineer. *Note:* Altering plans *before* you begin to build is really dirt cheap.

To build an all-concrete pond, follow the steps for the liner-with-concrete-block-walls pond (check out "Creating a Pond with a Liner and Concrete-Block Walls" earlier in this chapter) until the walls are installed and you're ready to place the drains. When you reach that point, follow these steps:

1. Rake the dirt on the bottom until you have the 2- to 6-inch per foot slant toward the center of the pond; then place the drains along the central depression.

2. Bury each drain until only 6 inches is above ground level; add a trench from the base of the drain to the nearest external drainpipe.

3. Cut a length of 3- or 4-inch PVC pipe to fit between each drain and its corresponding external drainpipe; then place the pipes in the trenches.

4. Connect the pipes with the drain on one end and the external drainpipe on the other.

5. Fill the trenches with dirt, add the wire braces and rebar at regular intervals along the pond floor, and order the concrete for the pond floor.

   This last step doesn't take a great deal of concrete; a 6-inch-thick floor for a 6-x-9-foot pond only takes 1 cubic yard.

6. Space out the concrete on the pond floor as you dump each bucket.

   This timesaver places the concrete in an almost even layer, thereby minimizing your effort to spread the concrete across the pond floor.

7. Run a bevel between the sides and the pond floor as you trowel the concrete into place on the pond floor, to eliminate the usual 90-degree angle between floor and walls, where debris will collect.

8. Let the concrete floor cure for a day before you walk on it.

9. Once the concrete has cured for a day or two, you'll need to seal it, just as you'd seal the concrete walls of a converted swimming pool. (Concrete is extremely alkaline, and it will affect your water chemistry for years unless you seal it.)

These sealers are not products you can buy at a home improvement stores. They are nontoxic epoxy coatings that you spray, brush or roll on. They are most easily purchased online. The manufacturer may list retail outlets that sell the product, but you have to go online to find the name of the retailer.

Identifying (And Adding) Other Construction Components

Now that you have the pond shell, what's next? You need to install a filter, but is there anything else you really ought to consider? But of course — and Figure 7-4 gives you a quick preview of some of the various components, which we explain in this section.

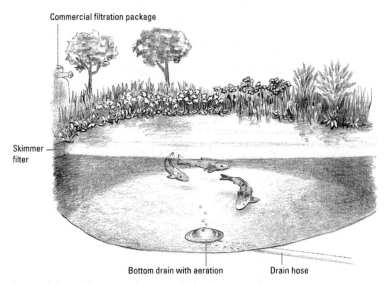

Figure 7-4: A schematic of a completed outdoor pond.

Installing the filtration unit

Chapter 6 discusses the two main options you have when adding a filtration unit to your pond. If you decide to go with an above-ground filter, you need a second trench for the filter outflow. The outflow pipe can be plumbed to

✓ A small waterfall that trickles into the pond

✓ A bog garden that empties into the pond

✓ Returns that you install in the pond corners

If you go with a gravity-fed filter, you need one trench for the PVC pipe that connects the external drainpipes to the first filter unit and another trench for the outflow pipe from the water pump. Like the above-ground filters, the water from the outflow can enter the pond through a waterfall, a bog garden, or outflow pipes in the pond corners.

 Pick a site for your gravity-fed filters adjacent to the pond but not in your line of vision of the pond. Granted, the pond filter area is covered, but when you place it on one side or the other, you're not forced to look at it every time you look at the pond.

Whether you have an above-ground filter or a gravity-fed filter, we offer these guidelines:

- ✔ **For obvious reasons, be sure you buy a water pump or water pumps powerful enough to do the task.** Your pump(s) should have an hourly rate equal to half the capacity of your pond.

- ✔ **Use sweep bends in the PVC pipes rather than right-angle turns to reduce what an aerodynamicist would call the coefficient of drag.** You don't want to slow down the speed of the water in the pipes, for either type of filter.

  For the gravity-fed filter with the pump after the filter, you're paying big bucks for water ejected from the pump at a comparatively high rate of speed. You want to use this speed to set up a current in your pond for your koi to swim against.

  For the above-ground filters, with the pump before the filter, the water flow rate is slower. You don't want to slow it down any more. Even at these slower flow rates, you do not want to create a back flow that will push against the flow of water going through the filter.

Adding lighting

The vast majority of koi ponds do not have underwater lighting. The owners feel that artificial lighting intrudes on the koi, who cannot escape the light. And the fewer electrical components that can go wrong in a pond, the better.

But if you like watching your koi swim at night, add-on lights are self-contained lights that are easily installed in any pond.

Skimmer units, protein and otherwise

The *skimmer* is a small surface-mounted filter system that slurps in
and filters water at the pond's surface. Skimmers are useful for
removing newly fallen leaves, and they're especially helpful if a
tree overhangs your pond. Specialized skimmers that remove dissolved organic compounds along with pond surface debris are
called *protein skimmers* or *foam fractionators*.

Protein skimmers are useful in koi ponds because koi are big fish
that cheerfully and freely produce copious quantities of fish slime,
milt, and other organic compounds. Some of this debris is dissolved in the water in the pond. Like the IRS, you can't see it but
you know it's always there. These floating dissolved organic compounds *(DOCs)* are positively charged at one end and negatively
charged at the other. They appear on the pond's surface as a thin
patch of scum or as persistent water bubbles. The protein skimmer
hooks onto these compounds by pulling water at the pond's surface across a bubble veil. The scum and bubbles coalesce and are
swept into the collection basket, along with other floating debris.

Place your skimmer where a prevailing wind can help push surface
detritus into the unit. If the skimmer is going to be plumbed into
the pump, dig a trench leading to the pump using PVC piping to
attach the two. ***Note:*** Skimmers may be powered by their own
pump, or they may be plumbed into the main water pump.
(For the latter, install a dual valve manifold in the pump intake.)

Turn off your skimmer when you feed your koi — or the skimmer
may end up with the majority of the pellets.

Finishing work

The hard part about finishing work is that you're so near yet so far.
These details are critical to the success of your pond, so keep on
pluggin' away.

Heating

If you decide to heat your pond during the winter, the heater will be

- ✔ Plumbed to the water line exiting the *pump* for gravity-fed filters
- ✔ Plumbed to the water line exiting the *filter* for above-ground
  filters.

A pond heater uses propane or electricity to heat a small boiler,
just like your own hot water heater. Water passes through the
boiler, is heated, and goes back into your pond.

But before we get into a discussion about the finer points of heating your pond, how do you know if you need a heater? Ponds in areas where the nighttime temperatures routinely dip below 60 degrees F need a heater. Pond temps that go below the mid 60s are an open invitation for an Aeromonas outbreak. Aeromonas is, as you see in Chapter 12, called "hole-in-side disease."

How much it costs to heat your pond depends on several factors:

✔ **Your pond size.** A large pond works to your advantage when you heat it up; the larger the body of water, the more heat it retains.

✔ **Your pond shape.** A deeper pond holds heat better than a shallow pond.

✔ **Your pond construction.** A concrete-block pond holds heat better than a liner pond.

✔ **Your pond orientation and exposure to the sun.** Sun heats things up, and even winter's weaker sun is a lot warmer than shade at that time of year. A pond in full sun stays warmer than a shaded or partially shaded pond, but you need to balance this with the more intense sun of summertime.

✔ **Your pond covering (or lack thereof).** A covered pond holds more heat than a pond with its surface area exposed to freezing air. You wouldn't heat a garage and then leave the garage door open, would you? If you need a pond heater, cover your pond.

To apply the coating, follow these steps:

1. **Mix the coating components and apply it with a roller.**

   You can use a paintbrush for smaller areas or places too convoluted for a roller. Texture-wise, it's like painting with thick cream or with one of the thick latex paints designed for basement walls.

2. **After the coating is dry, in two or three days, fill your pond.**

   No need to rinse your pond because the coating is inert, which means there's nothing toxic to seep into the water and from there into your fish's bodies.

   Be sure you read the last section "New Pond Syndrome and What to Do about It" before you let your koi take the plunge.

Coatings come in several colors and as a clear coating. Most koi-keepers use a black coating, which shows off the colors of their koi better. The dark green is also pretty, we think.

Applying fiberglass

An alternate sealant or coating for concrete is fiberglass. This section covers the basics, but if you haven't worked with fiberglass, we suggest you ask a pro because you're working with finely spun glass in a resin base. For example:

✔ The resin cures fairly rapidly, so you don't have much time to work with a mixed batch.

✔ The fiberglass cloth can shed minute fibers, which are very irritating to the skin.

✔ If you don't mix the components correctly, the styrenes can leach out into the pond.

To estimate the amount you need, start with the square footage of the area to be covered — all four walls and the floor of the pond — and add ⅓ more for overlap and irregularities in the surface. One gallon of resin soaks 15 to 20 square feet of mat, the fiberglass "fabric." (It's a bit like using sheets of newspaper and flour paste but a lot more permanent.) A standard small pond, 4 feet deep and 9 x 6 feet, has 174 square feet of surface area. It will need 230 square feet of mat and 15 to 18 gallons of resin.

To apply fiberglass, follow this procedure:

1. **Apply resin with a long-napped roller or a wide paintbrush to a section of the wall or floor of the pond (you'll be doing this in sections).**

2. **Soak a piece of fiberglass fabric or mat with resin by dousing it in the paint tray with the resin. Apply the wetted mat to the wetted wall or floor. Smooth it into place and add resin to cover.**

3. **Soak another mat and place it on the resin-painted wall or pond floor, next to the first. Overlap the edges 1 to 2 inches. Rewet with resin and smooth.**

4. **Continue this process until you've covered the entire pond surface, up to the lower edge of the capstone.**

5. **Sand the nonconcrete components (like the drains and water returns) with a fine-grit sandpaper to create a surface the fiberglass can cling to.**

6. **Soak mat strips in resin and wind them around all projections for a watertight seal.**

7. **After you've applied fiberglass to the entire pond, apply a final *gel-coat* of fiberglass to smooth the entire surface.**

Plan to complete the application of fiberglass in one day so you create a one-piece shell on the inside of the pond. This shell needs to cure for at least a week (up to three weeks in cool weather!) before you wash and rinse the pond. Then the pond is ready for water. Fiberglass comes in clear, green, and black. As a koi keeper, you'll probably want to opt for the black.

New Pond Syndrome and What to Do about It

Before you place your koi into your new pond, you have to make sure the pond is koi-friendly. Although you've followed every suggestion in building your pond, it's not going to be a great place to put your koi — at least, not at first. We offer some suggestions on how you and your koi can get through the adjustment period.

Aging the pond water and the biological filter

Few emotions are happier than building a new pond, having all the equipment installed and working, and, with everything in place, welcoming your koi to their new home.

While your first koi or two swim around, feeding, inspecting the pond, and adding their own personal seal of approval to the waters, your biofilter begins to develop its own population of nitrifying bacteria. Strains of "Oh, happy day . . ." begin to float through the air.

Everything looks perfect, but you can tell something's not right. The water values are just terrible. Although the koi are trying, there are no friendly bacteria in the biofilter, so the filter isn't working as it should. The ammonia level's too high, the nitrite level's too high, and the pH acts like it's on the end of a yo-yo. What's going on?

Any new pond (and its owner) is going to suffer new-pond syndrome as the pond becomes a living organism of its own. The sky-high numbers for ammonia and nitrite and the swinging pH values are absolutely normal, and they usually last about six weeks. But as you already know, *absolutely normal* doesn't mean *good*. That's why you only put a couple of very ordinary koi into a new pond. These are often called canary koi, and they are used as bellwethers. They tell you if things are going as planned with the water chemistry. You hope they survive the process.

What on earth is zeolite, and why do you want it?

Zeolite is an inorganic volcanic-rock derivative that absorbs ammonia. It comes in bags, and some koi keepers replace part of the biofilter media with a mesh bag of zeolite. However, we suggest placing the bag in your filter outflow, or even in your pond, so whatever bacteria you have in your filter can multiply and be fruitful.

Every morning, you haul out the old bag of zeolite and put in a new one, but stop! You can reuse the bags. All you do is renew the zeolite by soaking the bag in a bucket of saltwater overnight. Then, simply rinse and reuse the zeolite bag.

Buy two 20-pound bags of zeolite so you can alternate their use. Soak the used bag in saltwater overnight. Then rinse it the next morning and switch it out for the other bag.

Obviously, you don't want to do this every day for the rest of your life, but it's doable for a week or two as your new pond becomes established. Continue to test your water values daily so you'll know what's going on. After a week, you can check the values twice a week until they drift into the normal range.

You can speed up the pond-maturation process, increase your koi's comfort, and decrease your sleepless nights by trying one or all of the following suggestions:

- Partial water changes help (up to 10 percent of the pond's volume a day).

- Give the filter maturation a boost by adding nitrifying bacteria to the pond (you buy these in little bottles at an aquarium store, or in larger bottles from a pond-supply store or an online pond-supply vendor).

   Some of the bacteria will cling to your pond walls, but most will end up in the filter, which is where you want them.

- Add AmQuel Plus to bind up the ammonia and nitrites or add a temporary chemical filter by using Zeolite.

Chapter 8

Making It Pretty:
Landscaping the Pond

In This Chapter

▶ Planting in the pond despite those misbehavin' koi

▶ Surrounding your pond with complementary landscape

▶ Focusing at night: Pond lighting

▶ Adding those extra touches

▶ Considering your broader options: Patios and decks

*Y*our pond can be the focal point of your yard, but every focal point needs a frame. That's where the landscaping comes in. In this chapter, we deal with the added touches to both the inside of your pond and its perimeter. The goal is to add to your enjoyment of your koi and your pond without adversely affecting their natural balance.

We start where it all begins — in the pond — and work outward from there.

A Habitat Fit for Your Koi: Furnishing Their Digs

Living plants greatly enhance the beauty of an outdoor pond, increase its effectiveness as a functioning habitat, and attract birds, insects, and other wildlife. No matter how focused on koi you may be, at some point you will likely want to try your hand at water gardening as well. This endeavor takes a good deal of care and planning where koi are involved, but it is possible.

Avoiding the holey-plant problem

When you began thinking about a koi pond, maybe you thought it would be a great home for the fish *and* a lavish display of lilies, lotus, and aquatic plants. After all, you see a lot of Japanese paintings with koi enjoying their water lily and lotus surroundings, right?

Ahh, but that's where artistic license comes in. Remember: Japanese paintings are still lifes. If they were videos, the next scene would have the koi turning and ripping a chunk out of the nearest lily pad!

Koi love plants. When they reach a length of 10 inches or so, there's no aquatic plant these finny pigs can say "No" to. Lotus? Yum. Anacharis? Yum, yum. Vallisneria? Soup's on, mate (and it's vegetarian!)!

In fact, just about any of your old favorites from your aquarium or water-garden days are quite high on your koi's greens menu. And if they decide that the leaves are too tough, then your koi head for all the great-tasting, spaghetti-like roots and munch on those.

Not to worry. You have some opportunities to show off your koi and aquatic plants in same setting — you just have to keep them separate.

Fashioning a bog pond

One way to help your koi and plants enjoy a friendly coexistence is by creating separate subponds or bog areas that are about a foot deep. Two methods of creating this separation are

- ✔ **A low berm, or ridge, of soil:** This should be seeded with grasses or other plants, the roots of which will hold the soil in place.

- ✔ **A brick wall:** This need not be watertight, so you can either cement the bricks together or create a more naturalistic structure by fitting stones to form the wall.

These shallow bog areas can go anywhere around your pond, but most pond owners place them near the filter and run one of the filter outflows through the bog. As the water flows through the bog and into the main pond over a lower wall (see Figure 8-1), the bog plants feed on the nitrates from the pond water, and the nitrate levels in the pond decrease. The result? The plants flourish, the pond's water values improve, and the koi environment improves — recycling at its finest!

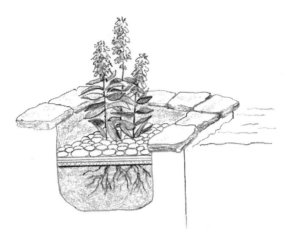

Figure 8-1: A bog pond keeps aquatic plants looking good.

You can find bog plant candidates at almost every garden store or online, and they generally range from 4 to 12 inches in height. Readily available types include those in Table 8-1; Figure 8-2 depicts some of them.

Table 8-1	Common Bog Plants
Common Name	**Botanical Name**
Swamp milkweed	*Asclepias incarnate*
Turtlehead	*Chelone lyonii*
Joe Pye weed	*Eupatorium purpureum*
Chameleon plant	*Houttuynia cordata*
Cardinal flower	*Lobelia cardinalis*
Golden creeping Jenny	*Lysimachia nummularia*
Pitcher plants	*Sarracenia sp.*
Blue-eyed grass	*Sisyrinchium angustifolium*
Spiderwort	*Tradescantia spp.*
Rain lilies	*Zephyranthes candida*

You can also add aquarium plants to your bog area if they're readily available. Two examples are Anacharis and Cabomba fish (give them a slightly deeper bog, if you can).

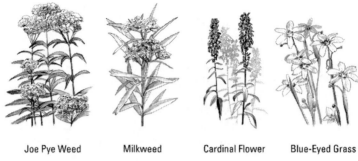

Joe Pye Weed   Milkweed   Cardinal Flower   Blue-Eyed Grass

Figure 8-2: Common bog plants.

Creating koi-proof plant containers

Another way to simultaneously enjoy plants and koi is by *containerizing* the plants in the pond. Several options are possible:

- ✔ **Floating life preservers for small plants:** Put small, live plants into these rigid foam disks (available at garden pond stores) that are about 14 inches across and have four circles cut out. Drop your plants — still in their 4-inch pots — into the holes. The pot rims support the plants, and the unit spins away across the surface of your pond.

  You can easily remove these floating planters if you wish to net out a koi, so they aren't quite the hassle that a heavier terracotta pot or planter can be. The drawback is, of course, that you can't put a very large plant into a 4-inch pot.

- ✔ **Heavy terracotta pots for larger plants:** Place larger plants in these pots and put the pots on a shallow shelf. Ideally, this shelf should be built in during the construction phase. However, temporary shelves can be created using cinder blocks or bricks, positioned so that the pots placed on them will be at or just below the water's surface. Preformed pools with shelves already built in are also available. Koi ignore a planted container or pot if they can't nibble on it, so this is one way you can add papyrus, cattails, iris, and other *emergent species* (plants that root in water but send stems and leaves above the surface) to your pond. Make sure the pot is tall enough so the upper rim is above the water level.

- ✔ **A shallow flowerpot for water lilies:** Plant the bulbs in the pot and add a cylinder of rust-proof wire or plastic mesh just inside the upper edge. The cylinder should be high enough to reach a few inches above the water's surface, effectively *jailing* the water lily.

As the plant grows, the mesh protects the stems while the emergent leaves flop over the top edge of the mesh. The effect will not be completely natural — because the mesh extends above the water's surface, the leaves will not float as they normally do. They will, however, survive and flower.

One downside of potted plants in a koi pond is the lack of water flow in the dead areas near and on the *lee* side (the side that faces away from the filter outflow) of the containers. Another problem is the logistics: You have to move the containers whenever you net out your fish, and like your fish, these plants will grow and the water-filled containers will get heavier and heavier.

A koi purist may feel koi are too magnificent to share a pond, but a lot of koi fanciers like water lilies and lotus enough to make some concessions for them.

Opting for plastic to avoid the hassle

Plastic plants (particularly those with trailing foliage) at the edge of a pond provide shelter and shade for koi fry and a hiding place for large, shy koi that are hesitant to approach during feedings. The plastic plants provide a more-or-less permanent shelter because koi try an exploratory nibble and then give up.

You may have to pull your plastic plants out of the water and let them dry out occasionally if you want to discourage algae from growing on them. Otherwise, plastic plants are maintenance-free.

Stepping over the edge (of your pond)

After the pond has its added attractions, but before you consider the extended landscape, check the edging of your pond. Is it raised 6 inches or so to keep any sort of runoff out of your pond? (See Chapter 7 for ways to build a raised edge during construction.)

Runoff (excessive water along with any chemicals it picks up along the way) can come from your side yard (where your son lovingly washes his car every Saturday morning), from your neighbor's prize-winning camellia garden, or from the street beyond your yard. But no matter where it comes from, runoff is bad for your koi.

If you don't have a raised edge, you can minimize runoff problems from reaching your pond by digging a small trench at those points where runoff enters and burying a black drainage pipe in the trench (a 4-inch diameter pipe will do). Some of these drainage pipes have holes along their length to enhance their draining capacity.

Creating the Landscape of Your Heart's Desire

Koi-keepers tend to go in one of two directions in landscaping their pond. Many of them go the Japanese garden route, and others opt for a more jungle-like environment.

The two popular styles: Japanese and just plain wild

Part of the appeal of a Japanese landscape is its simplicity. It has few elements to detract one's attention from the pond, and this understatement is on purpose. The following list identifies some of the traditional elements that contribute to the overall appearance:

- ✓ The negative spaces are as important as the plantings.
- ✓ Asymmetrically placed plants, paths, and sculptures give a feeling of motion within the contained space.
- ✓ Monochromatic designs of dark green foliage, dark stones, and white gravel and sand invite contemplation.
- ✓ Color is only a temporary accent via blossoms or grasses that change color with the seasons.
- ✓ Plant shapes are enhanced and controlled by pruning with close attention to diagonal, horizontal, and vertical directions.

Other koi-keepers prefer lush greenery over control, and they enjoy an environment that grows with the seasons. They see a wild landscape as a natural backdrop for their koi, a landscape that can take care of itself and leaves the owners with more time to spend with their koi. This approach is, essentially, the opposite of the Japanese garden in all aspects. Plants that are added are allowed to grow as they will, and native plants that establish themselves aren't controlled unless they cause a problem (for example, poison ivy).

Obviously, we can't give you a one-size-fits-all way to deal with a pond landscape. But we can give you some practical guidelines for any style of garden and show you how to play with colors and textures.

Putting fish first and landscape second: Controlling the sunlight

Sunlight is good for plants in the landscape, but direct sun isn't all that good for koi or their ponds. Sunlight triggers algal growth, particularly the unicellular type that turns your pond into *pea soup* (that's a genuine term, as in *pea soup syndrome,* in the koi world). This growth can also make your pond uncomfortably warm for your koi.

Although you can add a UV sterilizer to your filter to minimize algal growth, consider sheltering your entire koi pond or at least part of it from direct sun.

The easiest way to shade your pond is by adding a pergola. Most pergolas have lattice tops that provide some shade, but you can increase the shading by adding shade cloth (see Figure 8-3) that comes in varying colors, densities, and sizes. A typical custom-cut, 12-x-12-foot, 50 percent density, black shade cloth with grommets along the sides costs about $160. Pergolas can be bought or constructed in an enormous array of sizes, shapes, and materials, so it should be simple to find one that suits your particular pond. If overheating or lack of a shady retreat for the koi is your concern, locate the pergola over a section of the pond that gets the most exposure to the afternoon sun.

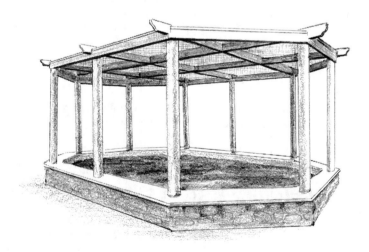

Figure 8-3: A pergola.

Finding plants that suit your fancy

Because your plant selection depends a great deal on where you live — ferns do well in Washington state and Florida, for instance, but not in Arizona — we suggest you shop locally. Of course, your local garden store may spring to mind, but don't forget your neighbors and natural resources.

The advantage of your local garden store for your plants is one-stop shopping. The store is likely to have three or four types of ground-hugging evergreens and other types of plants you're looking for, along with landscape accessories, pond equipment, and, last but not least, a new shipment of koi. (Turn your face resolutely from the bins of koi. This is landscape-project time, not koi-buying time. But look at Chapter 2 if you're wondering what to call those black and white koi, the ones with the really long fins.)

The advantage of plants from your neighbor is that they ought to do okay in your yard as well. And you're likely to find that neighbors enjoy sharing their plants, particularly the ones they've done well with.

You may be able to collect local plants to add texture to your koi landscape. For example:

- ✔ In the Southwest, you may be able to dig and pot nonprotected cacti and succulents.
- ✔ In northwestern and northeastern states, as well as in temperate parts of Europe, you can find some beautiful and tolerant-of-transplanting species such as aroids (philodendrons), Jack-in-the-Pulpits, marsh marigolds, and many ferns.
- ✔ In the Southeast (especially Florida), you can find tropical ferns, bromeliads, honeysuckle, and passion flowers.

Check the applicable laws before collecting any native plants. Many are now fully protected in parts or all of their ranges.

Pond-edge plantings: Balancing heights, textures, and colors

When you begin selecting plantings for the koi pond, think of stair steps — the lower plants next to the pond, the knee-highs a bit farther back, then the waist-high bushes, and finally the trees or a hedge and fencing. You can vary this order a bit, of course, by bringing a taller plant to the pond edge to soften the lines.

After mentally sorting your plants of choice by height, factor in the sunlight. Landscape plantings for a sunlit pond at almost any latitude include the following:

- ✔ At the pond's edge, English ivy or a compact or dwarf sansevieria
- ✔ At knee height, day lilies and zinnias (Crocus, jonquils, and daffodils also work for northern climes.)
- ✔ At waist height, mallows, cannas, and pussy willows
- ✔ As a hedge, shrubs such as boxwood, Japanese garden juniper, and bayberry

Plants that do well with just three or four hours of sun a day include the following:

- ✔ At the pond's edge, woodfern or royal fern
- ✔ At knee height, ragwort or sage
- ✔ At waist height, plantain lily or lady fern
- ✔ As a hedge, azalea or rhododendron

Within this category of partial sun lovers are the many varieties of ornamental grasses. These plants are attractive year-round, acknowledging winter by a color shift in the seed heads or stalks. See Table 8-2 for a listing of popular grasses that can provide varying heights for your pond landscape. Figure 8-4 shows what a few of them look like.

All the ornamental grasses in this list like semimoist gardens, and as a general rule, the taller the grass, the more water it needs. Your local extension agent can advise you on which ornamental grasses work in your area and what invasive species to avoid.

Table 8-2	Varieties of Ornamental Grasses		
Generic Name	*Botanical Name*	*Height*	*Notes*
Variegated bulbous oat	*Arrhenatherum elatius bulbosum*	6 to 12 inches	Grows in white-striped tufts
Velvet grass	*Holcus lanatus*	Up to 12 inches	Soft gray-green foliage

(continued)

Table 8-2 (continued)

Generic Name	Botanical Name	Height	Notes
Autumn moorgrass	*Sesleria autumnalis*	Up to 18 inches	Olive green foliage; bears purplish bloom spikes that last through most of the winter
Morning light	*Miscanthus sinensis*	Up to 6 feet	Narrow leaves edged with white
Bamboo	*Bambusa, Chusquea,* or *Dendrocalamus*	Up to 40 feet	Self-clumping; very slow spreading

Autumn Moorgrass   Bambusa Multiplex   Velvet Grass

Figure 8-4: Various types of grass.

Bamboo has 1,500 varieties to choose from, and their mature size can be as short as 4 inches. Many originated in mountains and are very cold-hardy.

Spreading bamboo propagates by underground runners that pop up anywhere from 2 to 10 feet from the parent plant. Bamboo in the genus *Pleoblastus,* for instance, look great on paper. Some of them stay very small, from 18 inches to 3 feet, and they're hardy to 10 degrees F. But they're runners. If you buy a *Pleoblastus,* confine it in a pot, or you may rue the day you bought the plant.

For ponds in temperate climates, you may choose to have all or most of your plants naturalized and in the ground. But just as you pot some types of bamboo, you can pot other tropical plants to create a beautiful garden during warm months and then move the plants to a protected and warmed indoor spot for the winter months. Tropical beauties such as New Guinea impatiens, various bromeliads, some orchids, peace lilies, and philodendrons can provide immense seasonal beauty to your koi garden.

When you're considering plants for texture and color, plan for groups of like plants that you accent with one or two plants of a different foliage type or foliage color. This uneven balance has more impact than the one-of-these, one-of-those gardens. For textures, use evergreens, grasses, and leafy shrubs; for colors, consider dwarf red maples, hostas, and caladiums.

Setting the Mood with Lighting

Lighting extends the useful time you can spend with your koi, and that's a good thing. By adding light to your deck or patio, you can share a very early breakfast or an evening meal there; accent lights in the koi garden provide additional depth to your night views. But the lights in your koi pond may just please you most because you can see your finny friends as they glide around in the evening. Adding lighting is no big deal, even after your construction and landscape's complete. This section sheds some light on two varieties: submersibles and accent lights.

Lighting up from down below: Submersible lights

Most add-on submersible lighting units are mug-sized black boxes with a light fixture sticking out of the top of each box. Because the lights are wired in sequence, you simply lower the boxes into place and plug in the electrical cord.

Although you have your choice of clear or colored light bulbs, koi-keepers tend to snicker at the colored bulb route. After all, you already own some of the most spectacularly beautiful fish in the world — but hey, if you want colored lights, go ahead.

Turn the pond lights out when you go inside so your koi can sleep. When you can't close your eyes, darkness makes it much easier. (In case you didn't know, koi lie on the bottom of their pond to sleep.)

Lighting your koi from above: Accent lights

Several varieties of accent lights are on the market. Your pond or lighting store should be able to provide you with some ideas for consideration.

The prettiest we've seen are just decorative — not big enough to shed a lot of light. These LED lights sit atop long plastic sticks that you stick in the ground. Their stems light at the top and then wave in the breeze.

Lanterns are another form of accent lighting that seem to fit in every koi garden. They stand alone and are either wired for electricity or literally candle powered. Two examples are

✔ Lanterns that light pathways or serve as exclamation points in the garden (usually 3 feet tall or higher)

✔ *Snow-viewing* lanterns that are placed next to the pond (usually knee high). Much favored in Japanese gardens, snow lanterns, or *yukimidoro,* have a wide roof that collects snow, which is then illuminated by the light chamber below. In warmer seasons, the illuminated lantern casts an interesting mix of light and shadow on the water's surface.

Keep taller plantings away from these lower lanterns so you can enjoy the light and not trip over them.

Adding the Finishing Touches: Garden Accessories

Garden accessories include the statues, benches, and other non-growing elements of the pond landscape. Sometimes the accessories are functional, like the filters disguised as Japanese lanterns, so their location is predetermined. Other accessories, such as statues and gazing balls, are just for fun, so you can place them where you'll enjoy them the most. This short section offers suggestions on two of the larger accessories in your landscape, statues and benches.

Planting a statue

When you're shopping for statues for your koi garden, keep the following suggestions in mind:

✔ The emphasis is on the koi pond and the koi, not the backdrop; keep statuary less than 4 feet tall and soften their impact by adding a few plants beside them.

✔ Select pieces that accent your pond and don't detract from it.

A statue of a small boy kneeling beside the pond with his hand outstretched as if feeding koi is a good accent. A casting of Rodin's *The Kiss* may prove to be a distraction!

Not all statues are created equal in terms of outdoor durability. Look for materials that stand up under outdoor use, such as resin, Durastone (a cementlike product), or bronze. Bronze, as the top of the line, develops a great patina in the koi garden. Unfortunately, the weight of a bronze accessory can make installation a bit of a challenge.

Positioning a bench

Place benches in the shade so you can avoid the direct sunlight and still see your pond. Benches with a back invite sitting more than those without, and two benches that are close to each other make it easier for your friends to join you in admiring your fish.

The all-metal styles are attractive but unyielding — you're apt to end up with the imprint of the cast roses on your body when you stand up! Designs that use wooden slats for the seating and back have a bit more give to them, but you'll have to replace the slats eventually.

Going the Extra Mile: Adding a Patio or Deck

As you begin to plot out where to add plants and lighting, remember to leave a large, open area next to the pond, both as a work space (filter changes and repair, an area from which to net fish or perform routine maintenance, and so on) and as a lounging area.

Patios — Simply beautiful

As with building a pond, your finances, construction skills, and time limitations will be the deciding factors in determining how you'll proceed when it comes to patio construction. Considering pond-side surfaces, patios are, of course, the easiest to build and the simplest to change. Patio bricks, called *pavers,* come in all sizes, shapes, and colors, and they're readily available from home improvement stores.

Buy pavers a few at a time or all at once as your budget and time permit. Their real advantage is their building-block capacity that allows you to move your patio around, if and when you decide to add another pond or enlarge your present pond.

You can do the job all with one kind of paver, or you can formulate designs with pavers of different shapes and colors and then edge the patio with paving bricks of the same or contrasting colors. In reality, the patio can be as simple or as intricate as your pocketbook and energy level allow.

Bear in mind that patios are not solid, permanent surfaces. Therefore, the surface may settle or shift during wet weather, and plants can grow up through the spaces between the stones. Most troubling are tree roots that lift the stones as they grow below. Therefore, be sure to plan your location carefully, and consult an expert if you are at all unsure.

Decks — Naturally versatile

You may decide that building a pond-side deck is easier than lugging pavers. A deck is a bigger investment and is more difficult to modify at a later date, but it's a wonderful addition to your pond. We suggest you build your deck from treated 2 x 4s because they're easy to work with, resist warping better than larger widths of wood, and are available at every home improvement store. Just don't use treated wood for a pond overhang.

Why do we think decks are better? Pure and simple: They're far more versatile in terms of shape, materials, size, and other construction-related options. In addition, water never pools on a deck, they're easy to clean by sweeping, and their wood construction is slightly more forgiving than pavers when you drop a breakable item.

Besides the versatility in their construction, decks are equally versatile in their placement. You can situate your deck so it stops short at the side of your pond or, with a bit more planning and effort, you can build it to extend a foot or two over the edge of your pond. If your pond lacks underwater lights, add lights to the underside of the overhanging deck. In the evenings you'll be able to watch your koi as they swim in and out of the lights.

Chapter 9

Maintaining Your Pond

*Y*ou've gone to considerable time and expense in designing and constructing your pond. Now that the pond is ready and a half-dozen test koi have moved in, you invite some friends and neighbors to celebrate with a barbeque cookout. Everything's perfect.

But the next day you step outside, look at the pond, and wonder, "What do I do now? Can I keep it going?"

Taking care of a pond is like taking care of any complex organism. As long as you follow the rules, are ready for a few exceptions to those rules, and pay attention to pond chemistry, you and your koi are headed for a long, happy association. This chapter helps you maintain your pond year-round by walking you through the regular, routine tasks and explaining how the seasons affect pond care. We also guide you through the basics of water testing and how to interpret your results.

Maintaining Your Equipment

Everything wears out, and in keeping with the "no surprises" concept in pond-keeping, you want to know when to replace different items of equipment. See Table 9-1 for specifics. Knowing the typical life of a filter or a pump gives you a heads-up so you can check out the new technology and do some comparison shopping.

Table 9-1	When to Replace Your Pond Equipment
Item	*Replace at*
Water pump	3 years
Filter	2 years
Air pump	5 years
Air hoses	Replace when you replace your air pump
Liner	20 years
Concrete	Essentially never, barring frost heaves or tree root incursions

Testing for Proper Water Chemistry

You can't tell whether the chemistry in your pond is right simply by looking at the water. Even if it looks clean (koi-keepers use the term *gin clear*), the water can be laden with bad components, like ammonia and nitrites, and shy of critical elements, like oxygen. So even though your filter and water pump, air pump, and pond skimmer are working together to rid the pond of the physical and chemical waste, you need to monitor the water quality to make certain your equipment's doing the job right.

All you need is a pond thermometer and two or three water-testing kits. You need to test for ammonia, nitrite, salt, pH, dissolved oxygen, and chlorine/chloramine. *Note:* You can buy multitest kits that test four or five of these items, but you may need to buy separate kits for chlorine/chloramines and dissolved oxygen. Pet or garden-pond stores have these kits, or you can purchase them from an online vendor (searching under *outdoor pond test kits* will yield good results).

The kits are easy to use and take only a few moments to give you readings. For a new pond, test the water twice a week until the values stabilize (about six weeks). After that initial period, test your pond water once a week.

Be consistent by testing at the same time each day. Water chemistry values change as the day progresses, so testing your ammonia values, for instance, at the same time each day gives you a more accurate comparison. (Most koi owners test their water around 4 p.m., just before they feed their koi.)

Log your water-testing readings, noting the day and time for each one. The numbers or values help you track your pond's chemistry so you know when you need to make adjustments. We use a small spiral notebook that we keep in the box with the water test kits. (The notebook looks awful, but the data's good, and any day now we're going to spring for one of those field notebooks with the waterproof paper.)

The following sections explain the values you need to track.

Ammonia

Your goal on ammonia levels is zero, but your readings may change depending on the time of day you take them. The ammonia levels rise a couple of hours after you feed your fish as the fish process their food and excrete the leftovers into the water. As the pH naturally rises through the course of a day, the ammonia is temporarily converted to ammonium as each ammonia molecule takes on an additional hydrogen atom (conversely, when pH falls, the extra hydrogen atom is plucked off the ammonium, converting it back to ammonia). This cycle explains why you want to test for ammonia at the same time of day (or go crazy trying to figure out what those ammonia levels really mean).

You can lower high ammonia levels by dilution, in other words a partial water change, which we describe in the section "When You Need to Change the Water," later in this chapter.

But when the readings are consistently too high, you need to figure out the reason.

✔ Is your pond new? *New pond syndrome,* as it's called, is characterized by changing water chemistry readings that are too high or too low. This problem may take six weeks to stabilize. This is a natural process, and, if your pond was set up properly, should pass without incident. Do monitor your koi for signs of stress, however, and perform a partial water change (see "When You Need to Change the Water," later in this chapter) if they appear to be in trouble.

✔ Is your pump doing the job you thought it would, or do you have too many fish for your biofilter? Ammonia values can spike even if you've had your pond in operation for years. (Those little rascals grew, didn't they, and how can you get rid of fish that know your voice and respond to their name?)

To check the gallons-per-hour of your pump, attach a flow meter (available at an outdoor pond supply store) to the output and check it after 15 minutes. By multiplying the 15-minute reading by 8, you can determine if the pump is pumping enough water to circulate the water in your pond every two hours.

Depending on your biofilter media (see Chapter 6 for info on this essential piece of equipment), you may be able to switch to a newer high-surface-area biomedia that increases the surface area of your biofilter. As a basic figure, plan on 24 square feet of biofilter surface for every pound of koi (the average 12-inch koi weighs 0.7 pound, or about 11 ounces), so the 24-square-foot surface accommodates approximately one 12-inch koi, with a small safety margin.

pH

The perfect pH range for a koi pond is 6.8 to 7.2, but koi can do quite well with a broader range, from 6.5 to 9.0. When your pH reaches the lower end of that range, however, you need to worry about your biofilter as well as your koi. The friendly bacteria in a biofilter quit working if the pH goes below 6.0. As the bacteria begin to die off, their vital role in converting ammonia to less toxic nitrites and nitrates will cease. Ammonia levels will skyrocket, often very quickly, and your fish will become stressed and may die.

Don't take any single pH reading to heart. Your pond is a dynamic system, and its pH changes during the passage of a day, with lower values in the morning and higher ones in the afternoon. A heavy rain can nudge your pond toward a lower, acidic pH, and some pond additives push the numbers toward the higher alkaline side. If the fish look fine and other chemistry values are okay, relax. Koi are adaptive as long as the pH changes aren't sudden or extreme.

Your biological filter and weekly water changes help narrow the range of your pond's pH values, but don't be surprised if you get a lot of uninvited advice about pH. Well-intended people will insist (in gentle, soft voices) that adding baking soda is an easy, safe way to lower the pH. Keep in mind (and whisper it gently back to these nice folks if you want) that pH, ammonia, and nitrite are all interconnected. Using a sledgehammer like baking soda on pH is a good way to throw your water chemistry values seriously and immediately out of whack. You don't need to manipulate your pond chemistry values that badly. Skip the baking soda.

Nitrites

Like ammonia, nitrites are byproducts of digestion, and you want them to be as low as you can get them. The best nitrite level to shoot for is zero, but this may take a while if you're working with a new pond that hasn't settled down. (The cyclical chemistry of new ponds includes rising nitrite levels as ammonia levels decrease.)

Trying to figure out this chemistry balance can be confusing to a new koi-keeper, especially considering that each pond is unique in this regard; don't hesitate to call on a more experienced keeper for advice. You should also check your local public aquarium — the staff or volunteers at such institutions are often happy to help serious hobbyists. Test for nitrites at the same time of day, so you have similar readings to compare.

Your filter and its friendly bacteria generally take care of nitrites, converting them to nitrates, which are essentially harmless to your koi. You can help lower nitrite levels by partially changing the water each week or by letting the water from the filter run through a plant-filled sluice on its way back to the pond. Plants use nitrites as a food source and will contribute favorably to your water quality.

To make use of plants, arrange your filter's outflow to pass through a plastic pond or wide PVC pipe stocked with aquatic or *emergent plants* (those that grow with their roots in water and stems and leaves above it). Water hyacinth and water lettuce are particularly hardy (if given lots of sun) and amazingly efficient at removing nitrites and other impurities from the water. Because of their aggressive growth rate, water hyacinth are not legal in all states, but a wide variety of other plants will work equally well. Employees at outdoor pond and garden supply shops should be able to guide you. Please also see Chapter 8 for more information on pond plants.

Dissolved oxygen

The amount of oxygen in your pond water is important, and although you'd expect it to stay steady, it's a dynamic, moving number. Oxygen is used by the friendly bacteria in your filter, by your fish, and by any decomposing organic material in the pond.

Oxygen is replaced at the surface of the pond at the *water-air interface* (the area where air and water meet). To increase the pond's absorption of oxygen, simply increase the surface area of the water. We're not talking about stretching water, just exposing more of it to the air. Splashing and bubbling via air pumps and airstones, foam fractionators, and waterfalls all do the trick.

Adding oxygenation devices to your pond is a good idea if you have low oxygen readings, but if your readings are consistently low, you need to figure out the reason. The following are possible causes:

- ✔ Ponds with poor water circulation (due to an awkward pond shape or a water pump that's too small) usually have a *dead space* (nonmoving water that sinks to the bottom of the pond). This nonmoving water isn't exposed to air and can't pick up oxygen.

✔ An *algal bloom* — a sudden explosion in the population level of algae in the pond — can cause a rapid drop in oxygen levels. A number of factors can precipitate a bloom, some of which are related to the particular algae's biology and a bit complex to go into here. Often such blooms are associated with hot, sunny weather and a spike in nitrite levels from fish waste, the presence of a dead animal, or fertilizer washing into the pond.

An overcrowded pond and hot weather can deplete water of its oxygen. (Fish respire faster in hot weather and, as a result, remove more oxygen from the water.)

✔ Do you have too many fish for the size of your pond and the size of your pump and filter? (See Chapter 6 for a simple calculation of the best ratio.)

✔ Ponds at high altitudes (Hello, Denver!) are behind the oxygen curve to start with; the oxygen level is lower at high altitudes than at low altitudes. If you live in such an area, be sure to consult with local experts as to the water pump needed for your pond. In all likelihood, you will need one that is stronger than those recommended in Chapter 6.

When You Need to Change the Water

Partial water changes (and adding a dechlorinator) are a natural part of housekeeping for koi-keepers. The following are two obvious benefits:

✔ They're an easy, inexpensive way to maintain or clean your pond's water chemistry because they dilute all the bad values that result from koi waste.

✔ They help moderate your pond's temperature, cooling the sun-heated pool in the summer and warming the chilled pool in the winter.

Water changes are most important during the summer when the fish are active and eating heavily. You should do a 20 to 30 percent water change once a week in the summer. You can lessen the frequency a bit during early spring and fall (every 10–14 days), but once per week is the best overall policy.

Before you begin the water change, buy a flow meter for your hose so you know how many gallons you're putting in your pond, rather than guessing. The meter also helps you know the correct amount of dechlor to add and (if your pond is salted) the amount of additional salt you need to bring the readings to the original level. Direct the overflow to your lawn or garden. For ponds with salted water, divert your filter's outflow into your wastewater system because the salt is harmful to most plants.

 An alternate method to using a flow meter is to mark your outdoor hose spigot at a quarter-turn and time how long it takes to fill a 5-gallon bucket when the spigot is turned to that marking. That way, you can add the hose to your pond, turn the spigot to the marking, and set a timer for a measured water change.

Perhaps the easiest way to effect a partial water change is to redirect the outflow from your filter so that the water exits the pond. Another useful method is to use a small submersible pump. You may already have one on hand to operate a waterfall, or you can purchase one specifically for water changes. (It's always good to have one on hand anyway — if your main pump fails, the submersible can be used to circulate and oxygenate the water until you replace your main unit.)

To change the water, simply attach plastic tubing (a variety of widths and lengths are available at pet and pond stores) to the pump's outflow port and pump out 20 to 30 percent of the pond's water (if possible, direct the water to a garden or somewhere else where it will be of use). The replacement water should be dechlorinated and about the same temperature as what's already in the pond (unless you're trying to raise or lower the temperature).

You can also use hand-held siphons (the water is pumped by rubber ball into a length of plastic tubing) or siphon the pond water out by filling a hose with water and submerging one end in the pond. However, these methods require gravity's help, so you'll need to have a low-lying area right next to the pond.

For small ponds or in an emergency (or if you enjoy the exercise), you can also use a 5-gallon bucket to remove the appropriate amount of water.

Maintaining a Stable Temperature

Koi do best at 70 to 82 degrees F. However, nothing is ideal. Sudden, unexpected temperature drops can stress your koi. We remember some fall days in Colorado when the temperature dropped from 65 degrees in the morning to 21 degrees in the afternoon. When you get caught by one of these switches, add salt (available in bulk at outdoor pond supply stores) to your pond at the rate of 3 pounds per 100 gallons for a 0.3 percent reading (roughly a third of 1 percent) to help your koi deal with the temperature drop. Although salt dissolves rapidly in water, avoid dumping it in one heap. Rather, mix the salt with water in a clean plastic pail, and pour this into the pond at your filter's outflow. You can keep track of the amount of salt in your pond, especially after a partial water change, with one of the tests in your testing kit or you can buy a digital salt meter. Either method will yield accurate results.

To help you keep your fish comfy cozy, this section offers ways to deal with colder and warmer conditions.

When the weather gets cold

Koi-keepers who live in the extreme southern parts of the United States (in the United States Department of Agriculture zones 9 and 10) don't need to worry much about pond temperatures. Cold weather in these areas means less than 60 degrees and it rarely lasts more than a day or two. Partial water changes (remember to use a dechlorinating chemical preparation) or a pond cover can keep the pond water warm.

The rest of us, left out in the cold so to speak, have the choice of covering or heating our ponds or doing neither.

Covering the pond

If you live in an area with no snowfall, then building and covering a simple frame around your pond is a feasible project for the do-it-yourselfer. The process entails building a wooden or metal framework around your pond and covering the frame with 6-millimeter plastic sheeting, acrylic panels, or even bubble wrap. Be sure to use rustproof products, such as copper screws or plastic ties or strips, to attach the cover material to the frame. You need about a foot of space between the pond and the cover for air exchange. Remember to create an access panel of some sort (a simple way to do this is to secure one corner of the cover with a length of plastic tubing that can be easily untied) so you can check the water temperature. See Figure 9-1 for a sample of this pond cover.

Areas that normally get snowfall require a pond cover with a bit of a slant to the roof to avoid the weight of snow buildup. Building a cover like this can be as simple as making two of the four support legs longer. Koi pond covers are available in knock-down (KD), easy-to-assemble kits for round ponds up to 30 feet in diameter. See Figure 9-2 for more details. (The manufacturer says one person can set up a koi pond cover in 30 minutes with no special tools.)

Figure 9-1: A simple pond cover.

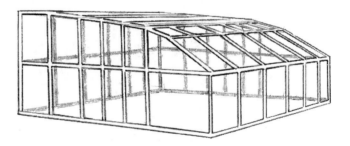

Figure 9-2: A slanted-roof cover for a koi pond.

Figure 9-3 shows a lower pond cover with bubble wrap in place. Multiple layers of wrap provide additional insulation.

Bringing koi indoors

Many pond keepers in the extreme northern area of the United States with ponds less than 5 feet deep generally bring their koi indoors during the winter (for the basics of an indoor pond, see Chapter 10).

Letting a deep pond freeze on top

Other northern koi-keepers with ponds that are too deep to freeze solid prepare their pond for the winter by doing the following:

- ✔ Prepping their fish, making sure none of them have health problems going into their wintertime slowdown

✔ Consider turning off the filters (many experts insist the filter be left on; ask your koi friends what they do)

✔ Adding an *ice porthole* so gas exchange can take place

An ice porthole is a bottomless wooden box about 2 feet x 2 feet with a hinged top. You set the box at the edge of the pond with the bottom edge of the porthole extending a foot down into the water. A 100-watt light bulb set into the top of the box provides enough warmth to keep ice from forming inside the box. Air exchange occurs at the water's surface inside the box. The electric cord connected to the bulb should, of course, be rated for outdoor use and can be plugged into the outdoor outlets that power your filtration system.

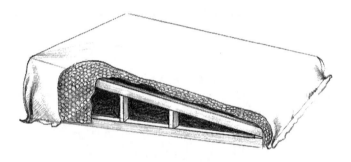

Figure 9-3: A simple pond cover that uses bubble wrap as the cover.

With these basic winterizing steps, most koi get through the winter and the equally hazardous spring warm-up.

Heating the pond

Some owners choose to cover and heat the koi pond over the winter. These owners point out the following advantages:

✔ They can interact with their fish all year round.

✔ Owners have no worries concerning fish that have been weakened by winter's cold temperatures, fasting, and the resultant metabolic changes.

✔ The fish stay active, are fed regularly, and can digest the food because they're warmer.

✔ The fish grow all year and maintain their weight better than koi who overwinter without heat.

Heated ponds bring sizzling sales

The trend toward heating over the winter is growing. In Japan, koi were traditionally overwintered in mud ponds, and the annual pond draining and harvest of the koi was a big event. Beginning in the 1970s, however, breeders found that the growing popularity of the hobby supported the expense of heated winter quarters for their koi. They had higher survival numbers, particularly with the yearlings. (The first winter was considered a great winnower of yearling koi.) In addition, the bigger fish didn't falter during the winter, they got even bigger and fatter during the summer, and they commanded higher prices in October during the traditional koi sales event. For these big-number breeders, heated ponds pay off.

But is heating your pond right for you? We can't guess what your heating costs may be (both in setup and in operating costs) because each pond is different; geographical area, size, and shape of your pond are all factors. You may want to talk to a couple of koi-keepers in your area and representatives from firms that build and install pond heaters, just so you have an idea of the cost of heating your pond.

If you know how many watts the system requires, you can figure out your electricity costs with these steps:

1. **Divide the number of watts by 1,000 to get kilowatts.**

2. **Multiply the kilowatts by 8,760 (the number of hours in a year) to figure how many kilowatts you'll use a year.**

3. **Multiply that product by your utility's charges for a kilowatt hour to find out the cost of running the heater for a year.**

Dealing with hotter temps

As the days heat up during the summer, check your pond temperature in the afternoon, when the heat is highest. If the water temperature creeps up to the 80s, you need to act to protect your koi:

✔ Make a partial (20 to 30 percent) water change, adding cold water to gradually reduce the pond's temperature.

✔ Sling a shade cloth up over your pergola framework to reduce the heating effect of the sun.

> ✔ Activate a waterfall feature or pond bubbler. This action will help to increase your water's dissolved oxygen content (warm water holds less oxygen than does cool water, and also increases the koi's rate of respiration).

Keeping Predators Away

Oh-oh! You're missing a koi?

This is fair warning: Other sentient beings on this earth enjoy koi almost as much as you do. In fact, they may enjoy koi more than you do. To you the colorful fish are living gems. But for those other admirers, whether two-footed, four-footed, six-footed, or no-footed, the koi are a feast in the most literal sense.

The kinds of koi predator you need to reckon with will depend on two factors: your pond setting and the size of your fish. Koi-keepers in rural areas or in wooded urban areas find raccoons and herons to be their major predators. Urbanites add cats to that list and move herons down to third place.

Larger koi are safer from predation than smaller koi simply because fewer creatures can tackle them.

 Your predators' success depends to a large extent on the steepness of the sides of your pond. Ponds with shelves for potted plants provide a ready-made table for nabbing koi because the innocent but curious fish like to come up and see what's going on. Vertical sides, on the other hand, provide a safeguard against predators; the fish can quickly move deeper into the pond and beyond reach.

When Rover comes over

We have to admit that predation can occur when you least expect it. We had never thought much about domestic dogs being koi predators until a koi-keeper told us about her cocker spaniel. The pond was new, and her dog spent a lot of time looking into the water, evidently fascinated by the koi that swam at his feet.

The koi may have been equally curious. One day the owner came out to find her dog standing over a 14-inch koi he had just lifted from the water. Both dog and koi seemed surprised. The owner put the koi back in the pond and quickly trained the dog to stay away from the pond.

Moral of the story? If Rover seems curious about your koi, introduce them to each other so he'll understand that these are pets, too. Use whatever method has worked with your dog in other training situations to accomplish this.

These are additional suggestions for keeping your koi safe:

- ✔ A fence — even a low fence — around your yard helps deter many predators.

- ✔ By keeping brush and other natural cover away from the pool's edge, you can deter most snakes.

- ✔ Vigilance on your part in combination with a free-ranging dog and a bird-netting pond cover can thwart the efforts of predatory wading birds. If the netting droops to the ground, it also prevents most large frogs (bullfrogs are the most serious threat) from gaining pool access.

- ✔ Net out turtles and large frogs that move into your pond. Take them to the nearest patch of suitable habitat and release. (Be very careful how you handle large snapping turtles!)

- ✔ A number of aquatic insects will prey upon small koi. While dragonfly larvae and water scorpions can take only fry, giant water bugs will attack fish of 4–5 inches in length. All of these insects (especially the giant water bug, fondly referred to in some locales as the "toe biter") can administer painful bites, so use a net to capture and release them in a local pond.

- ✔ Treat snakes with caution (but not fear and loathing) and call a removal service if you don't feel qualified to remove and relocate them yourself.

The one creature that you're most likely to have recurring problems with is that cuddly-appearing (but ferociously defensive), food-washing, masked marauder of the evening — the raccoon. Raccoons attempt to capture koi of any size and injure those that escape.

Beware the nighttime bandit

Raccoons aren't just smart, they're street-smart as well. They've adapted to life in the inner city and in the forested outskirts. After they locate a food source, they return to it time and again. Although most raccoons run from dogs and people, some — especially if they're very hungry or very well acclimated to people, stand their ground and choose confrontation over retreat.

Raccoons may carry rabies and distemper. Persistent raccoons must be trapped and physically relocated miles away or destroyed. Look in the phone book for a pest exterminator who deals with wildlife.

Caring for the Pond through the Four Seasons

Getting a running start on pond care each season is like entering data into your tax software all year long — you have a lot less stress when the deadline hits. The following sections walk you through pond maintenance for each season of the year.

Falling into a slower routine

Your primary goal in autumn is to remove extraneous organic matter from your pond and filter. Anything organic decomposes very slowly during the winter, but when spring hits and the water warms, the bacterial bloom will overwhelm your koi.

Other chores to take care of before the snow flies include

- ✔ Hosing off the filter mats or the bioballs or turning the backwash valve on your bead filter.

- ✔ Installing your leaf netting (a net cover to prevent leaves from entering the pond) before the leaves begin to fall and making sure your cover or frame is accessible and ready to install.

- ✔ Feeding your koi a high protein diet until the first cold spell, and then switching to the wheat-germ-based diet (see Chapter 11 for more on these foods).

- ✔ Trimming any plants that dangle into the pond. The cold weather will kill the foliage and the debris will end up in your pond.

- ✔ Checking your koi for health problems and correcting them. Their immune system slows down after the pond cools.

- ✔ Installing an ice porthole or heater, if either are required.

Settling into winter

After the leaves on local trees have all fallen, take the leaf cover off. Depending on your setup, you have different tasks at this point to prepare your pond and koi for the coldest season. The following points cover each of those arrangements:

- ✔ **Ponds with heaters:** Set the thermostat at 62 degrees. Your fish will eat a bit at this temperature, but not with the eagerness that they show in the summer. Offer food once per day, and carefully monitor the amount they eat and make adjustments as necessary. Please see Chapter 11 for more details.

✔ **Unheated ponds:** Stop feeding your koi when the water temperature is below 52 degrees. (Their digestive systems are working too slowly to digest the food, and the bacteria in your biofilter can't keep up with an ammonia/nitrite spike.)

Keep your filter running to deal with fish waste, but turn off the aeration system in the pond because the movement chills the water.

✔ **Uncovered ponds where the access to the pond is through an ice porthole:** Check the porthole daily to make certain the light bulb is still on, and replace the bulb before it reaches the allotted hour-life (see the side of the bulb package for this number).

Opening the porthole to check on your chilled koi in midwinter can be a bit traumatic because your koi are lying semicomatose on the bottom of your pond. Some koi are inclined toward one side, and those that are swimming are moving in slow motion. This is normal behavior for very cold koi.

When the temperature hits 60 degrees, you can begin to feed your fish. Use wheat germ–based food (see Chapter 11) and feed only enough to be consumed in two minutes. (Wheat germ is easier for koi to digest than the more complex proteins.)

Make a 10 percent water change every week or two weeks.

Spring into (careful) action

The days are getting longer, the sky is warmer, spring is right around the corner, and all of your wintertime worries are over. No, sorry to say. April is the cruelest month, and it isn't just because of love. This is the time of year that overwintering koi die. Their metabolisms have been drastically altered to deal with the low temperatures and lack of food, and any koi that were not in tip-top shape in the fall are likely to be in a vulnerable state by spring.

At the end of winter, chilled koi (and their immune systems) begin to perk up. That's the good news.

The bad news is that your koi are behind the curve when it comes to waking up. All the bacteria and parasites that have spent the last couple of months slumbering (no, they're not dead, just resting) in the bottom *mulm* (the sticky layer of organic material such as unfiltered droppings, odd bits of leaves, and dead plants) of your koi pond are awake *and* hungry. Like a herd of very tiny

Tasmanian devils, they're scrounging around for food, and mulm is just the start of what they'll feed on. Bacteria will move into any breach in the koi's skin and immediately start multiplying, and the external parasites will begin feeding and reproducing. They're more awake than your koi's immune system. Keep an eye out for ailments such as hole in the side, anchor worms, or fungus. (See Chapter 13 for more on ulcers and parasites and how to deal with them.) Watch your koi for *flashing behavior,* curving the body to scrape along the pond bottom or sides.

Most koi-keepers either feed very lightly or don't feed at all until the water edges upward past 60 degrees. Then the feedings should start small. (We're not trying to protect your koi's delicate digestive systems. Koi are really just fancy digestive tubes, with just a two-hour delay between feeding and excreting.) The goal is to avoid an increase in ammonia and nitrite levels while your biofilter bacteria become active.

As the water temperature creeps past 70 degrees, you can gradually increase the amount of food, but be stingy! If your koi take more than a minute and a half to eat, you're feeding too much. Feed small amounts twice a day, and test your water for ammonia and nitrite content at least twice a week. Make partial water changes (5 to 15 percent) weekly to help keep nitrite and ammonia levels down.

Easing into summer

It's summertime and the living is, well, weedy. The increased levels of sunlight may trigger an exuberant *hair algae bloom,* a weed that looks like green, slimy cotton candy. (If you run your fingers through that floating filamentous gunk in your pond, you'll see what we mean.) This algae is commonly known as *blanket weed.* In addition to being ugly, blanket weed is an oxygen stealer at night.

Discourage blanket weed by

✔ Shading at least part of your pond; blanket weed grows like crazy in direct sunlight.

✔ Using a commercial blanket weed killer, one that's safe for use with koi. These work by removing phosphate and other key nutrients from the water (which blanket weed needs) so the weed starves and shrivels.

✔ Adding barley straw to your pond. As the straw decomposes, it discourages blanket weed. (Tropical-fish keepers from way back recognize barley as a prime source of *infusoria,* tiny micro-organisms that are an important food source for many newly hatched fish.)

You can buy barley straw pads packaged just for this purpose at your local pond or aquarium shop or online. Or, if you need a 50-pound bale, purchase it as stock feed at your local feed store. Because each pond is unique when it comes to blanket weed, you should consult a local retailer or pond owner as to the appropriate amount of straw to use. (We put a chunk of the bale into a nylon mesh bag used for laundering delicate washables, add a rock for ballast, and hang the bag in our pond.) Replace the barley straw pad every three months during warm weather.

You can also buy barley straw extract from some outdoor pond stores, or via the Internet, and not have to wait a couple of days before the blanket weed diminishes. Your retailer can guide you as to the appropriate use of this product in your particular situation.

✔ Using an electronic device that disperses a mineral that kills blanket weed. *Note:* The manufacturer apologetically explains that the device is not suitable for use with invertebrates or mollusks, so kiss goodbye, metaphorically, any dragonfly larvae or snails you may have in your koi pond (Where have they been hiding? Koi *love* snails, and not platonically.).

As temperatures rise, the oxygen-carrying capacity of water drops. On hot days more koi are near the surface of the water. The koi that are gasping at the surface are seeking air. Add aeration via water bubblers, fountains, or a waterfall. The increased aeration these provide allows the fish to obtain more oxygen. A partial water change of 20 to 30 percent can also help by temporarily lowering the water's temperature (please see Chapter 9 for more details).

Summertime is the best time to bring out your high-protein koi foods. Your koi are hungry, having awakened from their wintertime rest during the spring months, and they want food, glorious food.

With these rapacious appetites comes a big increase in ammonia and fish poop production, so clean your mechanical and biological filters weekly.

When you're shopping around, keep an eye out for end-of-the-season bargains. For example, filter material goes on sale in late summer. You can stock up and save a bundle (which you'll immediately spend on koi, because this is when they come out of the mud ponds in Japan). The downside, of course, is finding a place to put the items until you need them. But isn't that why car trunks and deck-side storage benches were invented?

Chapter 10

Keeping Koi Inside

For most people, an indoor pond is an alternate, second choice to an outdoor pond. Either the indoor pond is seasonal (for colder months), or the home is in a metropolitan area where an outdoor pond isn't possible. Some koi-keepers have just one pond, in a screened-in pool cage or similar area, so that it's both outdoors and indoors, but they live in areas where the daytime temperatures are always 70 degrees F or higher. There are, of course, a few areas where the weather makes it possible to have one pond, a pond that is both outside and inside.

Outdoor ponds seem to have all the pluses:

✔ Koi are much easier to take care of outside.

✔ Their colors are brighter because of sunlight.

✔ The fish are healthier because they have more swimming room, vertically and horizontally.

Yet you can design an indoor pond to provide many of the good points of an outdoor pond.

More than anything else, an indoor pond makes sense when it comes to your pocketbook. Taking care of koi in an outdoor pond during the winter is expensive. Although the cost of a cover and a heating system are one-time expenses, the utility costs aren't.

In contrast, an indoor pond adds modestly to your utility costs. Of course, the cost of installing an indoor pond can go from affordable to extravagant, but for most koi-keepers in northern states, the enjoyment is well worth the cost.

In this chapter, we discuss the do's and don'ts and the ABCs of indoor koi-keeping. In addition to the questions of humidity, equipment needs, and logistics, we guide you through the setup of your aquarium, water-quality issues, and the anticipated arrival of your koi. Finally, we add our advice on potential problems: what they look like, how to avoid them, and how to solve them if they do occur.

Addressing Humidity and Its Effect on Your Home

The first question we get regarding indoor ponds is usually, "Doesn't all the moisture from the indoor pond wreck your house?" Our answer: Absolutely not.

Instead of causing problems because of increased humidity, an indoor koi pond helps alleviate the wintertime dryness that makes human noses and hands red and itchy. The moisture also decreases the chance of you shuffling your feet across the carpet and pulling a 2-inch static spark off the tip of your spouse's nose (which may or may not be a good thing!).

If you renovate a room for pond installation, avoid possible damage by using water-resistant green board for the walls rather than ordinary sheetrock. Concrete backer board (the material used as an underlayment for ceramic tile) is even better if there's a chance that the water will come in contact with the walls.

However, adopt a zero-tolerance attitude toward any bit of moisture on the floor next to your pond. A small leak can cause a ghastly amount of damage, and leaks rarely stay small. (Our personal experience is that little leaks become big leaks on Sunday afternoons or immediately as you leave for a three-day weekend.)

You can easily disperse the humidity that builds up in your pond room with ventilation. *Note:* An exhaust fan vented outside or even to your attic isn't a good idea if it's 40 degrees outside because you're tossing heat out along with the moisture. Instead, vent the fan into a hallway to help circulate the damp air throughout the house.

 You can also go slightly higher-tech and buy a home dehumidifier that can roll from one room to another. These units pull the moisture from the air; then once a day or so, you empty its water receptacle.

Plan C: You can just not worry about it. We don't.

Planning Ahead for Your Indoor Spectacle

Designing and building an indoor koi pond isn't all that different from constructing an outside pond. You start by planning for the largest pond that your space and budget will allow, figuring in the size and potential size of your koi as part of the process.

Finding a container for an indoor pond is surprisingly easy. You can use any of the following:

- ✔ A big aquarium (for baby koi)
- ✔ A show tank
- ✔ A stock tank
- ✔ A preformed pond
- ✔ A semi-permanent pond made from a liner and landscape timbers
- ✔ A permanent indoor pond

The costs increase in that order as well. Table 10-1 gives you a side-by-side comparison of each of the options that are suitable for adult koi. See the next section for info on using an aquarium.

Table 10-1		A Comparison of the Types of Indoor Ponds			
Type of Pond	**Material**	**Cost**	**Pros**	**Cons**	**Where to Get One**
Preformed ponds	Vinyl	$2,100 before shipping for 4-ft. deep, 11 ½-ft.-long, 1,100-gallon pond	Fitted for a bottom drain; adding siding (even stucco) creates a permanent look	Requires a good deal of space and is semi-permanent; can be expensive; same safety concerns as outdoor ponds (see Chapter 6)	Local pond dealer or online directly from manufacturer
Show tanks	Sky-blue polyester vinyl, cut and sealed into a pond shape; supported by an external framework of PVC pipes	$450 for a 6-ft. tank; $50 for a cover; add a filter, pump, and aerator	Quick to set up and break down; stores unassembled under a bed or on a closet floor; very affordable and functional	Looks like an add-on	Pond store or manufacturer
Stock tanks	Polyethylene	$100–$200 for 100-gallon pond or $200–$300 for 200-gallon; available in larger sizes	Box in to make attractive	Doesn't have a bottom drain	Local farm-and-feed store, manufacturer
Indoor custom-built ponds	Typically cement-block walls with cement floor, coated in-side with paint-on or spray-on sealant, liner and landscape timbers in 8-ft. lengths; floor slants to one side; filter drains at valley of the slope; walls are 2–4 ft. above floor to reduce digging and provide safety	Upwards of $3,000 for a small pond. Cost depends on size and design of pond, the amount of electrical and plumbing work needed, as well as any decorative tile work	Can be made to your specifications; theoret-ically can approach outdoor pond in size, beauty, permanence; may allow for land-scaping, decorative rockwork	Expensive; perma-nence can be a down-side; same safety concerns as outdoor ponds	Local contractor recommended by pond store or koi hobbyists

Considering the aquarium option

A large aquarium tank, 150 to 200 gallons, works as a winter wonderland for a few baby koi up to 6 inches long. The problem is that koi don't stay small, so the fancy-schmancy aquarium with a heater and filter and lights is only useful for a year before those cute baby koi outgrow it.

But an aquarium buys you some time if you need temporary housing while you complete the inside pond. Be forewarned: You'll put about $400 into a big aquarium and all its accessories, none of which will work in your inside koi pond.

Deciding on the setup type

As you decide which type of indoor pond best suits your needs, give some thought to plumbing. Plan to plumb a drain line right into the pond bottom or adjacent to the pond. Trust us on this: Filling and draining the pond or backwashing the filter is a lot easier if you've installed a drain in the setup process.

Figuring out how big to make it

The only concern you have regarding the size of your indoor pond and your koi is the fish load, meaning how many inches of koi will fit comfortably into the new pond. Simply put, the pond must be big enough to provide swimming room for the koi.

 In planning your indoor pond, the minimum depth of 4 feet is a given. So, to figure out how many koi you can adequately house, and how large a space you'll actually need around any pond, start with some basic numbers and work outward, using the compromise standard of an inch-and-a-half of koi per square foot of surface area:

1. **Start out with the smallest possible pond.** A small pond measuring 6 feet x 4 feet (and 4 feet deep, at least) can house 36 inches of koi.

2. **Adjust the measurements a bit to see how many more inches of koi you can add with that tweak.** For example, bump up the measurements by just 1 foot along one side, and you have a 6-x-5-foot pond that can house 45 inches of koi.

Because your indoor pond will probably be smaller than your outdoor pond, putting all those koi into a smaller pond is going to send the ammonia and nitrite readings through the roof (read that:

your fish will quickly become stressed and die). Consider the wise words of Dolly Parton, who once said that you can't put 10 pounds of potatoes in a 5-pound sack. Either accept that you will be keeping fewer fish than would be possible in a large, outdoor pond, or make plans now to redistribute some of your koi to pond stores or other hobbyists before the cold season sets in.

Although koi lovers sometimes don't have the space to accommodate their koi-keeping habit and may feel a bit self-conscious about the small size of their inside pond, you needn't be one of them. Take a deep breath — you can overcome that small-inside-pond syndrome. If you are in the fortunate position of having unlimited time and money, as well as a place to live during construction, you can follow the example of those unusually dedicated (extreme?) koi owners:

✔ Some such folks add on an outside pond and then increase the size of the house to encompass the pond.

✔ Other owners start with a pond and then build their house around the pond.

✔ Realistically, however, most people just find a corner in the den or the mudroom and build an indoor pond there.

Buying the necessary indoor pond equipment

The decision to create an indoor pond and the process of doing so involves many of the same issues that face those seeking to establish an outdoor pond. If you are new to pond keeping, please read Chapters 6 through 9 before embarking on a plan to build an indoor pond.

If you already have an outdoor pond, you probably have much of the smaller equipment you need for an indoor pond. Just bring your koi nets, sock nets, koi bowl, water-testing kit(s), and the koi wheat germ diet inside. The nets and the bowl can be stored on hooks on a wall adjacent to the pond, and the rest fits inside a plastic outdoor storage unit that you bring inside for the season.

Or you can do what most koi-keepers do: Clean out the guest coat closet for your koi supplies. When company comes, toss their coats on your bed. Because many of your friends are going to be koi-keepers as well, they'll understand perfectly.

Discarding the crud: Filters

This is not the time to skimp on filters. Many kinds of biofilters are out there, all produced by different companies, but be as careful in the selection of this biofilter as you are for your pond.

You're best off biting the bullet and buying a three-chambered filter or a bead filter for your indoor pond. (For more info on these two types of filters, flip back to Chapter 6.) One area you can actually save money in is on a UV sterilizer; you probably won't need one for an indoor pond.

A submerged filter can't handle what your koi dish out, so don't even think about buying one. Also, don't buy a canister that promises to handle mechanical and biological filtration if it only has a couple of small filter pads and a double-handful of bio-balls. These small pond biofilters may be okay for water-lily ponds, but koi sure aren't lilies when it comes to producing debris.

Getting the water to go through the filter: Water pumps

Pump designers choose between cheap, easy-to-produce pumps and pumps where efficient design is more important than production cost. So, you're not likely to find a cheap pump that is also very effective. As water quality and overall clarity is especially important in indoor situations, we suggest that you do not skimp on costs when choosing a pump.

An important factor in pumps is the power requirement. Sort your top choices for a pump by amperage. Ignore the pumps on the high end of amperage use (any that use more than 8 amps) because they literally drink electricity (note that we did not say *sip*). If a kilowatt-hour in your area costs a dime (what a deal you're getting!), you can multiply $100 times the number of your pump's amps to guesstimate its annual cost to run. For instance, a water pump that uses 12 amps costs about $1,200 a year to run, or about $100 dollars a month.

Of course, the cost of a high-amperage pump (12 or 13 amps — and yes, you should flinch when you hear those words) is a bit cheaper upfront (about $800) than a lower-amp pump. A pump that needs only half the amps may have an initial cost of $1,400, but it'll cost you a lot less to run (multiply 6 by $100 and divide by 12 to get your monthly expense of $50). When you're writing out a check to your local utility each month, the thought of saving $50 because you bought the right kind of water pump can be very appealing. In just one year you'll make up the difference of the more expensive unit ($1,400 − $800 = $600 ÷ 12 = $50).

The size of your pump will determine its ability to clean and oxygenate the water. Look for a water pump that can move your pond's volume through the filter about every two hours.

Giving your koi some oxygen: Air pumps

The smaller surface area of inside koi ponds means lower gas exchange. When you add in the chance for overcrowding, your koi are going to need some help.

Solve the problem by putting in an air pump and an airstone. Two benefits from higher levels of oxygen are

- ✔ The fish will be able to breathe naturally, that is, without gulping for air at the surface. They will, therefore, be more likely to remain healthy and behave normally.
- ✔ The friendly bacteria in your biofilter work more efficiently.

Position the airstone in front of the filter return so the oxygen-laden air gets pushed around the pond (and you get more oomph for your airstone buck).

Look for an air pump that can deliver at least 1 cubic foot per minute through ¼-inch or ⁵⁄₁₆-inch tubing. This flow will operate a 12-inch airstone or two 6-inch airstones, enough for most indoor ponds. When you buy the air pump, buy the tubing and a manifold at the same time so you can put more than one airstone on a single air pump.

Because this pond is indoors, you don't need to worry about weatherproof housing for the air pump. An indoor air pump that can pump a cubic foot a minute costs about $100, and a metal manifold costs about $70. Expect the pump to last about two years.

Bringing your koi out from the dark: Lighting

Light quality is an important but often overlooked consideration in the design of indoor koi environments. Although koi do not absolutely require full spectrum light, the subtleties of their colors are certainly shown to best advantage under it. The fish also seem to be more active under such naturalistic lighting — perhaps full spectrum light may someday be shown to confer health benefits to koi, as is the case for many reptiles. In any event, your viewing pleasure and the appearance of your home will be enhanced if you choose your pond's lighting wisely.

It is recommended that you add banks of full spectrum fluorescent plant bulbs over your pond, but that can be pretty bright, and the shop-type fixtures are better suited to a garage workbench than your pond room.

Some koi keepers install a wall of glass blocks or large double-paned glass windows next to the pond and add insulated drapes for cold days and nights. But when the drapes are closed on cold days, you need additional lighting.

Incandescent bulbs that give off UVA and UVB light are available from reptile dealers and some pet shops. Although they look like sunlamp bulbs, these UVA/UVB lights are made from clear glass. And because they're so bright, you need to place them in *reflectors* (metal units that hold the bulbs) so the light is directed down into the pond. (Reflectors are available where you buy the bulbs.)

 Place the UVA/UVB bulbs on one end of your indoor pond. They not only light up the whole pond but also provide the kind of lighting that encourages plant growth (please note that some bulbs sold as "plant bulbs" do not emit sufficient UVA/UVB — check that the label specifically notes UVA/UVB emission).

Koi may be startled by light suddenly flooding a dark room, so be sure to turn on the room lights first, then the pond lights. A timer can be used to keep the lights on a fixed schedule — 10 to 12 hours of light per day works well. A timer can also be used to program a small lamp or room light to come on a half hour or so before the pond light and to stay on a half hour after they go off. This will provide a "dawn/dusk" period, and will eliminate the risk of stressing the fish. If you plan on breeding your koi, you should use a light timer to mimic local seasonal fluctuations, such as short winter days that lengthen as spring approaches.

Incidentally, koi look gorgeous in full spectrum light.

Getting Down to Business: Setting Up Your Indoor Pond

The initial stages of planning your indoor pond are as important as the actual physical process. Maintaining koi indoors can be a time-consuming and expensive prospect, and mistakes made early on will be compounded over time and difficult (and expensive) to correct. Therefore, read and plan carefully at this stage so that you have a thorough understanding of all that is involved before you actually get your hands wet (pun intended).

In case you're a bit wary, take it from us that setting up an inside koi pond is actually easier than it sounds. Whether you go for a permanent or a temporary pond, you'll find working on a smaller scale fun because everything is so reachable; the filter is just around the edge of the pond, and the bottom of the pond is just 4 feet down — you could reach in with a fine fish net or siphon to pick up any dirt.

But first, the easiest setup of all: the aquarium.

Starting out simple with an aquarium

An aquarium is the least expensive way to keep koi indoors and is, on the surface, a simpler route to follow than is pool construction. We say "on the surface" because there are some potential pitfalls that you must consider. As mentioned in the "Considering the aquarium option" section, koi will quickly outgrow most aquariums, so you must either plan for an eventual larger enclosure or resign yourself to finding new homes for your pets at some point. Also, because tanks are smaller than ponds, any mistakes that you make in terms of water chemistry (allowing ammonia levels to rise, for example) will be magnified and more serious than they would be in a large pond. Therefore, always purchase the largest tank that your space and budget allow (although you can keep small koi in a 55-gallon tank for a short period of time, a 100- to 200-gallon tank is really the smallest that you should consider).

Location

Deciding where to put your aquarium is an important decision that is usually made based on available space within the home. However, you need to consider several other important factors, especially the weight of the tank. When filled with water, a 100-gallon aquarium with its associated equipment approaches 1,000 pounds in weight. The floor on which it rests must, therefore, be strong enough to support it over time. Ideally, the tank should be located over support beams. If you have any doubts in this regard, consult an architect.

If you plan to place your aquarium on a stand, you should purchase one with adjustable legs. This allows you to compensate for uneven spots in the floor. The stand's surface should be smooth and free of bumps as even tiny irregularities can cause stress fractures and leaks in the aquarium over time. A cork or foam sheet placed on top of the stand is an important added safety measure. You may also wish to purchase appropriate home or renter's insurance, just in case a leak does occur.

Although sunlight through a window may add to your viewing pleasure, be aware that such light can affect water temperatures and stimulate the rapid growth of algae. Keep in mind also that koi can detect sound via water vibrations, and so may be stressed by loud stereos and televisions. "Busy" rooms with slamming doors are best avoided as well. The noise concerns go both ways, so don't locate the aquarium where the sound of the pump's motor or of flowing water will disturb you or others.

Your tank should be placed near a source of electricity. Ideally, the socket should be off to one side and out of the range of spilled water. If, as is likely, a floor drain is not available, you will need to run a siphon hose out a door or into a toilet (don't use sinks where food is prepared) when doing water changes and other routine maintenance. You also need to consider a source for fresh water and space for your filter and pump.

The pump and filter

A wide variety of pumps and filters are suitable for use with koi aquariums. These are rated by the size of the aquarium that can be filtered (be sure to read the product information carefully or consult a knowledgeable retailer). In choosing one, it is better to go with a model on the stronger end of the scale, because koi produce a good deal of waste and will easily overwhelm an undersized system. Of course, don't go overboard and buy a unit that is far too powerful for your tank, or the currents generated may interfere with the fish's ability to swim.

Please see Chapter 5 for a list of basic supplies that you will need to have on hand.

Setting up a preformed pond

A preformed pond may be the easiest way to add an indoor pond. There are a few drawbacks, however. Normally, preformed ponds are buried in the ground, and the surrounding dirt helps the pond support the weight of the water.

If your pond isn't strong enough to be self-standing when filled, you'll need to find a way to support the pond, which means building a wooden box around the pond that is strong enough to support the weight of the water-filled pond.

If the preformed pond has a bottom drain, you'll need to raise the pond high enough to hook up the drain to the water pump. Most koi-keepers just reinforce the area under the raised pond with 2-x-4s but leave an access area to the drain open. The air pump will feed air out through the top of the drain, or you can attach the air pump hose to an airstone and drape the hose over the edge of the pond.

If your pond doesn't have a drain in the bottom, you have two easy options:

✔ **Buy an add-on bottom drain.** Tetra makes a *vacuum attachment* (the rest of the koi world calls it an *add-on bottom drain*) for $45. It rests on the bottom of the pond, looking a bit like the vacuum wand for your canister vacuum. It hooks up to your water pump with a length of 2-inch flex hose (about $2.25 per foot not including any fittings).

✔ **Drape your pump intake and filter outflow pipes over the edge of the pond.** This approach is simpler than adding a drain, but it isn't so pretty. Add a prefilter (a foam filter-intake cover) to avoid catching one of your koi in the intake hose.

Figure 10-1 shows the various components of an indoor preformed pond.

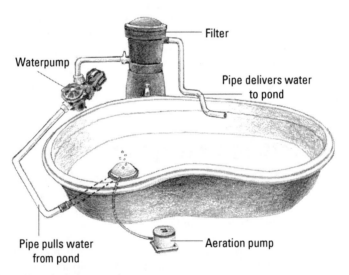

Filter

Waterpump

Pipe delivers water to pond

Pipe pulls water from pond

Aeration pump

Figure 10-1: An indoor pond setup.

Building and setting up a timber-and-liner pond

Landscape timers and a liner make for an easy-to-assemble, easy-to-take-down pond. You simply buy enough timbers to make the pond as high as you want it; four timbers, stacked atop each other, are a foot high, so each side of a 4-foot-high pond will need 16 timbers.

Constructing the pond

Landscape timbers are 3 inches high, 4 inches wide, and 8 feet long. If you make your pond 8 feet square, you won't have to cut any timbers. You simply fasten the stacked timbers together with 4-foot lengths of rebar, inserted through holes you drill in the timber. You'll need three lengths of rebar per side, one for each end of the time, and one in the center, for a total of 12 4-foot lengths.

1. **Using a 7/8 drill bit and an 8-foot length of 1 x 4, drill holes in the timber, 2 inches, 6 inches, 44 inches, and 48 inches from one end. Drill a fifth hole 2 inches from the far end.**

   This piece of timber will serve as a template, so you can drill all the timbers and the holes will match up.

2. **Use the template to drill these holes in every timber.**

3. **Lay the first course of timbers in a square, so the end of one piece abuts the side of the piece next to it.**

4. **Add the second layer of timbers so the corners are inter-locked, like a log cabin.**

5. **Repeat the layers, making certain the corners overlap.**

6. **When your layers are about a foot high, insert the rebar into the timbers so they are locked together, then continue to place the timbers, threading them onto the rebar.**

   There will be rebar at each end, and one near the center.

7. **Continue the courses until your pond is just one layer short of 4 feet high.**

Installing the drain line

Ask your local plumber to install a drain, unless your skills extend to modest plumbing. The drain can be as simple as the drain in your laundry room — a 3-inch PVC pipe, covered at floor level with a removable metal grate and leading to your back or side yard. You will use this drain when you flush, clean, or drain your pond, and when you backwash your filter. To get rid of the backwash, simply attach a 2-inch flexible hose to the backwash drain, stick the other end down into the drain, and open the filter's valve.

Backwash is loaded with nutrients, and it's a good fertilizer. But if there's salt in the water, you may not want it on your lawn; for this reason and perhaps for local regulations, your plumber may rec-ommend the drain be tied into your sewage line.

Incidentally, an indoor pond can be a good place to use your filter outflow for a small waterfall if you can position it so any splashing is kept within the pond. This added attraction also helps aerate the water.

Adding the filter intake and outflow

Now you need to place your filter and your water pump near the pond and hook them up. You need three sections of PVC or flexible swimming pool hose, 2 inches in diameter, or whatever size your filter and water pump take. If you use PVC, be prepared to cut it and add PVC preformed joints as needed.

You need one piece of hose or PVC pipe long enough to reach from the bottom drain to the water pump, one long enough to go between the water pump and the filter, and the third long enough to reach from the filter over the side of the pond and down into the pond. Follow the manufacturer's directions on securing the hose or PVC pipe to the various components.

1. **Check your filter to make certain the filter media is in place, and move the filter to the site you've chosen next to the pond.**

2. **Place your water pump adjacent to the filter.**

3. **Attach the intake hose/PVC pipe from the bottom drain to the water pump.**

4. **Attach the hose between the water pump and the filter.**

5. **Attach the filter outflow hose to the filter, and place the free end of the hose down into the pond.**

When you set up your indoor filter, some koi-keepers recommend replacing some of the new filter media with media from your outside pond and filling the filter tank with water from your outside pond. This step helps to establish the nitrifying (beneficial) bacteria in the filter. But beware: Using media and water from your outdoor pond also delivers any pathogens from that pond to your indoor pond. If you have any concerns about this, purchase a culture of nitrifying bacteria from your pond or pet store.

Adding the liner and water

If you've gone through the preceding sections, you're now ready for the final, glorious step: adding the liner and the water.

1. **Drape the liner into the pond, being careful to hold the corners neatly, and bring the upper edges out over the**

top landscape timber. You can cut slits in the top edge of the liner to make it fit around the rebar.

2. **Staple the liner onto the top of the timbers.**

3. **Thread the final landscape layer over the rebar to conceal the liner edge.**

4. **Add water.**

With this style of indoor pond, it's important that the water in the pond not come into contact with the treated landscape timbers. Keep the level of the water in the pond at least 4 inches below the top edge of the liner.

A good way to settle your indoor pond water is to put a few goldfish or inexpensive (read *ugly*) koi into your indoor pond a few weeks before the other koi. These trial fish will, by their behavior and adjustment (or nonadjustment!), bring to light any water-quality problems and will help feed the beneficial bacteria and mature your indoor pond water naturally.

Monitoring Water Quality

The drawback of indoor ponds is, of course, the size. This smaller pond system is chemically far more fragile than an outdoor pond. If you have an outdoor pond and think you've been very careful with your water readings this summer, ramp it up a notch. You have to be twice as vigilant and twice as concerned about small chemical changes in your indoor pond because the impact of these will be magnified in the reduced water volume.

Your vigilance on the indoor pond's water chemistry takes two factors into consideration:

✔ This new pond will have all the typical new-pond problems. Don't think you're getting away from them just because you're a seasoned pro with outdoor ponds.

✔ Your old nitrite-gobbling friend, algae, isn't going to grow on the walls of an indoor pond the way it does on an outdoor pond. Indoor ponds don't get enough sunlight for algae, so you may need to use a product like AmQuel Plus (the *plus* is important) to reduce nitrite levels.

Do the following to transition to a chemically balanced pond (please see Chapter 9 for details):

✔ Test your indoor pond for ammonia, nitrites, nitrates, and pH at least weekly or until the readings level out.

✔ Partially change the water (10 percent) every week to lower the ammonia and nitrite levels until the water chemistry settles down.

✔ Use a product like AmQuel Plus to remove nitrites.

Check out Table 10-2 for the correct chemistry levels for your indoor pond.

One of the simplest but most important ways to maintain your indoor pond's water quality is by not overfeeding. Koi, poor things, have no stomach. Their throat leads directly to their gut, so they have very little pause time, if you understand, between feeding and output. Koi don't need a great deal of food, and they can fast without bad results for a month or more. Bottom line: Feeding lightly is a good idea for the water quality of an indoor pond.

Table 10-2 Desired Values for Indoor Pond Water Quality

Component	Range
pH	6.8–7.6; ideally 7.4
Ammonia	As close to zero as possible; if pH is higher than 7.4, the toxic effect of any ammonia whatsoever is greatly increased.
Nitrites	Close to zero; above 1 part per million (1 ppm) stresses your fish
Nitrates	Close to zero — nitrates are a byproduct of filtration. A low level is okay because nitrates are a food source for pond plants or bog plants.
Chlorine/chloramines	Zero
Alkalinity	120–240 ppm
Salinity	Near zero unless fish are being treated for parasites or infection.
Dissolved oxygen	Decreases as water temperature gets above 80 degrees; 8 mg/L is ideal when water temps are about 77 degrees.

Adding the Finishing Touch: Releasing the Koi

You can add koi to your indoor pond after you've

- ✔ Filled, drained, and refilled the pond
- ✔ Treated the water for chlorine and chloramines
- ✔ Checked the pH level and temperature to make sure your fish won't undergo drastic pH or temperature changes

You may not want to put your prize Bekko in at this point. Instead, test drive your indoor pond by putting in a few goldfish (if you haven't already included them to help mature the water) or a few koi for a day or two and watch for any obvious signs of distress.

Before you add all of your koi, double-check those koi-load factors to be sure that your pond and its filtration system can support the fish you plan to keep in it (see Chapter 3). Then add your koi and call your koi friends to come over and admire your new indoor pond.

How to Tell When Something's Wrong (And How to Fix It)

No matter how much you read, plan, and prepare, problems will inevitably arise. You can prevent problems from becoming disasters by being alert and detecting them early, and by knowing what steps to take. The following hints will help you recognize and deal with the most commonly encountered difficulties.

- ✔ **Closely observe the fish.** Are they gasping at the surface of the water? Are they staying near the surface and not venturing down into the bottom of the pond?

- ✔ **Check your water chemistry values, especially for ammonia or nitrite levels.** A partial water change may help deal with the problem temporarily, but if the values go up again, you need to identify the cause and deal with it.

- ✔ **Check your dissolved oxygen levels.** Are they at least 5 milligrams per liter? You can increase the oxygen levels by using a small waterfall or one or two airstones.

  Can the problem be (gasp!) too many fish? Maybe the answer is a bigger indoor pond.

✔ **Check your pond for leaks.** The sooner you know about a leak, the better. You can buy a battery-operated leak detector (Skylink WA 318 is one) that consists of a sensor and a receiver for about $25. You place the sensor on the floor near the pond. When water touches electrodes on the bottom of the sensor, the sensor sets off a chime and a flashing light in the household receiver. The receiver can be located up to 300 feet away from the pond.

Prepare for the what-if of a pond leak. You may never need it, but thinking out a procedure ahead of time can save you time and headaches.

If you can't self-diagnose your pond problem, call an experienced koi-keeper to look at your setup and your fish. He may be able to see something that you don't — and it's a good way to find out more about your fish at the same time.

In the case of a total pond meltdown, your koi need help fast, and that likely means a koi buddy to the rescue. Friends like this arrive in the middle of the night with loaner show tanks or stock tanks, or they help you scoop your koi up and take them home to their own quarantine tubs, or they fill your bathtubs, dechlor that water, and move the survivors. They'll even call around and see who has room for what. There is no substitute for koi buddies. Lacking them, you should keep empty stock tanks or inexpensive plastic wading pools on hand. Be sure to have enough extra liquid dechlorinator to treat the water that you'll be adding to these enclosures.

Other supplies you'll need *just in case* include

✔ **A wet/dry shop vacuum** (Although the biggest versions can handle only about 10 gallons before you have to dump out the water, they take the water off the floor faster than you can mop.)

✔ **A dozen rolls of paper towels**

✔ **One or two buckets**

✔ **Big sponges**

✔ **A mop**

Part III

Caring for Koi and Keeping Them Healthy

"Notice their bright colors? That comes from a good diet, a healthy environment and a little airbrushing."

In this part . . .

Mares eat oats and little lambs eat ivy, but how about koi? With more than 20 kinds of koi food at the pond store, how do you know which ones to buy?

This part explains koi nutrition, recommends the best choices of commercial foods, and even tells you how to make your own koi food. (And *you* can eat it — it's loaded with good stuff.) We also give you the lowdown on koi stress, including its causes and how to avoid it. Finally, we key you into koi illnesses: how to spot and treat them and which ones you can't stop (that's why quarantining is important).

Chapter 11

Koi Nutrition 101

*J*ust like people, koi like to eat. And very much like people, they cheerfully consume diets high in fat or crammed with carbohydrates without a real concern for how they pan out in the long run (or long swim, as the case may be). Some foods that koi love to eat, like white bread and cooked rice, provide carbohydrates but not full nutrition, and the koi tend to load on weight with no real nutritional benefit.

The good news is that you can provide a healthful diet through commercial foods, and you don't have to pick up a single earthworm or cook up a batch of greens unless you want to. In this chapter, we tell you what koi need to eat, how to find commercial fish foods to fill those dietary requirements, and how you can supplement those commercial foods with foods from your garden or grocery store. We even tell you how to make your own koi food cakes (if you feel like cooking!).

Eating Right: It's All about Variety

No single food item provides total nutrition for koi, which is why a variety of food items is so important. Whether the food items are fresh (fresh from the ground, fresh from the sea, fresh from the field) or part of a dried or frozen commercial mix doesn't seem to matter. The important factor is the mix of ingredients.

Ideally, a wide variety of plant- and animal-based foods should be provided. The specifics of the koi's natural diet are not completely known and vary from location to location throughout their enormous range. Commercial diets also vary in their ingredients, including such diverse items as fish meal (made from 4–5 species), shrimp meal, krill, dried insects, corn, wheat, soybeans, rose hips, spirulina, oats, rice, and alfalfa. By combining these foods with various vitamins and minerals, several formulas have been devised that provide all the nutrients needed by captive koi. You can, of course, furnish a wholly fresh diet to your koi (and have no life other than koi-feeding), or, like serious koi-keepers, you can take advantage of high-quality commercial koi diets.

Making the Best Commercial Food Choices

Koi-food companies have spent years and hundreds of thousands of dollars to develop diets that appeal to koi and still offer complete nutrition in a packaged, dry form. But how can you tell whether the food you're buying is really a complete diet? Do federal standards exist like the ones for baby food?

Like cuts of meat, generally speaking, you get what you pay for with koi food. So, the not-so-good commercial brands exist alongside the good commercial brands and the very good commercial feeds. How can you tell which is which? Stick with us, dear reader; we walk you through it in this section.

 Koi-food manufacturers spend a lot of money on package design because they want to catch your eye. If the label's attractive, it helps entice you, the consumer, into picking the container up — and that's half the battle. An attractive package can also entice you to spend more than you planned and distract you from your real goal, which is to buy good nutrition for your koi.

What to look for in koi food

 When you're purchasing koi food, size matters. Look for pellets that are keyed to the size of your koi. Young koi (4 inches or less) need a pellet small enough to eat right away, so they don't have to wait for it to fall apart. Look for pellets about one-eighth inch across for small koi. Quarter-inch pellets are fine for adult koi.

When you're sure you're looking at the right size of food, you still have some choices to make, and it's easy to get confused.

Basically, you want to pay attention to the variety of ingredients and to the levels of vitamins, minerals, protein, and fat. To narrow down your choices, read the contents list on the container to ensure that these important nutrients are at appropriate levels (as described later in this chapter), and that the food draws its ingredients from varying sources.

Some details to note about koi food products:

✔ The list can include vitamins and items as common as ground corn and as arcane as rose hips. Specifics as to the actual value of each may be lacking, but experience has shown that such foods are good for koi and readily accepted by them.

✔ Some ingredients can meet more than one nutritional guideline. (For instance, wheat germ can provide vitamins, protein, and carbohydrates, and oils can provide energy and vitamins.) Koi nutrition is not an exact science, so don't worry about ingredients that seem to overlap. Reputable companies use formulas that have, over time, been shown to provide koi with fairly complete nutrition.

Koi are pretty simple creatures, so you don't need to buy 18 kinds of koi food and still wonder about the nutritional value. You just need to stick with diets that meet the guidelines set out here and add a few of the extra items that we will discuss in the following pages. The following sections lay out the essentials for your koi's diet.

Protein

Protein is one of the most important contents because fish need it for energy, growth, and tissue repair.

The best sources of protein in a koi diet are fish meal and soybeans. Animal protein (from chicken for example) is not as digestible. Fish sources may include whitefish meal, anchovy meal, herring meal, and shrimp meal.

The protein content may be 25 to 36 percent of your koi's diet, depending on the season and the age of your koi. Consider the following information as a guide:

✔ **During the summer:** Protein should be 30 to 36 percent of the diet when the energy needs of your koi are higher (during the active summer months).

✔ **During the winter:** Protein should be nearer 25 percent of the diet when koi are less active and their metabolism slows (in the fall and early winter). In southern states where the weather remains warm, your fish will not enter a dormant stage, so plan to feed them a higher protein diet year-round.

✔ **When they're young (under 3 years of age):** Protein should be 30 to 36 percent of the diet.

Look for a food that lists protein first on the ingredients label. (All manufacturers list contents from highest to lowest according to their dry-weight quantity.)

If you prefer to stay on the middle ground and not veer into high or low protein levels, buy plant-derived protein sources, like wheat germ pellets. These sources generally provide enough protein (and they're a good source of vitamin E). You can give these to your koi throughout the year, but they are especially important during the cooler seasons.

Carbohydrates

Carbohydrates are another energy source. They're also good sources of fiber and a main component of vegetables and fruit. (See the later section on fiber for more info on fiber in the koi diet.) If koi don't have carbs for easy-to-obtain energy, your koi break down protein instead, which leads to a vastly increased output of ammonia. However, you need to strike the right balance because too many carbs can lead to chubby koi. The correct amount is not firmly established, but 60 to 70 percent is safe. Suitable sources for carbs are plant-based foods such as wheat, corn, soybeans, and rose hips.

Lipids

Oils and fats (or simply *lipids*) are another source of energy and a good source of fat-soluble vitamins like A, D, E, and K. Koi derive lipids from animal-based foods such as fish meal and shrimp meal, as well as from fish oil and wheat germ oil.

An ideal koi diet consists of 3 to 10 percent fat. The high end is for fast-growing young fish, and the low end is for adult fish. The fat content of the diet should come from easily digested sources, such as wheat germ, during the colder months when the fish's metabolisms are operating at a reduced pace.

Vitamins and minerals

Vitamins and minerals are important components of a koi diet (as they are for any living organism). Little is known of the exact levels required by koi, but those included in long-established commercial foods can be trusted.

Fiber

Fiber is the vehicle that carries the food components through the digestive system where they are then absorbed. The longer the food's in the gut (within limits, of course), the more time the fish has to absorb the nutrients. This is obviously the advantage to fiber in the diet. However, the less fiber, the less bulk in the excreted feces, which is important when you're raising koi in fairly high numbers because less bulk means less strain on your filtration system. In practice, however, your best option is not to attempt to regulate feces composition via diet. Rather, feed a standard commercial diet and use adequate filtration for the number of koi you have. If you feel you must reduce the volume of the feces that your fish produce, use a lower-fiber food, such as wheat germ pellets, as the main portion of their diet.

Good sources of fiber are ground corn, oats, wheat germ, and similar plant-based foods. The fiber provided by these generally makes up about 5 percent of commercial diets, which seems to be an adequate level. Fiber content should, like other foods, be reduced in the cooler months. Recommended winter foods such as wheat germ pellets have a fiber content of 2 to 3 percent.

Sinking versus floating food

Koi foods are either floating or sinking. Sinking foods do just that, making them seem like a good choice for fish that are usually *bottom feeders* (fish that swim along the bottom of a pond or stream, taking up mouthfuls of this and that and spitting out what doesn't taste like food). But pond koi are another matter entirely. Because display-quality koi can cost hundred of dollars, you most likely want to see these living jewels. So, feeding your fish floating food simply increases your opportunity to enjoy your treasure chest. Floating food is also practical for three reasons:

- ✔ It helps you keep track of how much food you actually drop into your pond.

- ✔ The food disperses over the surface of your pond, giving each fish a chance to feed.

- ✔ It gives you a chance to interact with your fish, to see who's feeding and who isn't, and to check out who may have scale or other health issues (see Chapter 13 for info on what to do about health and scale problems).

Because koi fry understand from day one that food comes from the sky and stays on the pond surface, your koi already know how to eat a floating commercial diet. Koi just out of the egg are often brought up on flake food by the breeder and then graduate to floating pellets.

Does this stuff ever go bad?

Don't rely on the old sniff test to see whether your koi food is still good. You can't really tell whether it's gone rancid because they all smell pretty bad even when you open them!

Although few fish foods are dated, try to buy a quantity you can use within four months. Also, buy from a store that has a high turnover rate so you're not buying food that's been on the shelf for a couple of months. Some brands actually have *use by* dates on the package, which makes it easier to tell whether the product is fresh.

If you want to be extra-cautious (because you're new to koi-keeping or have some very expensive koi in your pond), you may want to store the open container in your refrigerator to slow down deterioration. Some koi-keepers buy a six-month supply, decant a month's worth into a container, put the rest in freezer bags, and store the bags in their freezer until needed.

In fall, when the pond waters cool, we suggest you use sinking pellets. Koi are less active in cooler water, so the sinking pellets are easier for the koi to feed on. Just don't go overboard in quantity because your fish won't be nearly as hungry as they were in the warmer months. (We talk about seasonal feedings and food quantities later in this chapter.)

When you use sinking pellets, broadcast them over the surface of the pond so they're dispersed as they sink. The quantity is the same as for floating pellets.

Adding Some Simple (And Lively) Treats

Although the commercial diets provide good nutrition to your koi, you can offer snack foods in limited quantities from your grocer, your garden, or your local bait store that your koi will obviously enjoy. If you feed treats daily, reduce the amount of commercial food. Feeding a diet composed entirely of fresh foods is not recommended because it's extremely difficult to provide the dietary variety necessary for good health.

Try these as treats in spring or summer:

- **Romaine lettuce:** Cut the head into quarters and toss them into the water. It may take a while, but your koi put their lips and mouths to good use as they shred and devour the lettuce.

✔ **Oranges:** Slice a whole orange into six sections, but leave the skin on. Your koi can slurp out the pulp. If you want to prolong the process, cut across the orange to create floating orange slices. You'll see a bobbing-for-apples action, only in reverse.

✔ **Earthworms:** Toss these into the pond, one at a time, and watch what happens when your koi discover them. This is one of the best natural foods you can provide, and even if you overfeed, it doesn't affect the water quality.

Earthworms are especially useful as a conditioning food before spawning or as an end-of-winter appetite wakeup. You can dig these from your garden — maybe — or you can buy them from bait stores. We buy ours by the 500-lot from a mail-order fishing supply company and store them in our refrigerator.

✔ **Live crayfish:** When you toss a few live crayfish into the pond, you'll be reminded of the koi's closeness to their wild brethren, the carp.

✔ **Freshwater *glass* shrimp (also called *grass* shrimp):** Add a half cup to your pond and watch your koi take on the treat.

Note: Other people feed live tadpoles, but we like tadpoles too much to feed them to our koi.

Live foods are only an addition to the commercial diet. They don't offer a nutritional diet by themselves (and they're too expensive to be a steady diet anyway).

Avoiding Foods that Do No Good

Koi have extremely hearty appetites, and it therefore comes as no surprise that they will consume foods that are not necessarily good for them. The foods discussed in this section are tempting to use because they are quite easy to come by and relished by koi. However, they serve little purpose in the diet and should be avoided.

Most of us can remember going to a goldfish or koi pond sometime in the not-so-distant past and maybe tossing cubes of white bread to the gaping mouths. White bread provides very little nutrition and lots of carbohydrates — not good for your koi.

Whole meal bread is slightly better than white bread, but it may cause eye protrusion *(exophthalmia),* an ugly sight and one that can leave even experienced koi-keepers clueless as to the cause.

Making your own koi cakes

Adult or subadult koi (8 inches or longer) may benefit from a home-cooked meal, or rather, koi cubes. These will provide a variety of fresh ingredients not usually found in commercial diets. In addition to being a welcome change of pace for your koi, the cubes are another way of introducing variety into the diet. The following is the recipe for this delicacy:

1. **Chop each of the following ingredients separately in a food processor or a chopper (we use a small electric chopper).**

   10 ounces frozen, chopped collard greens

   5 ounces frozen green peas

   5 ounces whitefish or imitation crab meat

   ½ green pepper, chopped

   1 tablespoon each: freeze-dried tubifex worms (available at any pet store), wheat germ

   1 teaspoon montmolinite

2. **Combine all ingredients and then puree them.**

3. **Add the pureed ingredients from Step 2 to 2½ cups of cold water. Mix well.**

4. **Combine the following ingredients in a separate bowl and mix well:**

   1 teaspoon liquid vitamins, like you'd buy in a pet store

   8 packages unflavored gelatin

   2½ cups boiling water

5. **Stir the hot mix into the cold mix.**

6. **Spray mini ice-cube trays or mini muffin tins with an aerosol oil spray, fill with the final collard mixture, and freeze.**

   The frozen cubes will thaw rapidly when you put them into the pond and can be used as a replacement for the usual diet on a random basis. Feed as you would other food — as much as the fish will consume in 5 minutes or so.

Trout pellets are another food to avoid — some people are tempted to feed them to koi because they're cheap and large. These pellets are a high-protein food designed for rapid growth in trout. You want your koi to grow at normal rates so they become well shaped as opposed to bloated.

Supplying Supplements

Koi-food sales are big business, and the food manufacturer who can make a convincing case for food supplements is richer than one who can't. Some manufacturers promote rapid growth or brighter colors, while others push the concept of treats for special occasions, in celebration of an event, or as a reward.

Do your koi need these supplements? You can answer this question yourself. You know if you're raising fry, or if your brightly colored koi could benefit from a color supplement (see the nearby sidebar, "Color-enhancing diets").

Do koi need treats? Probably not. Koi don't need to be motivated the way humans do. On the other fin, maybe offering treats makes you feel as if you're providing a better diet or a more interesting life to your fish. Or maybe offering these food items results in more time and interaction with your fish. If so, go ahead. But like the labels say, offer these foods in moderation, as an occasional treat.

Color-enhancing diets

Color-enhancing diets are foods with supplements — like carotene (the stuff that makes carrots orange and flamingo feathers pink) or spirulina (green algae that boost red and yellow coloration). People like to feed these enhancers because they think their fish will be brighter and hence easier to spot in the pond.

Both of these additives enhance red coloration. If you select a food with spirulina, remember that most koi-keepers only give their koi spirulina supplements in September because this plant-based food is readily digested when the water temperature drops. (Don't feed it when the pond temperature drops below 40 degrees F because your koi won't feed at such temperatures.) Just to confuse the issue, other keepers use spirulina to brighten up their koi a month before they enter their koi in a show.

Although brighter fish colors may sound attractive, think for a moment about your fish before you go that route. Color enhancers add a pink blush to a koi's white skin — not what you want, for instance, when you've spent big bucks for a Shiro Bekko, a black and white koi. On the other hand, if your prize koi are all Hi Utsuri (red and black koi), feeding a color enhancer may turn those fish into knockouts. Use color enhancers just once daily.

Feeding Koi through the Seasons

One of the charms of the koi pond is that you don't have to feed the koi year-round. Koi stop feeding and digesting their food when water temps near 50 degrees F. But just because it's 50 degrees outside doesn't mean your pond is that cool. Your filter circulates the water in your pond twice every hour (or at least it should), so your pond doesn't have much of a *cool sink* (a calm, undisturbed area where cool water can collect) at the bottom. As a result, your water may be warmer than the air temperature because it can pick up heat from the sun while being moved about by the filter's pump.

Of course, if you heat your pond, the air temperature has less effect on the water temperature.

Use a pool thermometer to check the temperature at the bottom of the pond in both heated and unheated situations. Monitoring the water temperature will prevent the surprises that can arise because of sudden weather changes or heater failure. Two types of thermometers are

- ✔ A digital version with a probe at the end of a cable for pond use

- ✔ A submersible thermometer tied to the end of a nylon cord

   Make the cord long enough so the thermometer hangs near the bottom of the pond. (For obvious reasons, be sure to secure the out-of-pond end of the cord to a structure at the edge of the pond!)

You want to know the temperature near the bottom of the pond in case you lose power some cold, wintry day. If the bottom of your pool dips below 50 degrees, you have to take action (see Chapter 17 on what to do when your power goes out).

Following are koi-feeding guidelines keyed to water temperature:

- ✔ **Over 75 degrees:** Feed floating pellets two to four times a day, as much as the fish will consume in 5 minutes or so.

- ✔ **70 to 75 degrees:** Feed floating pellets two to four times a day, but add koi cubes or a treat such as earthworms or crayfish twice a week to bulk up the fish for cold resistance.

- ✔ **55 to 70 degrees:** Feed wheat germ pellets twice a day.

   When the water temperature falls below 59 degrees (15 degrees Celsius), koi metabolism also falls. Provide a food that's readily digested because the friendly bacteria in the gut (that digest the food) also slow down. Because your fish aren't active, they don't need much protein.

> ✔ **50 to 55 degrees:** Feed wheat germ pellets once a day.
>
> ✔ **50 degrees and below:** Do not feed when water temperatures remain at 50 degrees or less.

Establishing the Timing and Right Amounts for Feedings

Koi seem to be willing to eat any time food hits the pond surface. But when koi are fed until they're stuffed, their excretion rate increases, which in turn increases ammonia levels in the water. High ammonia levels and the bloom in the bacteria that eat the unconsumed food can overwhelm a filter that had been perfectly satisfactory. The water becomes foul, and your fish are in trouble as they try to extract oxygen from the icky soup they now swim in. So go easy on the feedings until you see for yourself what quantity to offer. You can feed less at each feeding and increase the number of feedings if you're concerned about your koi going hungry.

Rather than measuring out a specific amount of food to feed your koi at every feeding, use the time rule: Toss some pellets into the pond and wait five minutes. If the food's gone, toss in some more pellets and wait another five minutes. You're looking for the amount of food that the koi eat in five minutes. The basic amount we recommend to begin with is a teaspoon of food per 5 inches of fish per feeding.

For a very basic maintenance diet, koi need at least 2 percent of their body weight in food a day. But most koi owners agree that capturing and weighing koi puts more stress on them than simply tossing in food and making sure it's gone within five minutes.

If you feed them, they will grow

One of the interesting facts about koi is that they never stop growing. The growth rate slows as the fish reach sexual maturity at 10 to 12 inches, but koi continue to grow throughout their lives unless something intervenes (like the pond becomes crowded or the water quality deteriorates). This fact explains why the 1-meter koi looms out there like a big juicy tempting plum.

Because koi generally grow less during the winter and more during the summer, you can actually figure out how old a koi is. They add growth rings to their scales. Alas, if koi are in warm ponds year-round and fed year-round, the rings are harder to count.

Feeding times

Most koi-keepers feed their koi in the morning, using the theory that filter can pull the waste from the pond before the fish submerge to the bottom of the pond at night. In actuality, any daylight hour is a good time to feed your koi, but try to stick to a schedule. You'll soon find your fish gathering near the feeding station just before feeding time, getting very excited as you approach. Keep in mind that smaller amounts of food given more frequently put less strain on your filter.

Even during the warmer months you may have a reason not to feed your koi every day. Koi that are going to be shipped or exhibited in a show are not fed for several days before the ship or show date. The lack of food ensures the koi don't excrete while in their shipping container so they don't have to breathe contaminated water.

Hand feeding

Many koi-keepers enjoy feeding their koi by hand. They put the pellets in their hand, sit by the pond, and lower their hand into the water until the pellets are floating a few inches above their hand. Koi will shove each other out of the way as they suck in the food, and occasionally they'll sample — and discard — your hand. Don't worry, it just tickles.

Using automatic feeders

Automatic feeders are one way to make sure your koi are fed. These feeders work either on a timer or on demand, where the koi nudge a pendulum on the feeder base.

For fry, the timed feeder is best because they're too small to activate the demand feeder, and they need food at regular intervals. Timed feeders can be activated by solar panels (which need only light, not direct sun), by spring-loaded built-in timers, by computer signals, or by electricity.

Select the one that works best for you (and for your budget). Adult koi seem to enjoy working the on-demand feeders, and you can set the feeder hopper to dispense a smaller amount of food upon each activation if you're worried your koi will make pigs of themselves.

Chapter 12

Diffusing Koi Stress

*S*tress is an unavoidable part of life for any living creature. It's simply a reaction to something uncomfortable or new, which translates at first blush to *possibly dangerous*. A creature's avoidance reaction is a lifesaving gesture; fish in the wild simply swim away from the perceived problem or anxiety source. But koi under our care can't leap out and go searching for greener pastures, so to speak. If ammonia levels in the pond are too high, those fish are stuck. And being stuck topples their anxiety into stress.

In this chapter, we help you notice when your koi are stressed and help you understand the factors that most often cause that stress. We also tell you how to alleviate or remove those stressors. In most cases, fixing the problem just requires a bit of work and forethought on your part.

How Can a Fish Possibly Feel Stress?

Human stress has two sides — emotional and physical. Although it's difficult for us to understand the emotional life of a koi, or any other animal for that matter, the physical aspects of stress operate very similarly in both humans and animals. Basically, when an animal perceives a dangerous or disturbing situation, his body releases a variety of chemical messengers to help deal with the problem (enter the *fight or flight* reaction). The threatened creature is physically prepared by his various hormones and chemical messengers to take appropriate action in the form of defense or escape. A number of bodily functions are affected — eyesight sharpens, running speed increases by adrenaline, digestion is suspended to allow blood to flow to the brain and limbs, and so on.

These reactions are necessary to the survival of all creatures. Problems arise, however, in unnatural situations — captivity, in particular. The creature's system is being flooded with chemicals that are preparing it to escape, but it has nowhere to go. For example, if ammonia levels in the pond are high, the koi must deal with the adverse effects of the ammonia as well as the conflicting signals within their own bodies.

Although useful in crisis situations, the stress chemicals cause severe health problems if they are released long term, especially if the animal can't react appropriately — where, for example, the koi's body is being primed to swim quickly, but it can't. Another health issue is the fact that, in times of stress, the body shuts down functions that aren't essential to immediate survival. The most common areas are digestion and reproduction, and, over time, these can be severely impaired.

Of even more concern is the long-term effect on the immune system — animals under stress sicken and die from ailments or micro-organisms that may normally be of little consequence. Stress is one of the most serious aspects of fish health but isn't well understood and is easily overlooked. Providing your koi with a suitable, stress-free captive environment is a vital step in ensuring their good health.

Signs Your Koi Are Stressing Out

Because koi aren't exactly big talkers, how on earth can they tell you anything, much less mention that they're stressed? You don't always need words to detect stress.

A huge part of detecting stress is observance. You simply watch your fish and let their behavior tell you how they're feeling.

The signs of illness in koi are both specific and nonspecific. The nonspecific signs are behavioral, and the specific indications are physical symptoms. The following examples are typical stress behaviors and indications to watch for:

- Failing to snorkel near the surface when feeder is near
- Jumping
- Lying partially on its side
- Remaining near the bottom of the pond

✔ Rubbing against items in the pond, as if to dislodge something from the skin

✔ Staying by itself; not joining with others to feed

✔ Swimming lethargically or with a tighter, almost jerky rhythm

✔ Trying to hide under ledges or under waterfall outflows

Physical symptoms are changes in appearance that often point to a specific disease. They include

✔ Clamped fins

✔ Fin damage

✔ Pale gills

✔ Raised scales

✔ Swollen areas of the body

✔ White spots on the body and gills

You can use mechanical ways to find out whether the problem is with your pond or your fish's health. For example, you can test the water for ammonia levels, or you can net and bowl your big Yamabuki ("yamabuki" is short for the Japanese term "Yamabuki Ogon" and refers to koi that are bright yellow in color) and see whether its gill covers have a problem (for a description of gill lice, see Chapter 13).

Sources of Stress and How to Fix Them

Pretty much all the stress that koi experience is human-caused. This is one of those blanket statements that points the finger of responsibility right at you, the koi owner. You put a pond in and okayed the design and the filtration system. You selected the koi — and the number of koi for the pond. And you decided to enter that 24-inch Shiro Bekko (a white koi with black markings) in the next koi show.

The good news is that, when you know your koi's stressor, you can take steps to alleviate the problem.

All this responsibility may seem a bit daunting, but don't let it weigh you down. Koi are too beautiful and too enjoyable to allow you to be discouraged, and most times, your koi are just fine as long as you provide them with adequate food and care. In this section, we look at what, specifically, causes stress in koi and how you can avoid or remedy stressful situations.

Water quality

The quality of your water (or lack thereof) is the biggest source of potential stress for your koi. Day in, day out, night in, night out, your koi breathe in water, extract oxygen, and push the water back out. But in fish, gills have a dual role — in addition to allowing for respiration, they are also excretory organs. As a result, fish excrete ammonia across their gill surface and release it into the water. Therefore, a water-quality test should be your first reaction to any abnormal behavior (lethargy, rubbing, disinterest in food, and so forth) that your koi exhibit.

Water in a clean pond dilutes the excreted ammonia, and then the bacteria in the biological filter (see Chapter 6) gobble it up. But in a dirty pond, or a pond with a nonfunctioning biological filter, the ammonia levels build up. Ammonia levels increase after the koi have been fed, and they really go up when koi are overfed. The higher the ammonia level in the pond, the more difficulties your koi have trying to push their ammonia out across their gill surface and in breathing in general.

In people, ammonia irritates lung tissue. Irritated bronchioles can't absorb oxygen or exchange carbon dioxide. Fish have a similar reaction. Exposure to environmental ammonia makes the gill coverings swell. The rate of water flow across the gill surface decreases as does the gas exchange rate (the flow of oxygen into and carbon dioxide out of the body). Your koi may try to dislodge this irritation by rubbing the sides of its face/gills against a hard surface. Unless you pull out your water test kit (see Chapter 5) and discover the high ammonia content, you may think your koi has parasites (see Chapter 13).

Low oxygen levels

Check your pond's dissolved oxygen levels, although fish that can't get enough oxygen from the water generally will be at the water's surface, gasping. While you're trying to ID the reason for the lower oxygen levels, add a compressor and a couple of big airstones to your pond to make your koi more comfortable while you nail down the cause of the problem. In addition to the airstones, do a partial water change and add a trickle feature to your filter outflow. The trickle feature can be a waterfall or a fountain, or you can let the water from the filter roll down a flat surface before it enters the pond — anything to increase the surface area exposed to the air. Now you can look for the cause of the problem.

Watch out for triggers you can't control

You can be as vigilant as possible, but sometimes happenings outside your control affect your water quality. For instance, it rains after your neighbor fertilizes his lawn, so some of that fertilizer runs off into your pond. Careful planning in the initial stages of pond construction — locating it away from an area bordering on a neighbor's lawn, for example — can go a long way in preventing such problems. But don't expect to be able to foresee everything. Plan as best you can, but remain alert and be prepared to take emergency action when necessary.

The oxygen levels can be depressed because of hot weather, pond additives such as potassium permanganate or an algaecide like AlgaeFix, or too many koi in your pond.

Crowding

Koi don't deal well with crowds because a crowded pond affects water quality. All your tests may tell you your pond's water quality is within acceptable parameters, but if you have too many koi in your pond, those fish are living in a narrow band of water quality. Anything that decreases that water quality has an immediate effect on the fish. One small change (for example, the weather gets hotter, causing the water to contain less oxygen, or sudden cool weather causes the warmer lower layer of water to rise, bringing with it fish waste that had settled to the pond's bottom) and suddenly all your fish are affected.

How do you avoid crowding your koi? Use our formula of 1 ½ inches of koi per square foot of pond surface. A 9-x-9-foot pond has 81 square feet of surface area and can be home to a total of 80 inches of koi — or eight 10-inchers.

Keep in mind that these fish are going to grow at least 4 inches per fish per year. Now, a sensible person would just sell off a fish a year to keep the total inches to a reasonable level. But real koi nuts like us just build a bigger pond!

Moving your fish

Who doesn't get stressed out by the idea of a big move? Even the hardiest of souls gets a little rattled with all the packing, unpacking, unfamiliar surroundings, and so on.

Again, your koi are no different. Netting and moving your koi stresses them. When you move your fish, you're moving your fish literally into new waters. The pH is different, the water temperature may be different, and the levels of dissolved gases (including oxygen and ammonia) are different. Even the light levels are different, especially at a new site.

A koi's reaction to a move will be influenced by many things, including the length of the process, the degree of difference in the two environments, and the fish's individual character. Upon introduction to their new home, your koi may swim about quickly for a short time, and then remain fairly still in deep water or under cover. This is a normal reaction to stress, and should pass within a day or so. They will also likely not eat for the first day or two. If they are not behaving normally within two to three days, you should check your water quality and make adjustments as necessary.

Moving your koi to a new place with little or no stress is a fairly simple process, but not a fast one. If you're bringing in some new koi or moving them from an old pond to a newer, bigger pond (koi ponds only get bigger), you need to acclimate your fish to the new water. Follow these steps:

1. **Add some of the new pond water to the water in the plastic bag or transport dish and then wait five minutes.**

2. **Test the water in the bag for ammonia and nitrite level, and check the temperature. Add some more water and wait again.**

3. **Repeat these steps until your test kit and thermometer show no difference between the two waters.**

For more precautions when adding new fish, see Chapter 5.

After your koi are in their new digs, keep an eye on them for a few days, even if they're by themselves in a quarantine pond. The stress of the move makes them susceptible to almost everything: particles floating around in the water, subclinical conditions, you name it.

If at all possible, provide a darkened area for your new koi. Koi adjust better to change when they feel secure, and they feel secure in darkened areas. Some koi owners put their plastic koi bags — the ones used for shipping koi — into black plastic bags before the bag/koi combination goes into the shipping container, or *styro*. If your pond doesn't have darker areas in the deepest portion, try to shade part of the pond to create a darker area.

Temperature extremes

Koi are very tolerant carp temperature-wise. They can live in out-door ponds in water temperatures of 36 to 85 degrees F. But keep in mind that the temperature in these ponds should fluctuate slowly, giving the fish a chance to acclimate.

When the water's too cold

Your pond thermometer should read above 50 degrees. Much colder than that, and your water freezes — "Goodbye, koi," and "Hello, fish popsicle."

Normally, semidormant koi in a winterized pond between 36 and 50 degrees stay in motion, swimming very slowly or pausing and remaining upright in the pond. In ponds where the water tempera-ture is above 50 degrees, koi move around more readily and feed. Koi that are too cold are lethargic, lie at an angle on the bottom of the pond, and don't feed. If the water remains below 50 degrees for too long, they may die.

You can use several methods to correct a too-cold pond, beginning with temporary quick fixes and moving toward maintenance for getting through the whole winter in good shape:

- ✔ **Make partial water changes, providing the temperature of the new water is warmer than the pond water.** Don't change more than 30 percent of the water and be sure to dechlorinate as you add the water.

- ✔ **Add a pond heater.** For a smaller pond (less than 1,000 gal-lons), you can use electric heating tubes. They look much like your standard aquarium heater, but are larger, more durable, and use more current.

  You can also opt for a gas unit that's part of the pond construction and hooks up to your filtering system.

- ✔ **Cover the pond with a plastic tarp or an insulated pool cover (leave one corner uncovered to allow for gas exchange) to prevent heat loss.** By monitoring the water's temperature after the cover is in place, you should be able to adjust what parts of the pond are covered and how long the cover is in place.

Refer to Chapter 9 for detailed information on how to winterize your pond.

When the pond's too warm

If your pond thermometer reads above 82 degrees, you don't have much of a margin of safety. Your koi are probably rolling near the water's surface, gasping for oxygen.

One reason koi ponds need to be at least 3 feet deep is for temperature stability. Ever notice how warm the water in a kid's 8-inch-high swimming pool gets on a summer's day, especially when the pool is in the sun? The deeper a koi pond is, the more stable its water temperature can be. And with less direct sunlight, the koi pond can stay even cooler.

Although koi are fine in water that may reach 85 degrees, you're pushing the envelope. Temps this warm stress your koi because warm water holds less oxygen, which makes koi work harder to breathe. This extra work makes koi sitting ducks, as the saying goes, if one of them gets a scrape or if the ammonia levels rise.

To cool your pond immediately, add cold water to your pond (usually, the temperature of the water as it leaves the tap is suitable). Again, add no more than 30 percent of the pond volume, and dechlorinate as you add the water.

If a too-warm pond is a chronic problem for you, try shading part of or the entire pond with woven bamboo screening. You can use bamboo window shades (available in home improvement stores) or the woven shade cloth that gardeners use to shield plants from the sun. See Chapter 8 for more on landscaping the pond.

Other potential causes

Koi may indicate their discomfort by jumping. If the ammonia and nitrite levels in the water are okay, there has to be another reason for the acrobatics.

Do you have a submersible pump? Submersibles have been known to short-circuit, and when this happens, your fish are going to feel it. Don't bother to get the pump fixed; you and your koi are better off if you replace the submersible with an in-line pump.

Are your koi new to the pond? Koi may jump if the pond is new to them. Sometimes differing water chemistry values, although acceptable, are different enough from what the koi is used to, and the fish feels, well, jumpy. Adding some koi tunnels on the bottom of the pond or some floating pieces of Styrofoam to the pond will give them a place of refuge and increase their security level.

Chapter 13

Spotting and Treating Common Koi Ailments

*T*his is the chapter we hope you never need, but if your koi get sick, this information can help you figure out the problem and its remedy. Our goal is to help you avoid the loss of even one koi.

Koi can seem delicate when you realize everything that can make them sick — the quick change of their pond's temperature, below par water quality, new koi that haven't gone through a 30-day quarantine period, and so on.

The amazing part is that after you know the cause and make a few corrections, the koi get well (if the condition hasn't gone on too long). Usually. We add the qualifier because koi with koi herpes virus (KHV) don't get well. This virus has no treatment and the disease is highly contagious to other koi.

Everyone understands that when an expensive koi gets sick, the effort to save that koi is worthwhile. But we think all koi, even those that aren't drop-dead gorgeous, deserve the very same effort. So in this chapter, we give you all you need to recognize a sick koi, to identify (or at least narrow down) the problem, and to start treating your beloved pet.

Empowering You, Because Koi Vets Are Few

Koi vets in the United States are few and far between. In fact, koi vets are rare around the world.

Part of the reason for the low number is the low number of koi-keepers (compared to dog and cat owners, for example). And part of the reason is that people don't know about koi. Think about it. Koi don't need to be walked, they don't need shots, and they don't bring home fleas. What's not to love about koi?

The demand for small-animal care is a lot greater than the demand for koi medical care, so veterinary colleges spend very little time offering courses in fish care of any type. Veterinarians learn koi-keeping details after graduation, from other veterinarians, advanced courses, books, koi-keepers, and koi breeders.

Don't fret, though. This chapter provides a load of guidance to help you diagnose and treat your sick koi. If you also want to seek professional guidance, consult one or more of the following sources:

- ✔ **Your local veterinarian:** Although only a dozen or so koi veterinarians practice in the United States, almost every veterinarian can help when problems crop up in your pond.

- ✔ **Fish farms and aquariums:** Tropical-fish farms in Florida often have a veterinarian on staff. Commercial aquariums, like the Tennessee Aquarium, employ their own veterinarian. These veterinarians may be able to answer your questions.

- ✔ **Koi health specialists:** The lack of formal veterinary training has led to another specialization, koi health specialist. Any serious hobbyist can take this certificate program. The United States has two programs: one is operated by the Mid-Atlantic Koi Club (MAKC, www.makc.com) and the other by the American Koi Association.

- ✔ **Other koi fanciers:** Talk to other koi-keepers because most likely they've been there, done that, and they're great at sharing their expertise.

  Search online through the Mid-Atlantic Koi Club (see earlier bullet) or the Associated Koi Clubs of America Web sites for contact information. If you're not handy with the Web, ask your local public librarian to help you make the search.

Before you contact someone about your koi's ailment, be prepared to answer the questions that you wil be asked:

- How old is your fish? (Younger koi are more susceptible to KHV and spring viremia of carp [SVC] viruses.)
- How long have you had the fish?
- When did you notice that something was wrong?
- Is the fish eating?
- What size is your pond?
- How many fish are in it?
- What are your water chemistry values?
- What type of filtration do you use?
- Have you added any new fish to the pond?
- Has the fish been treated with any medications?
- How is the fish acting?

Taking a Close Look: The Do-It-Yourself Koi Exam

The diagnosis of koi ailments is a tricky business, and serious problems are best left to a veterinarian. However, it is, in some respects, an art as well as a science, and therefore as you gain experience you may learn to recognize certain problems.

Catching your koi

In order to closely examine your koi, you will first need to contain it within a small place. This can be quite difficult or easy, depending upon the size of your pond, the koi's temperament and state of health, and your own skill. You may want to practice netting and bowling your koi when your fish are healthy, so that you will be prepared in the event a fish falls ill.

Examining your sickly fish

Signs of injury and disease in koi range from very obvious to quite subtle. A comprehensive physical exam, as described in this section, offers the best chance of detecting your koi's particular ailment.

Surveying his overall appearance

Although netting and bowling your koi adds to its stress, you need to examine him to identify the problem and treat the illness. Once he's in the bowl:

1. **Look for external parasites.**

   (See the section on parasites later in this chapter to help you ID and deal with them.)

2. **Look for any open wounds, or abnormal appearance to the body or fins.**

3. **Lift your koi out of the water using your wetted hands, and check for lesions or open wounds on his underside.**

4. **Put him back in the bowl when you're done, and gently pour out most of the water in the bowl so you can take a swab or a scraping.**

Taking a swab or scrape

Taking a swab is not as traumatic as it sounds. Follow these steps:

1. **Drag and roll a wet cotton swab over the gill covers, or along the base of the dorsal fin, or along the base of the tail to gather some of the mucous that coats the fish's body.**

   Always swab from the head to the tail, working in the direction the scales grow.

2. **Roll the swab along the surface of a microscope slide, add a drop of pond water and a cover slip, and examine the mucous (after it's on a slide, it's called a *smear*) under a microscope.**

   As an alternative, your veterinarian may furnish you with the swab, a tube, and a mailer envelope to send the specimen to a lab to identify possible bacteria.

If the swab is inconclusive, or if external parasites are suspected, your veterinarian may suggest the slightly more invasive *skin scrape*. To take a skin scrape, do the following:

1. **Scrape a blunt object, like a glass slide, along the body to gather some of the mucous.**

   This step is the same as Step 1 for the swab, but because you need to apply a bit more pressure, have someone hold the fish while you gently but firmly scrape off some mucous.

Always scrape in the direction of the scales; never run against them. Because the scraping peels off external parasites between the scales, scrape where you think your koi is most stressed, near the gills or near the fins, for instance.

2. **Add a droplet of pond water and then a cover slide. You're ready to examine the scraping under the microscope.**

Inspecting the small stuff: Enter, the microscope

When you first look at a smear or a scrape under the microscope, you may feel as if you're in uncharted territory. The micro-organisms that you might encounter exhibit a bewildering array of shapes, with many appearing to be straight out of a horror movie. However, with a bit of experience, you may be able to at least identify some of them in a general way, and this can help point the way toward an effective treatment.

✔ Compare what you see under the microscope with the drawings in this book. (See those illustrations throughout this chapter.)

✔ Go online for more information on koi parasites. (Check out www.koicarp.net or search under **koi parasites**.)

✔ Ask a more experienced koi-keeper to guide you through this smear-making and slide examination process that we describe in the previous section.

You really will get better with practice.

Dealing with Mild Traumatic Injuries

Koi encounter few traumas in the pond; they just don't have many opportunities bang up against something. Nonetheless, they still manage to get into a few scrapes.

Some injuries are seasonal and relatively minor. In spring, for instance, actively breeding koi tend to lose scales as part of the jostling during courtship. The female in particular may lose patches of scales and have a split fin or two. The only necessary treatment is a week or two of R&R in the warm waters of a hospital tank and away from other koi.

Because butterfly koi have delicate fins, the fins of very young koi may have *dragging* damage from the rough bottom of a pond.

Three-tenths of a percent salt solution (three pounds per 100 gallons of water in your pond) helps the fins heal, but see "Fin rot" in this chapter for more information on this condition. As fungus can take hold on damaged fins or skin, keep an eye on these koi while the fins heal.

Kinked spine also seems trauma-linked, but it can be the result of a poor diet (very obvious in younger, fast-growing koi), exposure to high levels of organophosphate insecticides (as a human, you don't really want these near you either), or electrocution. Many times the damage to the spine is permanent and euthanasia is the logical answer. Koi owners who can't bear the thought of killing one of their favorites usually hand feed the affected koi.

Electrocution can occur wherever there's electricity; when you combine water and electricity, the chances of something going amiss only escalate. Electrocution fries the nerve axons, causing some muscles to become permanently contracted and other muscles to become spasmodic. Because muscle control is gone, the electrocuted koi swim in a jerky fashion. When the fish are challenged or stressed, the swimming motions can become even more erratic until the fish loses the ability to swim altogether. An electrocuted fish drops weight — partly because he uses so much of his energy just trying to swim, but mostly because he can't compete with the other koi for food.

The Most Famous Parasites of All

Parasites are a common problem for all fish. When you mention parasites with koi, you generally mean the external variety. These parasites are always present and easily pass from one fish to another. The eggs or cysts may remain inactive and undetected until the weather warms up, but then the birds sing, flowers bud — and all of a sudden your koi are a-bloom with external parasites.

The problem with a parasitic infestation — other than obviously damaging your fish through the actions of the parasites themselves (feeding on blood and skin tissue, for example) and killing your appetite for cheese rollatini big-time — is that the condition sets up your fish for secondary bacterial infections.

The good news about parasites (and we do have some) is that a salt treatment kills many of them. Sometimes you have to add a secondary treatment, but salt's your number-one choice for *Ich, Costia,* and *Chilodonella.* (Check out more about these conditions and their treatments later in this section.)

Anchor worms

An anchor worm (see Figure 13-1) is a crustacean that looks like a worm. The females embed themselves in the skin of a koi, usually near the gills, around the eyes, on the fins, and on the base of the fins. A scraping and examination under a microscope can help you ID the varmint. Adult anchor worms are just under ¼-inch to ½-inch long and look like brown or black strands standing out from the koi's body. The site of attachment is usually inflamed, and the involved scales may be raised up a bit from their normal position. Young anchor worms look like white dots on the skin of the koi.

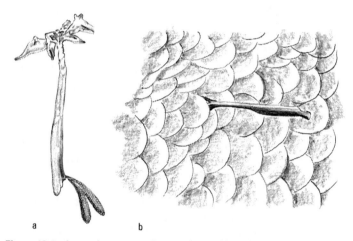

a   b

Figure 13-1: An anchor worm, alone and attacking a koi.

When you find them

Anchor worms are inactive during the winter but become active when the water warms to the upper 50s. Suddenly all your koi have anchor worms, and the fish may flash and leap in an attempt to dislodge the little pests. But the bigger problem is that the wounds caused by the worms are an open door to *Aeromonas* or *Pseudomonas* infections because the koi's resistance is just emerging from the wintertime slowdown.

You can assume that any koi you buy in late winter or early spring will come with a few anchor worms.

How you get rid of them

You can physically remove the worms by sedating your koi (see the section "Sedating Your Koi, Giving Injections, and Other First-Aid Tasks" at the end of this chapter), placing it on a wet towel on a table near the quarantine tub, and pulling off the anchor worms with tweezers. This is a very time- and labor- intensive job.

Fortunately, Dimilin, the trade name for diflubenzuron, is a proven, safe way to kill anchor worms in a pond. The dose is one gram per 1,000 gallons. Mix the powder with ½ cup or so of pond water and then sprinkle the treated water over the surface of the pond. If you can't obtain Dimilin, substitute *Program* (Lufernon), the anti-flea medication for dogs. It works the same way and, like Dimilin, is nontoxic.

To use Program, follow these steps:

1. **Pulverize one large-dog-size tablet per 1,000 gallons of water.**

2. **Add the powder to an empty gallon milk container.**

3. **Add water, snap on the lid, and shake to mix the two.**

4. **Shake the mixture as you distribute it around the perimeter of the pond.**

5. **Turn off your UV sterilizer and remove any carbon you have in your filter while using these medications. At the end of a week, turn on your UV sterilizer and replace the carbon in your filter.**

Depending on the temperature of your water, the treatment takes four to five days to eliminate the anchor worms or lice. We waited a week, just to make sure the problem was eliminated.

Apiosoma

Apiosoma is a protozoan parasite that looks like a vase with a fringe of *cilia* (hairlike projections) around the mouth of the vase. It's too small to be easily seen with the naked eye. Typical symptoms of this parasite include

✔ Heavy mucous production.

✔ Clamped fins.

✔ Respiratory distress.

✔ Head flicking (to try to dislodge the parasite — to no avail).

✔ Loss of appetite.

✔ Big head (the result of little appetite; the thin koi's head seems too big for its body) — this symptom indicates a heavy Apiosoma infection.

Treat Apiosoma with one of the following methods:

- ✔ Add salt to the pond at a concentration of 0.3 percent (three pounds per 100 gallons in your pond).

- ✔ Employ a salt bath with a 2 percent salt solution.

- ✔ Add a commercial anti-parasite to the pond (malachite green and Formalin).

- ✔ Add potassium permanganate at 1.5 grams per 220 gallons (1,000 liters).

Secondary bacterial or fungal infections are expected, so be sure to read about these in this chapter and be prepared to treat them as well.

Sometimes a concentrated salt bath is good for koi with a particularly stubborn affliction. In this case, you give your koi a salt bath as follows:

1. **Make a 2 percent solution (not 0.2, but ten times that!) by using 1 pound of salt to 5 gallons of water and making sure the salt is dissolved.**

2. **Place the koi in the bath and watch it carefully.**

   In two to five minutes, the koi loses its balance and falls to one side.

3. **When this happens, remove the koi and return it to the hospital tank or the main pond (see the section on hospital tanks later in this chapter).**

You can repeat this process after two days for a total of two baths.

Chilodonella

Chilodonella look a bit like transparent coffee beans under the microscope, with cilia lining the cleft underside of the beans. Like other protozoans, these are too small to see with the naked eye; they are diagnosed with a skin scraping. Irritation from Chilodonella can cause koi to drag their faces and bodies along the pond bottom or sides. These protozoans are most aggressive when pond temperatures are lower than 68 degrees F.

Symptoms of Chilodonella differ depending on which area of the koi is most heavily infested. For example:

✔ The koi may become lethargic and hold their fins clamped to their sides.

✔ The koi may remain near filter outlets because their gills are affected and can't function well.

✔ The skin may be covered by a grayish-white film, even covering the eyes.

✔ The koi have respiratory distress.

✔ Flashing and scraping are typical.

Treat Chilodonella with one of the following methods:

✔ A concentration of 0.3 percent salt

✔ Potassium permanganate at 1.5 grams per 220 gallons.

Treat topical damage caused by this parasite with propolis or malachite green.

Costia

Costia, more correctly known as *Ichthyobodo necatrix,* is a pear or "comma" shaped protozoan that moves by means of long, thin appendages known as flagellum (a second pair is used for feeding). Invisible to the naked eye, *Costia's* "jerky" swimming motions are readily observable under magnification of 200–400X. *Costia* attaches to the koi's skin and gills, and feeds upon the tissue there.

Koi infected by *Costia* will cease feeding, become lethargic and gasp for air, and will often excrete excess mucus.

Costia are best eliminated by treating the pond with potassium permanganate, which can be purchased at your pond store or ordered online. See the section on flukes later in this chapter for specifics concerning the use of this medication. Additional airstones should be added if the fish appear to have trouble breathing.

Fish lice

Fish lice, or *Argulus,* are crustaceans, like anchor worms. They look like small dots of clear jelly, with dark eyes on one end of their circular body and cilia at the other end. They pierce the koi's skin in order to feed and then inject an anticoagulant so they can feed unimpeded. The anticoagulant has a toxic effect on the koi, and may, by itself, be powerful enough to kill small koi. See Figure 13-2 for an illustration.

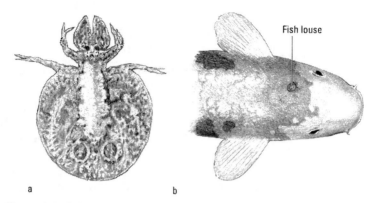

Fish louse

a   b

Figure 13-2: Fish louse, solo and pestering a koi.

Adult fish lice are large enough to see with the naked eye, ranging in size from just under ⅛ inch to ⅓ inch across. Infected fish or plants from an infected pond can bring the lice to your pond. Even something as innocent as a wading bird can transmit fish lice. (What are we saying? In koi-world, *innocent* and *wading birds* don't go together — all the more reason to discourage visits by any wading birds!)

The presence of fish lice is irritating for at least two reasons:

- ✔ Infected koi swim erratically, flashing and scraping against the side of the pond to dislodge the lice.

   Koi can damage their skin in this scraping process, opening an avenue for secondary infection.
- ✔ With a heavy infestation of fish lice, the koi cease feeding and become lethargic swimmers.

You can remove fish lice from anesthetized koi with tweezers and then dab the removal site with propolis. (See the section "Sedating Your Koi, Giving Injections, and Other First-Aid Tasks" later in this chapter.) Treating the pond with Dimilin and Program, however, is easier than removing the fish lice manually. Use the same dose as you'd use for anchor worms (see the earlier section "Anchor worms" for specifics on these treatments).

Flukes

Body and gill flukes feed on the mucous on a koi's body and literally hook themselves into place. Although they're very common on koi, they usually don't cause a problem unless the koi is weakened by another disease. Treat the flukes with potassium permanganate.

To treat a pond with potassium permanganate, follow these steps:

1. **Turn off the pond filter and dissolve one teaspoon per 1,000 gallons in a bucket of water.**

2. **Add the pink solution to your koi pond. (The water will turn pink, and that's good.)**

3. **If the pink coloration disappears within 45 minutes, add another ½ teaspoon per 1,000 gallons. If the color disappears after two hours, re-dose with ½ teaspoon per 1,000 gallons.**

4. **At the end of ten hours, change one-third of the pond water and turn the filter on. Repeat in seven days.**

If the infestation is severe and the flukes are on several fish, you may want to use *Fluke Tabs,* a medication available at most pet stores, that is specifically designed to fight this parasite. Check the instructions on the box, but generally you can use one tablet per 100 gallons of water.

Ich

Ich (also spelled *ick*) or *white spot* looks like little white spots on the koi's skin and generally appears when koi experience a sudden temperature drop. The infestation can only be controlled by killing the organism in its free-swimming stage, so be sure to follow the medication timetable carefully.

Symptoms of ich infestation are

- ✔ Koi may stop feeding and begin rubbing their bodies against the pond sides and bottom.

- ✔ They may produce so much mucous as a defense against ich that they take on a whitish tone.

- ✔ They may experience respiratory distress when ich attacks the thin, oxygen-absorbing skin that covers the gills.

 Ich is very contagious and has two life stages: a nonswimming stage on your koi, and a free-swimming stage. The only time ich is vulnerable — and therefore treatable — is the free-swimming stage.

The commercial anti-ich treatments are very effective. Several products are available, but be sure to follow the instructions provided by the medication.

Bacterial Infections: Bad News Anywhere

Bacteria attack a fish when the opportunity presents itself. Often this will occur secondarily to another disease or injury, or when the fish's immune systems are weakened by the stress of shipment, handling, poor water quality, or water temperatures that are too warm or too cold.

The exterior attack

When the bacteria sets in on the outside of a koi, the koi develop open wounds or ulcers that spontaneously appear

- ✔ On the mouth
- ✔ On the belly
- ✔ As holes in the fins
- ✔ As red streaks on the fins

Unless you provide treatment, the hole gets bigger and deeper.

Ulcers

The most common cause of external ulcers are two bacteria, *Aeromonas* and *Psuedomonas*. Although these bacteria are almost always present, they move in when your koi become stressed (particularly in the spring when water temperatures are around 60 degrees). Other typical symptoms are excessive mucous production and red areas around the edge of the ulcer.

Take the following steps to treat ulcers:

1. **Net and bowl the fish.**
2. **Clean the wound with hydrogen peroxide or mercurochrome.**
3. **Spray a multipurpose antibiotic like Polysporin on the wound.**
4. **Repeat Steps 1 through 3 two more times at three-day intervals.**

If you can move your koi to a heated hospital tank for this period, so much the better.

When more than one or two fish are affected, do one of the following:

- Treat by feeding an antibiotic-laced diet for two weeks. (Obtain the diet from your koi dealer or an online koi-product vendor.)

- Add potassium permanganate to the pond at the rate of 1.5 grams for 220 gallons (please see the "Flukes" section earlier in this chapter for details concerning treating koi with this medication).

Fin rot

During the warmer summer months, koi may seem healthy yet display signs of *fin rot* (also called *gill rot, mouth rot,* and *skin columnaris,* depending on where the rot attacks). Fin rot is actually caused by the combination of warm pond water and high ammonia and pH levels. (Can you imagine being in water so toxic that the skin on your appendages rots? Oh, ouch!)

These are the affected areas and their symptoms:

- **The fins:** The first signs are reddening of the fins, then white patches at the tips of fins where the circulation has been destroyed, then erosion of the fins.

- **The gills:** The gills become mucous-laden and then spotted with white; eventually necrosis develops.

- **Mouth rot:** This disease appears as a small, white spot near the nose that soon reddens and spreads.

- **Skin columnaris:** The first signs are small, white patches, then heavy mucous production; red patches appear on the skin and some scale sloughing may occur.

Koi with columnaris feed poorly, especially if the mouth is involved. They stay near the filter outlets or under the waterfalls, where the water has more oxygen.

Lower the ammonia level by doing one or more of the following:

- Partially change the water on a daily basis.

- Cool the pond to approximately 75 degrees F.

- Add an ammonia remover such as Zeolite or AmQuel Plus.

- Evaluate and upgrade the processing capacity of your biofilter, making sure it is large enough for your pond's water volume and the number and size of the fish in it.

When the problem's been solved, the fin rot stops and the fins can heal. Treatment for your koi consists of dabbing the sores with malachite green, followed by feeding propolis and an antibiotic feed such as MediKoi for at least ten days.

The inside attack: Internal infections

Internal bacterial infections are always serious, and the outcome is not guaranteed. The disease is called *bloater, pine cone,* or *dropsy.* In these cases the following occurs:

- The fish swells with the inflammation (sometimes more so on one side than the other).
- The pressure pushes the scales away from the body.
- The pressure on the fish's air bladder makes the fish swim awkwardly.
- The fish's eyes protrude.

See Figure 13-3 for an example of this disease.

Treatment for dropsy usually includes a stay in a hospital tank, if possible. Add salt for a 0.3 percent level and slowly heat up the tank or pond to 77 to 85 degrees. In addition, some koi owners offer one of the following:

- An antibiotic diet that's safe to use with salt
- A *probiotic* feed (feed that has friendly bacteria added)
- Very small amounts of plain yogurt that they hand feed via a syringe inserted into the mouth and down into the *alimentary cavity,* or what passes for a stomach in koi.

Preventing bacterial infection

You can forestall ulcers and dropsy by closely watching your pond's water quality and temperature and by adding a probiotic to the water. Probiotics are friendly bacteria. When you add a probiotic (KoiZyme is one) to your pond, you install friendly bacteria that will compete with Aeromonas or Pseudomonas for any available nutrients in the water (as in koi waste). The bad bacteria die. The good bacteria live.

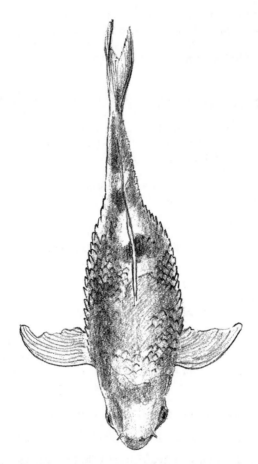

Figure 13-3: A koi with dropsy (also called pine cone or bloater) disease.

Combine a probiotic with a good filtration system, and you stop a lot of health problems in their tracks.

Swimmer's Gill (Or Skin): Fungal Infections

Fungus can attack any weakened portion of a koi, from the skin to the gills. It usually takes hold opportunistically, when the koi are stressed by injury, disease, shipping, poor water quality, or inappropriate water temperatures. Be sure that you always check for the presence of fungus when your fish suffer an unrelated trauma or illness.

Got fungus on the gills?

Gill fungus attacks the gills (go figure), and unless you're paying close attention, one day your koi's doing fine and the next day he's hanging around the waterfall. A short time later, he's belly up.

Gill fungus usually crops up in the spring either in ponds that don't have adequate aeration or in ponds whose fish-load has outgrown the filtration system. The koi act lethargic, feed poorly — if at all, and stay close to the surface of the pond. When you net and bowl one, the gills look like they have gray cotton growing on them.

Salt, in one percentage or another, is a classic koi treatment, or you can use one of the commercial fungus treatments.

Fluffy white fur isn't always a good thing

Cotton wool or *cotton ball* disease is a charming name for a nasty condition. It's caused by *Saprolegnia,* a fungus that grows when bad water quality stresses the koi. Expect to find it when the water contains quantities of uneaten food and when the pond has too many koi for its size.

The koi develop what looks like a fine-textured fur coat over their bodies that's actually mold growing on their skin. Sometimes the fungus looks like a pale-orange or ivory-colored layer, much like the mold that grows on items left too long in the fridge See Figure 13-4 for an illustration of what koi fungus looks like). As the disease progresses, the fungus grows longer, cottonlike tufts.

Treat this disease by correcting the conditions that lead to the out-break:

- ✔ Decrease the number of koi in the pond. (Show ponds work well as holding stations for the excess.)

- ✔ Improve water quality via partial water changes, an upgraded filtration system, an ammonia remover like AmQuel Plus or Zeolite, and increased aeration.

You can also use medication against the fungus. Adding *methylene blue* (a dye commonly used as a fish medication and available at most pet stores) to the pond at a rate of 1 teaspoon per 700 gallons helps kill the fungus, but individually treating each affected koi in a quarantine tub stops the progression of the disease much faster.

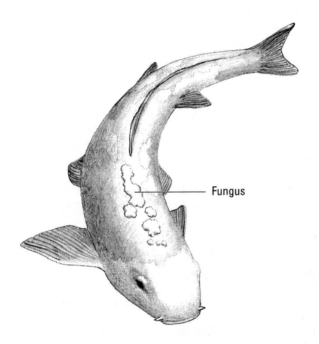

Fungus

Figure 13-4: Koi with a white fungus patch on its back.

Either sedate the koi or hold it so you can remove the patches of fungus with a cotton swab. Then dab the affected spots first with malachite green and then with propolis. (See the section "Sedating Your Koi, Giving Injections, and Other First-Aid Tasks" later in this chapter.) Return the fish to the quarantine tub and watch closely to make certain no secondary fungal or bacterial infection sets in.

The Three Greatest Viral Threats: Pox, SVK, and KHV

Diseases caused by a virus are tricky. Only a few vaccines have been developed to fight them, and those or koi are in the very early stages. With a koi virus, you and your koi pretty much have to take chances.

In addition to carp pox (koi's equivalent to the dreaded chicken pox), you need to know about two other viruses because they're far more life-threatening: spring viremia of koi (SVK) and koi herpes virus (KHV).

Forget the chicken — koi get carp pox

Carp pox appears as tiny, raised drops of paraffin on your koi's body or fins. The colors may be white, pink, or gray, and you can flick them off with your fingernail. Koi show no behavioral changes to indicate illness, but infected fish are carriers. The pox is a self-limiting disease, meaning it doesn't kill adult fish; however, it has a high mortality rate on koi younger than two months. There is no treatment, but research is underway for a carp pox vaccine. Adult fish in otherwise good health will survive, but you should isolate them from young koi and any new fish that you may acquire. You may, therefore need to set up a new pond, give infected fish to someone who maintains others with the disease, or resign yourself to not breeding or acquiring new fish.

Carp pox is most prevalent in early spring, when water temperatures are less than 68 degrees. If your pond suffers an outbreak, move the fish, drain the pond, and disinfect with 200 parts per million chlorine for one hour to sterilize surfaces; use a quaternary ammonium compound like Roccal at 500 ppm on nets.

Spring viremia of carp: Predator of koi at their most vulnerable

SVC is a virus that attacks koi, other species of carp, and goldfish. It becomes active in water temperatures of 40 to 68 degrees, when koi have essentially no immune system.

Symptoms include lethargy, awkward swimming, skin ulcers, and areas of hemorrhage adjacent to the ulcers. The body may bulge with *septicemia* (blood poisoning); bloody mucous may seep out from the vent. SVC is highly contagious and has a high mortality rate, especially for young koi.

There is no treatment for SVC, and surviving koi may become carriers of the virus. It is also a reportable disease. In other words, if it's been diagnosed by a USDA-approved laboratory by using a *polymerase chain reaction* (PCR) test (which is the only definitive diagnosis), federal officials must be notified. The feds will come to your home and require you to depopulate your fish and disinfect your pond.

If you decide against an official diagnosis, sterilize your pond by draining it and washing it down with a 500 parts per million chlorine solution. Allow the bleach solution to stay on the pond walls and floor for ten minutes before rinsing.

The quick, sneaky killer: Koi herpes virus

KHV is a DNA-based herpes virus that affects only the common carp and koi. The virus becomes active when water temperatures are between 64 and 81 degrees and it spreads via direct contact, exposure to fecal material, or infected water.

Koi with KHV become lethargic in their swimming, stay near the surface, and have difficulty breathing. Their gills become mottled red and white, indicating some hemorrhaging and blood clotting dysfunction. Death usually follows 24 to 48 hours after the symptoms appear. The diagnosis is confirmed with a PCR test, but the disease is not notifiable (in other words, federal veterinary officials need not be alerted).

Post mortem examination shows infections by bacteria and fungus on all skin surfaces, including the gill surfaces, so obviously KHV plays hob with a koi's immune system.

There is no treatment for KHV. You can prevent its spread by using a quarantine tub and by paying close attention to sanitation. For a pond where KHV has been confirmed, follow these steps:

1. **Empty and scrub the pond with a sanitizer** such as

   • A solution of 200 parts per million chlorine

   • A mixture of 0.26 ounces of Roccal Plus D to a gallon of water

2. **Rinse all surfaces.**

3. **Sanitize all pond equipment, nets, and bowls.**

KHV has been reported from the U.S., Europe, Israel, and Japan. The 2005 outbreak in Niigata was traced back to a single, borrowed, imported koi. The unfortunate result was the depopulation of at least five koi breeders' stock.

At koi shows, officials may decide to limit possible exposure to KHV by keeping all the fish belonging to one individual in his or her own show pond or ponds. Judges go from pond to pond, netting and bowling all the koi pertaining to the class being judged at that time. This is called the *English style,* as opposed to the Japanese syle of grouping all koi of a particular show class in a single show pond. Nets and bowls are currently restricted to one-container and one-koi use, and they're sanitized with Roccal between uses. Roccal can be diluted to 0.5 ounce per gallon and used to disinfect hands between handling koi.

Keeping your old koi safe from viral infection

Your best bet for avoiding KHV is to select your koi vendors carefully and use your quarantine tub for all additions to your pond.

You can *select* quarantine conditions that predispose new koi to developing SVC or KHV if either virus is already present. The advantage in this safety net is that only your new koi die, not your entire collection. Essentially, you simply change the temperature of the quarantine tub and wait for signs of SVC or KHV to show up.

Follow these steps:

1. **Place your new koi in the tub but don't turn on the heater. Keep temperatures of the tub in the low 60s for two to three weeks.**

2. **Turn on the heater, increasing the temperature no more than 5 degrees within a 24-hour period until the water is 75 degrees.**

3. **Keep the tank at that temperature for two to three weeks.**

If SVC is present, it will manifest itself when the water temperature's between 40 and 68 degrees; KHV will manifest itself when the water's between 72 and 81 degrees. Unfortunately, the infected fish will die. Be sure to disinfect your quarantine tub as described earlier before using it again.

Setting up the Hospital Tank

The hospital tank is much like the quarantine tub — an isolation tank where you can treat only the fish that need it. Always have at least two koi in a hospital tank, even if only one of them needs the treatment. Koi are not solitary creatures and the stress inherent to sickness and treatment will be lessened if they have company. A lower stress level will benefit the immune system and aid the fish in its recovery.

You can create a hospital tank out of a stock tank, a show tank, or a 150-gallon or larger polyethylene bin. A bottom drain fitting allows you to clean and drain it more easily, and they're usually salted to 0.3 percent.

Set the hospital tank up in a spot that's out of the sun and protected from adverse weather. Use the following equipment:

- ✔ **A filter:** Either a standard three-compartment filter or a poly-bead filter (see Chapter 3 for more on these filter types).

  Set the filter up to pull from the bottom drain or a retrofitted bottom drain; another variation is to place the inflow and out-flow pipes over opposite ends of the tank.

  Add a foam prefilter to the filter intake to protect your fish from being grabbed by the filter suction.

- ✔ **A heater:** 200- to 300-watt heaters are large enough for a 100-gallon tank.

- ✔ **A thermometer:** One used for an aquarium will work just fine, but pond thermometers are larger and easier to read.

- ✔ **An aeration pump with an airstone:** This equipment ensures adequate aeration and water circulation.

  Drape the airstone tubing over the edge of the bin and place it as near to the bottom of the bin as possible; the longer distance the bubbles travel, the greater the oxygen absorption.

Do not turn on the heater until you put your koi into the tank, and only increase the temperature 3 to 5 degrees a day — any faster is too fast for your koi to adjust to. Because the immune system of a koi is most efficient when the fish is warmed, keep the water between 78 and 82 degrees.

Cover the hospital tank with bird netting or with a fitted mesh cover. Distressed koi and koi placed in much-smaller-than-usual housing tend to jump.

Sedating Your Koi, Giving Injections, and Other First-Aid Tasks

At some point you may need to give your koi an injection, dab malachite green on an ulcer, or remove a bit of a fin or a specimen from the edge of a wound to ID the bacteria at fault.

In any case, you'll need to anesthetize your koi. You can do this safely and easily, but the process requires your undivided attention. Follow these steps:

1. **Gather the equipment:**
   - A koi bowl or child's wading pool with a few gallons of pond water aerated by an airstone
   - A nearby table covered with wet towels and a few more wet towels to prop up the koi
   - The anesthetic (three choices), added to the koi bowl or pond:

     Tricaine-S added to the water in the bowl at the rate of 200 milligrams per 2 pounds of koi

     Four drops of Oil of Cloves per gallon of water in the bowl

     Six drops of Eugenol added to the water in the bowl
   - A tuberculin syringe (you can usually get these at your local pharmacy in the section with diabetic supplies)
   - A broad-spectrum antibiotic: Baytril or Amikacin

2. **Add the koi and watch him until he rolls over.**

   This only takes a few minutes. The duration of the anesthetic effect averages 4 to 10 minutes, but is affected by a host of factors, and is therefore highly variable. It is best to review everything beforehand, so that you will be able to work swiftly and effectively. If the fish begins to recover before you are finished, do your best to complete the task at hand. Try to avoid a second period of anesthesia, but if you must do so, wait for 1 hour before putting the fish "back under."

3. **Lift the anesthetized koi to your table and prop him up with the towels.**

4. **There are two sites for injecting your koi. Pull the pectoral fin towards the fish's mouth, and inject the antibiotic into the fleshy lump behind the fin. The older method is to inject into the koi's belly, between the pelvic fins (see Figure 13-5).**

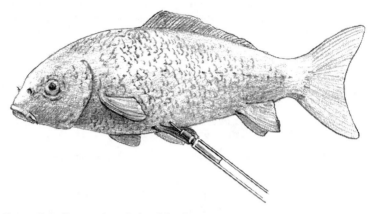

Figure 13-5: How to give a koi an injection.

To treat an ulcer:

1. **Prop the koi so the ulcer is uppermost.**

2. **Use cotton swabs to first dry the wound and then paint the ulcer with malachite green, changing the swabs as needed.**

3. **Add spray-on propolis (for its antioxidant qualities) over the malachite green.**

To remove a specimen:

1. **Take a pair of very sharp scissors to clip off the very edge of a fin or use a moistened swab to tease up a bit of the mucous and debris at the edge of a wound.**

2. **Place the specimen or swab in a specimen tube for mailing to a lab, and seal the tube.** (See the earlier section "Examining your sickly fish" for more about this process.)

When the operation is over:

1. **Place the koi in a blue bowl filled with fresh water from the pond. (The water should be heavily aerated.)**

2. **Keep the koi in the bowl until normal breathing is re-established. (Move him back and forth to put fresh water over the gills until he begins to move his fins or twitch his gills.)**

3. **Wait another minute and then put him back in the pond; watch him for a few moments to make certain he's capable of swimming under his own power.**

Part IV

The Big Leagues: Koi Breeding and Showing

The 5th Wave   By Rich Tennant

Are you thinking what I'm thinking?

Yes-that would look fabulous in the Koi pond.

In this part . . .

Who can resist the sight of a vendor's show pond all set up with a bunch of new koi, each as pretty as all get-out and priced at pretty reasonable rates? You stop yourself — just like a home movie where the film slips off the spindle — and you think, "I have koi. Why don't *I* do this?"

Well sure, you can breed your koi, but this adventure can be oh-so-much easier if you first find out how to raise the young before you dim the pond lights and start playing *Spanish Eyes* for your favorite pair of koi. The chapters in this part tell you what to expect during breeding and how to hatch and raise the young. We also give you some insights on showing your koi and enjoying the show.

Chapter 14

Breeding Koi

. . . .

In This Chapter

▶ Knowing the highs and lows of breeding koi

▶ Expecting the unexpected in breeding

▶ Preparing the koi and their breeding site

▶ Making baby koi — thousands of them

▶ Staging the hatching grounds

▶ Natural breeding: Baby koi made simple

. . . .

*W*hat if you want to get in on the ground floor, so to speak, when it comes to good koi? Breeding your fish and watching as the *fry* (hatchlings) emerge from the eggs is a real highlight of koi-keeping.

Breeding koi can be a complicated but fulfilling hobby. It certainly opens up a new world of knowledge, pond maintenance refinements, and koi behavior, and it offers you a ringside introduction to koi-keepers who regularly and successfully produce koi.

This chapter helps you decide whether you'd like to start a breeding program and what's involved if you do. We also give you a heads-up on the characteristics you can and can't breed for.

To Breed or Not to Breed: That Is the Question

Do you really want to breed your koi? Watching your fish reproduce can open up a whole new aspect of the hobby to you and will likely hook you on koi for good. You learn a great deal in the process and may even be able to add your own unique twists that can help future koi breeders.

Consider some of these pros for breeding:

- ✔ **It's a do-it-yourself way to get more koi.** At the same time, you have the fun of watching the young grow and see how their colors develop over time. (Let's see, this is year five, so the red [called *Hi* in koi terms] should be getting deeper and the Sumi should be spreading. . . .)

- ✔ **You can make some cold, hard cash.** Other koi-keepers like and appreciate koi, and most of them like to add to their collection. Of course, this is only a benefit for those who have a market (that is, can sell their koi) and can make enough money to at least break even.

- ✔ **The learning process is very stimulating and will probably spur you on to read, research, and speak with other hobbyists and professionals.**

- ✔ **The lessons you pick up from breeding koi are transferable to other fish species if you're inclined to expand your interests.**

- ✔ **Breeding is a great way to attract friends and family to your hobby and to share it with them.**

Breeding also has some negative points:

- ✔ It takes time.

- ✔ It takes money.

- ✔ It takes additional space.

- ✔ It's a boisterous sport; your fish, especially your female, may be damaged (see "Letting your koi have at it" later in this chapter).

- ✔ Most noticeably, it can produce tens of thousands of baby koi. Many die off before you make a single move toward *culling* (selective reduction), but you still need to cull, probably several times (see Chapter 15 for more on this process). At the least, you end up with a hundred or so 1- to 2-inch baby koi.

Predictions You Can Make (And Those You Can't)

Trying to predict what characteristics will be *expressed* (that is, be evident) in a particular breeding is complicated, mostly because we don't know what recessive genes a given koi carries. As a result, breeding between a selected pair of koi produces a hodge-podge of gene expression in the 5,000-plus young.

If you were to keep records and photos from breeding the same pair year after year, maybe you could get a sense about the young koi from that pair — but maybe not. Breeding koi is that unpredictable. You can only be sure of two facts: They'll all be koi, and only some of them will look like one parent or the other — many won't look like either.

Nevertheless, some characteristics in koi do breed true. Take a look at the following characteristics to get an idea:

✔ **Scale patterns:** Normal-scaled koi that mate with each other generally produce normal-scaled offspring, and mated pairs of mirror-scaled koi usually produce mirror-scaled young. Parents of both types, however, can carry the genes for other scale patterns, in which case the fry's scales will vary.

Leather-skinned koi pairs produce leather-skinned (predominantly) and mirror-scaled young.

When line-scaled koi are paired with line-scaled mates, the resulting young exhibit a variety of scale patterns.

✔ **Metallic sheen:** Metallic sheen is dominant over normal sheen when the parent koi are a white-skinned or black-skinned variety. If both parents have one gene for metallic sheen and one for normal sheen, they and their offspring look metallic.

✔ **Color and color pattern:** Koi color genetics are complex, and two koi that seem identical in color and basic pattern may arrive at that color and pattern with differing genetic mixes.

Unless you begin with a male and a female of one variety from a single lineage (like two closely related koi from a dealer who specializes in that variety), the patterns of the offspring are impossible to predict. So you can breed for a red and white Kohaku; you just can't breed for a heart-maruten on the head or for zigzag placement of the red along the body.

Pattern, alas, doesn't pass down from parent to offspring. You can't tell what colors are going to pop out until you have the growing fry in front of you. So what do you do? Start with strong, well-shaped, and well-colored adults of the same variety and hope for some surprises — which, given 5,000 variations, you're apt to get.

Don't let the unpredictability aspect throw you. It's part of the fun of breeding koi. The market for a breeder's affordable, handsome koi is much larger than the market for expensive offspring of Nishikigoi.

Preparing for the Dirty Deed

Koi are prolific breeders and are, as a species, well adjusted to captive life. This does not mean, however, that you can simply put two fish of opposite sex together, sit back, and wait for babies. (Although sometimes — especially in large, outdoor ponds — this is exactly what seems to happen.) If you (and your koi!) are to be successful, you need to plan carefully. Be sure that you have the time, patience, and space for this complex but rewarding endeavor.

The season for breeding usually begins in February and continues until May, depending on when the water temperature reaches 68 degrees F and when the fish (including the male) become more active and begin to feed. Because exact breeding times vary from place to place, season to season, and even among individual fish, have your breeding tank up and running at least two weeks before the earliest possible beginning of the local breeding season.

Formal breeding operations know how to eliminate as many of the variables as possible. But even as a newbie, you can minimize your challenges by making sure

- ✔ Your koi are as healthy as possible
- ✔ The breeding site is easy to monitor
- ✔ You use an easy method for changing the water
- ✔ You have enough room to move the adult koi in and out as necessary

Gathering the necessary tools

To help your koi successfully enter their parenting stage, some advance setup is necessary on your part. This section walks you through the details of the tanks and their essentials to make the breeding process as predictable and smooth as possible.

Selecting the breeding tank or pond

Most koi breeders set up one or more breeding ponds indoors or outdoors, depending on the springtime temperatures and the available space. Because the breeding tank often becomes a nursery after breeding (see "Setting up the nursery tank" in the next section), indoor tanks or ponds tend to be easier.

Polyethylene stock watering tanks or show tanks make good breeding tanks for koi. (Stock tanks are available from livestock/farm supply stores, and show tanks are sold in pet stores or pond supply stores.) Look for one that's about 200 gallons. This size (at least 4 x 4 x 2 feet) provides enough room for the female for a month or two before fertilization, then the female, male, and spawning brushes (for the less-than-12 hours for egg deposition and fertilization), and then the 2,000-plus fry.

Selecting the hospital tank

A second tank serves as a hospital for the female so she can rest up for a week or two after laying her eggs. A stock watering tank or show tank of at least 200 gallons will suffice. See Chapter 10 for details concerning this enclosure.

Supplies needed for each tank

Now that you have the tanks, they'll need to function just like your pond. So each tank needs its own

- Water pump
- Filter
- Air pump
- Airstones: *Airstones* connect to the pump and are made of a porous material. They diffuse air from the pump so it rises to the surface as a fine mist of bubbles. These bubbles disturb the water's surface and cause oxygen to be mixed into the water.
- Heater
- Net covering
- Spawning brushes: *Spawning brushes* are meant to imitate plants, the usual spawning site for koi.

  You can also use slender, smooth, tree branches (willows are a good, pliable choice) that you tie together at their ends and place into the tank. (If you use live branches, first wash them in soapy water, then rinse them, dip them into a solution of 10 percent bleach, and re-rinse to remove traces of insecticides and pollutants.)

Chapter 10 has more info on these supplies. *Note:* When you total them up, the supplies can get a little pricey. Consider checking out Amazon.com for used supplies to save on your setup investment.

Getting the breeding grounds ready for showtime

Before the weather warms, you need to prepare for the coming breeding season. As we mention earlier in this chapter, the onset of the fish's interest in reproduction is subject to many variables.

Your best guides are local koi-keepers who've been successful in breeding their fish.

Setting up the breeding tank

Reduce the water in the tank to expose about a foot of the tank sides; add airstones to agitate the water.

Place the spawning brushes in the water (they can float freely), and introduce the female. She'll likely nose about the tank for a while as she explores this new environment.

Setting up the nursery tank

The nursery (or incubator) tank should be up and running by the time the adults are ready for breeding. Keep it filled to about 6 inches below the lip so the fry can't jump out.

Add filtration and airstones. If you locate the nursery tank outdoors, you can simply put it online with the same filtration system as your koi pond. This step assures that the tanks are the same pH and temperature. Use an air pump to power up the airstones. As an alternative, you can use the breeding tank as a nursery tank.

Casting the stars of the show

In the excitement of your first breeding success, don't neglect to plan for the future. Although you can't imagine forgetting even one aspect of the event, be assured that time will blur the details. Keeping accurate records allows you to analyze and refine your methods in the future and can add to your overall understanding of this adventure.

Keep breeding records on your koi, even if the offspring seem only slightly better than average. Anyone who obtains one of your offspring and decides to breed his own koi will appreciate a copy of the lineage, if only to get an idea of possible dominant and recessive genes.

In all cases, keep photos with each record unless you have only a few, easily identified adults (in which case you can describe each accurately). By taking photos every six months (and labeling them!), you can easily provide a record of your koi's color development.

Telling the sexes apart

Adult koi are fairly easy to sex from the body shape alone. The females are plumper than the males, who look rather streamlined in comparison. Adult females also have smaller pectoral fins. But for younger koi, you have to rely on more subtle clues.

When breeding season starts in spring to early summer, the males (even as small as 5 or 6 inches long) develop a pebbly forward edge on their pectoral fins. The forward edge of a small female's pectoral fin is smooth. Although you can feel the difference with your finger, we've heard of koi fanciers whose sense of touch has dimmed, so they use their tongue to feel the pectoral fins. (Trust us; you don't have to do this.)

Females also tend to have larger, rounder pectoral fins than the males. (See Figure 14-1 for a visual of the differences between the sexes.)

Choosing the optimal fish

For breeding purposes, select adults on the basis of color, body shape, finnage, and scales. Fish are judged from above (no, not that kind of *Above* — from the tops of their bodies), so select koi that are prettiest from the top.

- ✔ **Number of each sex:** You can use just one or more males per female. (We talk about a single male in these instructions so you know what the young from a particular pairing will look like.) Many breeders use two or three males per female on the theory that competition makes the breeding more intense.

- ✔ **Age:** Select females that are 3 years old or older, although particularly robust females may successfully breed at age 2 or so. Males should be at least 2 years old, preferably 3, and they have no upper age limit for breeding.

  - Females need to be healthy and fully mature to endure the rigors of egg laying and to produce vigorous young. If you have any concerns in this regard, wait until your koi is 4 years old before pairing her with a male.

    Because breeding takes more out of a female, the oldest practical age for a female breeder is 5 to 8 years.

  - Males that are 3 years old or older are better able to joust with other males during breeding and not get damaged. They're also stronger than a smaller koi and better able to position themselves over the eggs to fertilize them.

    One breeder uses a male estimated to be 20 years old because he throws great babies.

- ✔ **Size:** Larger females can better tolerate the battering process involved with spawning, and they can produce more eggs. Although your first response may be, "Who in the world needs more than 50,000 fertilized eggs?" these eggs are also larger than those produced by a smaller female.

Larger eggs have larger yolks, which means larger fry and more nourishment for the fry in the first days after hatching. In addition, bigger fry can switch to a commercial diet earlier than small fry, which means they grow faster than the fry that must live off their yolk longer.

Grooming your koi for the rendezvous

Koi breeding is triggered by the lengthening *photoperiod* (the longer days in spring) and the warmer water temperatures (70 degrees is a good marker). *Note:* The Japanese believe that a full moon triggers egg laying, which may give you an indication of when to expect spawning.

Frequently breeders take the chosen female out of the pond in January and place her in the breeding tank to begin feeding and building up body weight.

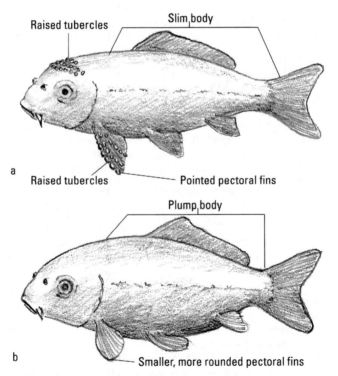

Figure 14-1: The difference between a male koi (a) and a female koi (b).

If your tank is indoors, be sure the room has a natural photoperiod. You can add timers to the lights to mimic normal, increasing day lengths; this trick helps nudge the female toward breeding readiness.

The male you've selected can stay outside in the pond (like a cold shower, only different) until the weather warms a bit.

Getting Down to Business

As is true for most fishes, koi engage in specific, if sometimes subtle, behaviors that signal their readiness to breed. If you want to recognize these and plan appropriately, you need to tune into your koi's normal behaviors. By carefully observing your fish over time, you can easily note changes that may indicate the onset of breeding behavior.

Beginning the breeding

Your first clue that egg laying is imminent is when the female begins to nose around the spawning mat and any other possible egg-deposition sites. She will be followed by the attentive and eager male(s), who is willing to do his part and fertilize any eggs the female may wish to deposit. At this point you can move the female to the breeding tank.

About sunset of the same day, place the male in the tank with the female, making sure to stretch the netting over the top of the tank.

Allow the fish to stay together through the night. The entire process should take about four hours. Eggs are usually laid in the morning, just before sunrise.

Stay in the same room for a time in case the male gets too aggressive toward the female, in which case you can remove him and substitute another male. Please note that this is a difficult call — especially for a novice — because normal mating behavior can seem pretty rough to the uninitiated. If at all possible, join a local koi club and try to observe breeding at a member's pond so you know what to expect. The male's presence may inspire the female to spend more time exploring the spawning brushes. This is normal behavior and requires no action on your part.

Letting your koi have at it

As the time of actual egg laying approaches, your koi exhibit a series of behaviors designed to synchronize the activities of both parents. Because fertilization is external, both male and female need to be in the same frame of mind if breeding is to be successful.

1. **As she prepares to release her eggs, the female releases a signal _pheromone_ (the sexy scent) that excites the male.**

2. **He then wrestles with the female, head-butting her, nipping her, and shoving her with his body as he pushes her toward the spawning brushes.**

   Her fins may be damaged in the process and she may lose scales or even flesh to the male's bites. The netting you use to cover the tank prevents both koi from leaping or being shoved out of the tank.

3. **Encouraged by the head-butts from the male, the female spews eggs from her vent.**

   The eggs are coated with a sticky mucous so they stick to the brushes and sides of the tank.

4. **The male, further signaled by the pheromone, releases his sperm (also called _milt_).**

   The milt, which looks like a milky haze in the water, is wafted by water currents over the eggs. The sperm enters each egg through a small pore called a _micropyle_. After fertilization, the micropyle closes.

5. **After she lays the first batch of eggs, the female pauses and snacks on a few eggs. The male does the same.**

   Then the female lays more eggs, the male nudging her as she does so, and he releases more sperm. They pause to snack on eggs, she lays more eggs, the male jostles her and fertilizes the eggs, then they pause to snack . . . and so on until she has released her entire supply.

   The faster the eggs are laid, the faster they can be fertilized and the male can leave to become less obvious. Even when all the female's eggs have been laid, the male continues to butt her in an exploratory way.

6. **When she's too tired to respond, he turns and begins eating the eggs. At this point, you can remove him so he can start handing out cigars to the guys in the pond.**

Reaping Your Reward: Parenting the Eggs Till They Hatch

Egg laying is an important milestone, but this is no time for you to sit back and relax. The care you give to the adults and the eggs from this point on greatly influences the future of the clutch.

In the beginning . . .

This is a busy time for the eggs *and* for you, the proud, new breeder. Do the following on Day 1:

1. **Make sure the filter is working in the nursery tank and double-check your water:**

   - Chemistry levels must be within acceptable limits.

   - The water temperature should be about the same temperature in the breeding and nursery tanks.

2. **When the female has finished laying, lift the spawning mats in a net and move them into your nursery tank.**

   (You're probably going to see lots of eggs; females generally lay from 20,000 to 50,000.) As an alternative, leave the eggs in the breeding tank and simply remove the adults.

3. **Move the female to the hospital tank (see "Selecting the hospital tank" earlier in this chapter). As always, take great care in transporting both the male and female.**

4. **Check the ammonia level in the nursery tank shortly after adding the eggs.**

   The protein from the eggs and the sperm may cause the ammonia level to jump.

5. **If the ammonia readings merit it (ideally, you're aiming for a reading of zero), do a very slow partial water change (20 to 30 percent over an hour), or use a product like AmQuel Plus to reduce the ammonia levels.**

   At this point the breeding tank water has a slight color or cast to it and a slight but distinct smell.

6. **Slowly add water from your pond at the top and siphon out water from the bottom.**

   Keep the flow rates equal so the water level doesn't drop and expose any of the eggs to air.

   The water change helps with the odor problem, and the odor will dissipate over time.

7. **Position the airstones to create a gentle current in the tank by distributing the stones evenly in the tank. The water filter should be off.**

8. **Sit back for a minute and admire the tank.**

   The eggs are scattered on the sides and bottom and on the spawning brushes and are quite visible, looking a little like pearl tapioca. In about two weeks, you're going to have a bunch of baby koi (and less time to sit!).

Because you aren't feeding any fish yet, the water quality should remain stable. A fine growth of green algae in the bin is a reason for joy, not despair, because the algae and the microscopic protozoans it harbors will be eaten by the tiny fry.

Moving on up

The first home for your hatchling koi will be the breeding tank or bin where they were conceived. This section walks you through your first six days as a koi breeder — when your progeny transition from fertilized egg to showing their first signs of life.

In a day or two, the eggs that aren't fertile turn white (and then develop a fuzzy fungus coat). The fertile eggs are clear except for two very small dots per egg, which are the eyes of the soon-to-hatch koi.

For the next few days:

✔ Keep the airstones fizzing.

✔ Siphon out or net out the unfertilized eggs.

Six days later, hocus-pocus: A lot of tiny, ¼-inch-long fry are jiggling about in the nursery. They have a bit of residual yolk, so they don't need feeding this first day.

If you have a high hatch rate and you're overwhelmed by the sheer numbers of fry pulsing through the tank, make your first cull (see Chapter 15) with these steps:

1. **Make a couple of passes through the fry with a fine fish net.**

2. **Discard the fry inside the net.**

 Cover the bin or tank containing your new fish with bird netting if there's any chance of bird predation on your young koi. As small as they are and as many as there are, a heron or egret may find a sampling worthwhile.

When the fish get to be 1 inch or longer, your neighborhood raccoons may stop by one evening. Raccoons are quite resourceful animals and are not thwarted by bird netting. If you expect to run into trouble with raccoons, keep your young koi in a container that can be fitted with a tightly locked cover.

Low-Maintenance Breeding: The All-Natural Love Pond

You don't have to go full-tilt to breed your koi; the second way is to let nature take its course (either by simply leaving your koi to their own devices or by furnishing a habitat that's suitable for baby koi making).

If you let nature take its course, be prepared to accept a tremendous attrition rate because of egg predation by adults and the spread of fungus from infertile to fertile eggs. Naturally, the outcomes of such breedings vary widely from pond to pond and season to season. One koi-keeper we know has only three or four new young koi in her pond every year as a result of leaving the adults to their own devices.

Sectioning off the in-pond romping grounds

If letting your koi enjoy free love just isn't your thing, but you don't want to hassle with the breeding tanks and such, you can section off part of your pond and create a nursery there. This nursery serves to confine the breeding adults to one area of the pond for a time so the eggs are in one location and therefore easily relocated. To create a nursery, follow these steps:

1. **Start by digging out that seine net you used last year to round up your koi for their winter pond and the spawning brushes you bought at the koi conference you attended.**

2. **Use the seine to confine the female and one or maybe two males to one end of the pond, and add the spawning brushes to that end of the pond.**

3. **Turn off the filter and the foam fractionator for a couple of hours.**

   This step helps the eggs stick to the spawning brushes instead of floating out of the spawning end of the pond.

4. **After courtship and spawning ends, use a net to move the egg-laden brushes to your nursery tank. Turn the pond filter back on, and return the male(s) to the main part of the pond after a few hours.**

By turning on the filter and the fractionator before you put the breeding male back into the main part of the pond, you avoid problems. The other male koi, invigorated by the scent of the female's pheromones in the water and on the male, get confused. They pummel the newly returned male to try to get him to release eggs. If the filtration systems run for an hour or so before you release the breeding males, most of the scent dissipates or is filtered out.

5. **Leave the female by herself in the spawning end for a few days or move her to a hospital tank with very high water quality for half a day or a full day. See "Selecting the hospital tank" earlier in this chapter for more about this tank.**

   This break lets her rest from egg laying and the enthusiastic attention of the males.

Preparing your pond for babies

Can you have a pond that's breeding- and baby-koi-friendly without a lot of extra equipment and effort? In a word, yes. You can make a few accommodations to help ensure the survival of some fry. They simply need food and shelter, so you need to provide a *substrate* (site) for egg deposition and hiding spots for the koi after they hatch.

To provide egg-deposition sites and shelter for the fry, position spawning brushes or mats or slender tree branches on the floor of the pond. Tie either device to a line that extends over the pond edge and anchor it to a brick or a rock. The line allows for easy retrieval after the young are large enough to fend for themselves.

The tiny koi don't need much space, but they're vulnerable to predation. Adult koi and such unwelcome visitors as predacious aquatic insects relish tiny fry, and raccoons and wading birds will consume those that survive and grow larger.

To provide a hiding area for the baby koi, plant ornamental grasses or pond-side plants that overhang the edge of the pond. If the pond has no place near the edge for living plants, tie leafy plastic plants together and hang them at the pond's edge with a line that's anchored by a rock. If the pond's edge is tiled, try looping the line around small suction cups stuck to the tile.

Chapter 15

The Small Fry: Bringing Up Baby Koi

In This Chapter
▶ Feeding the little buggers
▶ Culling: Population control
▶ Recognizing the best: Quality control

*W*hat can be cuter and more compelling than a group of 3-inch koi? At that size, they have a hint of the grown-up koi within. If you choose to buy them at this size, they aren't expensive. All you need to do is keep them alive over a winter or two until you can see how their color develops and their body shapes up. Almost anyone can raise 3-inch koi.

If you have the space and the time, raising young koi can be a lot of fun, if only for seeing how they color, recolor, and shape up.

And that's what this chapter is about — how to raise young koi, what to feed them, how to cull them (eliminate the weak ones), and finally, how to evaluate the success of your breeding program.

In a nutshell — or rather, in an air bubble — raising your koi is fun, but it's also a lot of work and expense. (The food for the first two months runs about $300.) The task also requires that you cull over 99 percent of the young (although with 30,000 fertile koi eggs, you quickly realize that housing and raising even 200 young koi is a real commitment).

Feeding Fry

The appetites of older koi are easy to satisfy. However, newly hatched fry have very specific nutritional requirements and, because of their tiny mouths, their food must be in a size that they can handle. The foods in Table 15-1 meet their needs.

Fry live on their retained yolk for the first 24 hours after they hatch, but after that, their survival depends on you. You need to tread the fine line between providing enough food and not polluting the tank (because you can't provide filtration).

The newly hatched koi need liquid or a suspended-particle food for the first day or so of life because they have tiny mouths. After a couple of days of this fine dining, the young are on a growth curve and are able to eat progressively larger, nonliquid foods.

Be sure you have all the necessary foods on hand when your fry hatch. You may not need all of them, but stock some of each so you can switch to another type if you run out of one food or if your fry no longer like one of them. The amounts in Table 15-1 are a good place to start, and you can tailor this list to fit your specific hatch size after you have some experience under your belt. If buying the different foods seems like a hassle, look for starter baby-koi food kits.

Foods for baby koi fall into three categories:

- **Commercial foods:** Those specifically created for baby fish, (such as liquid fry food) or foods for larger fish (such as blended freeze-dried krill) that you modify to be acceptable to tiny koi

- **Live foods:** Food such as baby brine shrimp that can be hatched from commercially available eggs

- **Foods from your refrigerator:** Foods that are part of a human diet such as hard-boiled eggs

Table 15-1	Fry Foods to Have on Hand
Food	*Amount*
Liquid fry feeder	four dozen tubes
Brine shrimp eggs for hatching live brine shrimp	15 oz. can
Frozen baby brine shrimp	1.75 oz.
Powdered fry food for egg layers	50-lb. bag
Hard-boiled eggs	cook a dozen and use as needed
Fish flake food	1 lb.
Freeze-dried krill, powdered in your blender	16-oz. bag
Frozen daphia cubes	16-oz. package

Food	Amount
Standard koi-food floating pellets, powdered in your blender	5 lbs.
Baby-koi sinking pellets	5 lbs.

A fry's feeding schedule

Growing fish need quite a lot of food, but overfeeding results in leftovers that pollute the water. Although commercial koi foods are marketed as a complete, balanced diet, generally the widest variety of food as possible is safer.

The first month

During the first month, you want to feed your koi four times per day. The liquid food dissolves in the water and is available to the koi for some time after you introduce it.

Monitor your koi during feeding and fine-tune the amounts of solid food that they need. If you find leftovers at the next feeding, cut back on your volume (but watch that you don't underfeed; large numbers of weak or dead fry are a sure clue). Only time and experience will help you gauge the right formula.

Add the new dietary items to each of the four feedings. Following are some tips and milestones for this first month:

✓ For Day 1, offer liquid fry food, one tube at a time. Simply squeeze the liquid food from its tube into the water. On this first day, also set up your brine shrimp hatchery. The specifics of setting up the brine shrimp hatchery vary from model to model, but all come with instructions and are simple to operate. Then again, you can use the production-line method we describe later in "Hatching brine shrimp."

✓ On Days 2 and 3, continue to feed the liquid fry food, increasing each feeding to two tubes per feeding. Once a day, add a netful of newly hatched brine shrimp (see the section, "Hatching brine shrimp" later in this chapter). The koi prefer the live brine shrimp to all other foods, so leftovers are rarely a problem. Generally, you're safe in feeding the daily output of your hatchery to your koi.

✓ After a day or two, your koi begin to associate human presence with food, and they wriggle to the surface of the water when you approach.

✔ For Days 4 and 5, continue with the liquid fry diet and newly hatched brine shrimp. Add ¼ cup of egg yolk slurry (see the nearby sidebar, "Making egg yolk slurry" for the recipe).

✔ For Days 6 and 7, continue the diet and add the powdered fry food.

✔ During Week 2, add in frozen or fresh daphnia and koi pellets that you've reduced to a powder with a blender, a chopper, or a rolling pin.

✔ At the end of Week 2, discontinue the egg slurry and the liquid fry food. Replace them with fish flake food and ground krill (tiny dried shrimp).

✔ Continue with this dietary mix for the rest of the first month.

At the end of this month, the young should be ¾ to 1 inch long. They are strong enough to swim against a filter current. Take these steps:

1. **Turn on the filtration system.**

2. **Transfer half of the baby koi into a second incubator bin and make sure the filter and airstones are working in this second unit.**

   By splitting up the fish, you ensure better water quality and larger, more robust fish (crowding inhibits growth).

3. **Cull your young koi (see "Culling: It Ain't Easy, but Somebody Has To Do It," later in this chapter).**

   As the koi increase in size, you can be a bit more selective in your culling — removing those that are weak or malformed, for example.

You may see some dramatic differences in the size of your young koi, even at the end of the first month. Some are cannibalistic, eating their smaller brethren. Net out these big pigs — discarding them or raising them separately — and continue this size-segregation netting monthly.

The second month

During the second month, continue feeding your fry four times per day. In general, feed as much as the fish can eat in about five minutes, but make sure that all fry are actively feeding during that time. If not, you'll need to spend more time feeding them, or you can separate the larger fish. You can feed every food item in the following list at each feeding to ensure that all the koi have a shot at getting a balanced diet:

✔ Continue with the powered koi pellets.

✔ Replace the fresh brine shrimp with frozen (the shrimp in the frozen blocks are adult and much larger, but they're easy to tear apart and consume).

✔ Add frozen daphnia to the diet.

✔ Depending on what brand of powdered fry diet you're using, you may be able to switch to a larger particle within that brand.

✔ Feed baby-koi sinking pellets once daily.

At the end of the second month, your young koi should be 1 to 2 inches long.

The third month

During the third month, you can decrease the feedings to three times a day (stay with an amount per feeding that they'll consume within five minutes or so) with the following changes:

✔ Offer the baby-koi pellets, powdered adult-koi pellets, and flake fish food.

✔ Cut the frozen daphnia to once a day.

Making egg yolk slurry

Peel three hard-boiled eggs and separate the yolks. Mash the yolks to a paste with a fork and add water to the yolks, starting with ¼ cup per yolk. You want the egg yolk soup to be liquid enough to use in a plastic squirt bottle (like a well-rinsed mustard or marinade bottle) or a turkey baster (nothing in the kitchen is sacred when you're raising baby koi!). Store the egg yolk slurry in your refrigerator between feedings.

Squirt a line of yolk slurry across the surface of the water in your baby koi bin, and watch the babies' response.

Because the fry are almost transparent when they hatch, you can see the yolk in their stomachs after they've eaten.

Note: Egg yolk is almost pure protein, which, if uneaten, rapidly fouls the water and puts the koi at risk. Don't dump the slurry in, willy-nilly. Feed a small amount at a time, watching carefully that the fry consume all of it. You can continue adding more, bit by bit, until the fish begin to lose interest. The standard rule is to feed what they can consume in five minutes or so, but adjust this to fit your specific situation. For example, you may have many nervous, slow feeders or many larger individuals that hog all the food.

Check the protein content of any food you offer your koi babies. They grow quickly and their protein content requirements are higher than those of the adults. Look for foods with about 40 percent protein content. Increase the protein content in your baby-koi diet if you see *whirling* (koi positioned head up, tail down in the water and turning in circles) or if cannibalism is rampant.

Monitor the water-quality numbers to make sure your protein skimmer and filter are taking care of the increased protein in the water. Even with the filters going, you need to make a 10 percent water change every week and remove the detritus on the bottom of the bin.

You can remove the detritus by one of the following methods:

- Sweep it toward the filter intake at the bottom of the bin.

- Siphon it up with a commercially available siphon. Most models come equipped with a rubber ball that is squeezed to fill the plastic siphon tube with water. Take care not to suck up any fry, and run the siphoned water through a net just to be sure.

  Uneaten egg yolk contributes to the gray-green sludge on the bottom of your tank. This material sticks to the bottom and is difficult to dislodge with a net, so siphoning is the only way to remove it. Use a tall bucket to collect the garbage.

  When you're done siphoning, net out any baby koi from the bucket and return them to their nursery.

  Flush the sludge into your wastewater system.

Hatching brine shrimp

Freshly hatched brine shrimp are minute enough even for koi fry. You can buy them frozen — a very expensive approach when talking about thousands of fry — or you can raise them.

Hatching brine shrimp is almost a mechanical process: Mix salt, water, brine shrimp eggs, and an airstone. Put a light overhead and wait 24 hours.

The best method for hatching brine is to have a production line. Set your production line up on a water-safe tabletop in your utility room, garage, or a protected spot on your porch. The table needs to be large enough for six water pitchers plus a bit of work space. You also need lighting for the area 24 hours a day.

You need these supplies:

- ✔ Six plastic 1-gallon pitchers

- ✔ 30 pounds of rock salt

- ✔ 40 ounces of brine shrimp eggs

- ✔ An air pump and enough valves and aquarium tubing to connect the pump to all six pitchers

Begin hatching three pitchers at a time using the following steps:

1. **Put 2 ½ tablespoons of rock salt in a pitcher.**

2. **Add water from your pond to within 2 inches of the top.**

3. **Add a tablespoon of brine shrimp eggs and stir to dissolve the salt and wet the eggs.**

4. **Put the pitcher on the left side of your table and add an airstone.**

5. **Follow Steps 1 through 4 for two more pitchers and set them along the left side of the table.**

The next day, set up the rest of the water pitchers and put them on the right side of the table.

The baby shrimp, known as *naupli,* will hatch in 24 hours at 85 degrees F. (They take two to three days at lower temperatures, but keep them at a minimum of 76 degrees.) When the shrimp in the pitchers on the left side hatch, you have three days of baby brine shrimp. Pour the contents of one pitcher from the left side of the table through a fine fish net (this water can be discarded) and empty the net into your koi tank as one of the daily feedings. You can set up the pitcher with rock salt and a new dose of eggs, or you can wait until you've emptied all three pitchers and set them all up at once.

Culling: It Ain't Easy, but Somebody Has To Do It

You have a lot of tiny koi when the eggs hatch, but the numbers diminish on their own, even with expert husbandry. (Some just seem to vanish, some get eaten by others, and some leap out of the tank.) But you're still looking at lots of baby fish. At one-month intervals for the first three months, *cull* (euthanize unwanted fish or find new homes for them) your baby fish.

Although culling may sound cruel at first, reducing the number of baby fish puts the nose-count down to a manageable level, work-wise for you, survival-wise for the fish left in your tank, and future-wise for trades or sales. The fewer fish you have to trade or sell, the more valuable each fish becomes.

Most breeders discard the culled fish, but other breeders dry them, grind them up, and feed them to the koi. That's a little grisly for our blood. If you don't want the young koi to die, at least not at your hands, ask a local pet store manager whether she's interested in feeder fish. Instead of asking for cash for these fish, which the pet store may sell at ten-for-a-buck, see whether you can trade them for fish food.

What to cull

After the fish are showing color (about the end of the second month), you can cull for the colors you want. You may also wish to remove aggressive fry and those that are weak, stunted, or deformed.

If you're breeding for Sanke (see Chapter 2 for a description of the various color morphs), look at the red-white-black koi in your tank. Discard the following Sanke:

- Those without red on their head.

- Those with red in the fins.

- Those that are more than one-third black — balance between red, white, and black is important for Sanke.

Also remember the following guidelines:

- Cull for solid colors; remove any solid whites or oranges.

- Keep all solid blacks because they may become Showa, the black koi with red and white markings. (On Showa, the red markings appear later, taking one to three years to develop.)

- Keep a young white koi that has red anywhere on its head because it may develop into a quality Tancho. (Large red markings on the head tend to shrink in size as the fish matures.)

  A good Tancho (the white koi with the red marking on the top of the head) has a rounded topknot (the colored area on the top of the head).

How much to cull

Whenever you cull, you want to seriously reduce your baby fish inventory.

The following numbers are guidelines that generations of koi-keepers and breeders have used:

- ✔ The first month, remove and discard 85 percent of your fish.
- ✔ The second month, remove and discard 80 percent.
- ✔ The third month, remove and discard 65 percent.

If you started with 5,000 fry, at the end of three months you'll have 52 healthy, lively, young koi that are 3 to 4 inches long. That's still a lot of fish. However, if you started with 20,000 fry and culled for three months, you'll have 210 fish, all of which eat, churn out ammonia, and grow about an inch a month. That's too many fish. Keep culling until you have a number that you can manage properly, given your constraints of time and space.

There's nothing wrong with being very selective about which koi you save; the singular purpose behind this entire adventure is to end up with a few very good koi.

Evaluating Your Young Koi

Deciding which fish to cull or show is a tricky process that becomes easier with experience. When your fish get large enough to seriously evaluate, keep this *backwards* rule of koi-judging in mind: Koi judges don't look for what makes a fish pretty; they look for the flaws, or rather the absence of flaws. Check out the sidebar "How the pros breed (and cull) their fish" for more about this refined koi selection.

An experienced koi breeder knows all about potential flaws and how to pick out the fish with the fewest flaws. Because this process is a bit more difficult for a beginner, follow these steps:

1. **Start with body shape.**

   A koi with a long back and a wide head is a good koi.

2. **Move out to the fins.**

   A koi's pectoral fins should extend well away from the body, with the rays fanned out.

3. **Check out that skin!**

Any white skin should be bright and unsullied. Any colors atop the white should be dense. The edges of markings should be distinct, and the color of the markings should be intense.

How the pros breed (and cull) their fish

Those who breed koi for a living have a more business-like approach to the process because they're selling lineage, not just pretty fish.

In Japan, breeding occurs in late summer. A female is placed in a spawning tank with a male, and they're both watched carefully. When the female koi begins to scatter a few eggs, she's removed from the spawning bin and anesthetized. She's then held over a stainless steel bowl and *dry stripped* (her abdomen is gently squeeze-rubbed to *strip* her eggs into the bowl). These eggs are divided among a series of bowls, depending on how many males have been selected to pair with this female. (One male initiates egg laying, but several may actually contribute to fertilization.)

Each male is anesthetized, and while he's out of it, his *milt* (semen) is removed through his vent via pipette. The milt is mixed with Ringer's solution, an isotonic solution that has the same salinity as fish blood, and each bowl is inoculated with one male's milt. The eggs are gently stirred. Fertilization occurs and the *micropyle* (the opening in the egg's membrane that allows for entry of the sperm) closes. The fertilized eggs are placed on spawning grass or brushes in a hatching bin, one male-female pairing per bin (so a few months down the road the breeder knows the success of each pairing). Water quality in each hatching bin is monitored for the next week and the infertile eggs are removed.

After the fry hatch, they go into *mud ponds,* a growing-out pond. For fry, a mud pond is just 2 feet deep but may contain 44,000 gallons of water. A mud pond that large can hold 180,000 to 200,000 fry, the progeny from 6 to 15 select pairings. The young are fed *infusoria* (protozoans raised in cultures of hay and water), powdered food, and daphnia twice a day. At the end of the first month, the fish are from ¾ to 1 inch long and the first culling occurs.

The first cull simply nets out and discards 85 percent of the fry from the water. Some Japanese breeders dry the discarded fish, grind them up, and feed them to their brethren.

A month later, the second culling removes 80 percent of the now 2-inch-long koi.

At the end of the third month, another culling removes 65 percent of the remaining koi. What had been 180,000 fry are now 1,890, and they're 3 to 4 inches long.

Half of these koi are sold on the market. The remaining 945 koi are kept over the winter. The following summer, half of these almost-yearlings are sold.

The remaining 472 go back into a mud pond (one deeper than their first mud pond) for the winter. That second summer, the koi are 12 to 14 inches long, and they have a ready market waiting for them. Just for the record, 0.2 percent, or one-fifth of a percent, of the hatched fry stay with the breeder through two winters.

Chapter 16

Koi Shows: Your All-Access Pass to Koi Kichi-dom

. . . .

In This Chapter

▶ Shows: More than just a blue ribbon

▶ Variety is the spice: Locating the shows

▶ Ready, set, go: Entering a competition

▶ Just for the fun of it: No koi, no pressure

▶ Stepping into the organizer's role: Your own koi show

. . . .

Showing koi isn't for everyone. Some people like their koi just the way they are and have no desire to see how their treasures compare to others. But other koi-keepers may just be more curious to see how their fish measure up. Maybe they want to see whether their wonderful little Bekko (the one they snatched from their pond-dealer's $19.95 tank) is growing into a very good Bekko. Or maybe they like trying to predict the judges' Grand Champion selection. Then again, maybe they hope that the dealer who had the gorgeous Ogon last year will bring in a Yamabuki Ogon this year. Or maybe they just like to travel a couple of times a month to meet a bunch of new friends with similar interests.

Koi shows accomplish two goals: They allow individuals to enter their prized koi in competition, and they allow vendors to reach a very select market with their koi supplies, books, and yes, koi for sale. So, even if you aren't up to primping your fish for judging, a koi show still has a lot to offer you.

In this chapter, you discover the ins and outs of koi shows — how they operate, what to expect, and even how to enter your own fish.

Showing Your Koi — Why Bother?

Of course, the prospect of winning a title or trophy has great appeal in any contest setting, but koi shows have so much more to offer than just awards. In terms of real pleasures and value, every participant at a koi show, whether you compete or not, comes out a winner.

You win gold in terms of knowledge

In addition to putting miles on your car and ending those weekends of working in the yard, koi shows teach you about koi. You discover myriad facts about koi-keeping and koi-judging. For example:

- ✔ **Inside tips on practical issues:** You discover more than you thought you ever could at the seminars and workshops that go along with koi shows. Typical sessions deal with setting up quarantine systems, operating a koi farm, and using salt against koi disease. Sometimes these are coupled with trade shows, where you can see and learn about new equipment, foods, books, and the like.

- ✔ **How koi are judged:** By observing the judges and talking with them and other hobbyists, you start to make sense of what is, at first glance, a confusing process.

- ✔ **The particulars about each judge:** You find out what koi characteristics are most important (this varies from judge to judge) — which judges, for example, look carefully at body shape and which ones look at pattern balance.

- ✔ **The reasons behind the results:** Why competition is so tough for Kohaku, for example.

You get to know your koi better

Showing koi that you've just purchased is a learning experience for you and your fish. You can't know ahead of time how well your koi will deal with the stress of the show. For example:

- ✔ Some varieties of koi lose their color intensity when they're under stress.

- ✔ Some try to hide or splash about in an agitated manner.

- ✔ Some (like the Chagoi) are friendly koi that just like people; nothing seems to stress them.

Realistically speaking, you need to attend one or two shows before you know how your new koi react to traveling and to the show itself. Travel is stressful, and many koi just don't deal well with it. (Review Chapter 5 for tips on transporting fish to make the trip less stressful on both of you.)

You can observe your koi carefully, both en route and at the show, to decide whether the experience is worthwhile for you and your fish. Particularly high-strung animals are best spared this ordeal. Let the behavior of other koi and the advice of more experienced people be your guide in making this decision.

You see what you're up against and what's in vogue

You need to see how different judges react to your new koi. You may think that your Aka Muji, a nonmetallic red koi, is extraordinary. But when three judges in a row pass it over, you have to face the fact that you have a very nice, very ordinary koi. See "The judging process" later in this chapter for more information concerning what the judges are looking for.

When you're at a show, look around to see what's being shown. If they seem to be the same old story, they probably are. Keep track of the following factors:

- ✔ **Variety:** The long-time top varieties of koi are the Kohaku, Showa, and Sanke, with the Ogon nudging in for fourth place.

- ✔ **Other factors:** Is there anything new in the way of color or shape? Perhaps something that points the way to a future trend?

- ✔ **Size:** No particular size is tops, mostly because koi tend to grow into the next size group every year or every other year.

Finding a Show Near You (Or Even Far Away)

The Web site or newsletter of your local koi club is a good place to start when searching for a local show. You can expand your search by checking with one of the bigger clubs, such as the Mid-Atlantic Koi Club (www.makc.com) or via a general Internet search. Koi magazines also list upcoming shows, as do the newsletters of general aquarium societies.

Showing Off Your Pride and Joy

After you've decided to show your koi, you have a number of questions to consider. And personal experience tells us that you'll enjoy the experience more if you understand what's expected of you and how the process works in general.

Local and regional shows in particular tend to be restricted to hobbyists. As a result, people who make a living from koi (let us pause for a minute to catch our breath from laughing — the idea of *making* money from koi seems outlandish!) may not be allowed to compete. They attend the shows as vendors only. If you're in doubt about your status, check the guidelines before you register for a show to avoid any problems. You can also contact the show organizer and ask about these limitations.

Registering for a show

If you decide to take the plunge and enter your Precious in a show, you need to plan ahead. Some shows have an entry deadline several days before the show dates. (This advance warning allows the organizers time to provide enough show tanks for the competing fish.) But the deadline for registration may be flexible; many shows allow for walk-up (swim-up?) registration when show tank space is still available. Bottom line: If the show's important, don't take that kind of chance. Be sure you determine these and other limitations from the show's announcement information or organizers so you can plan accordingly.

To get started in the registration process, consult the requirements posted on the Web site or magazine advertisement that announces the show. The show entry form includes

- ✔ **Your contact information:** Short and simple, just the way we like it.

- ✔ **Your show tank requirements:** You reserve one or more show tanks (6-foot or 8-foot) with the understanding that only your fish will be in your tanks (to prevent disease transmission).

  Generally, the show rules spell out the number of fish to be in each tank. Usually fish of each size class are assigned a certain number of points, and the tanks are designated to hold a certain number of *fish points*. For example, fish of 16 to 20 inches may be labeled as size 4 (4 points). So if a 6-foot-long tank can hold 25 *points* of koi, you can put six koi, 16 to 20 inches each, in that tank.

> Most show organizers don't require a head count ahead of time. They leave the number of fish per tank up to you.

> ✔ **Descriptions of your koi:** Although rare, sometimes the powers that be ask for the type and size of your koi.

You pay a registration fee (which can vary greatly from show to show) when you submit the registration form.

Paperwork with the registration probably reminds you not to feed your koi for at least three days before the show to keep the water in the show tanks and vats as clean as possible. Koi don't suffer from fasting over the entire event, even if it's several days.

A brief rundown of the affair

Most shows are weekend affairs with *benching* (setup) on Friday and early Saturday. The process goes something like this:

1. **A show official checks you in at the registration area and you're assigned a fish handler.**

   Please bring your own bowls and koi nets. Some onsite equipment is available, but you're wise to use your own for hygienic reasons.

2. **The fish handler helps you move your fish to your assigned show tank(s). After the bag(s) and tank temperatures have equalized, the handler physically transfers your fish into the tank(s).**

   The goal of the fish handler is to lift your koi out of the bag and place it into the tank without transferring any of the transport water to avoid spreading disease or parasites.

   You can dispose of the used bags and transport water, but you may want to keep yours for the trip home if you haven't brought extra bags. (Hint: To avoid problems because of ripped bags, bring along some extras.)

3. **A contest official visually inspects your fish for disease.**

   Fish that exhibit any symptoms of disease are not allowed into the show tank or vat.

4. **Using your net and bowl, a member of the benching team bowls each of your koi to classify, measure, and photograph it.**

   Your regular koi are measured from nose tip to tail-fin tip; long fins and butterfly koi are measured from nose tip to the base of the tail. See Table 16-1 for the group sizes.

5. You take the completed benching form and digital photos to the registration table to complete the entry process.

6. Judging begins Saturday morning. Depending upon the judges' dispositions, and, of course, the number and quality of the entries, this can be quite a tedious and protracted affair. Show officials generally announce awards at a banquet on Saturday night.

7. Takedown begins on Sunday afternoon, usually no earlier than 3 p.m.

The sponsoring club usually supplies oxygen and fresh water for bagging.

Table 16-1	Size Groups for Koi Shows
Group	**Koi Length**
1	Under 10″
2	10″ to under 13″
3	13″ to under 16″
4	16″ to under 19″
5	19″ to under 21″
6	21″ to under 24″
7	24″ to under 27″
8	Over 27″

Surveying the many ways to win

Prizes range from ribbon rosettes to trophies, with no two shows being identical in this regard. But koi shows do more than award prizes for the most beautifully configured koi. They recognize other categories including the best male, the most jumbo, and the show director's choice. Other awards are more lighthearted like the most beautiful eyes, longest tail fin, or most unique.

Part of the reason for separating koi by type and size is to have easily comparable fish. Some varieties don't develop their full range of colors until they near 12 inches, so comparing a 6-incher to a 12-incher isn't fair. And trying to compare a Koromo to a Utsuri Mono is like the proverbial apples to oranges game. Having lots of categories gives all competitors a better chance at winning.

Taking a sneak peek at Japanese koi shows

In Japan, koi competitions group the fish by size and classification, meaning all the size 2 Kohaku are together, and all the size 2 Utsuri Monos are together. Even though clear digital photos are part of the registration process, every koi-keeper can easily recognize his own fish.

The first Japanese point system to establish the value of a fish was fault-based: Each koi started with 100 points and then lost points for body shape, pattern faults, and color faults. In the 1980s the system switched to a positive approach: Points are now awarded for notable characteristics. With this system, a fish with great color can win over a fish with a good pattern, or a koi that swims with remarkable grace can still have a high score in spite of its other faults.

Japanese shows are a great deal more formal than American shows, and this formality acknowledges the judges' expertise by allowing them a great deal of leeway in selecting the finest koi. Judges use written ballots in selecting the show's Grand Champion.

As part of their always-positive approach, Japanese judges announce the show's Grand Champion first and then the lower prizes. This order is the opposite of U.S. shows, where they save the announcement of the Grand Champion for last.

Shows are generally prejudiced in favor of larger fish, meaning a 36-inch koi is more apt to win over a 30-inch koi only by virtue of size and age. However, larger fish are more difficult to transport, and many koi competitors just don't want to take a chance on losing their elder koi.

The judging process

The evaluation of each koi variety has set criteria, but the process is scarcely precise. For example, one judge may prefer the black on a Sanke scattered over the body, but avoid the red. Another judge may like a Sanke whose black is limited to four splotches that form two opposing V's over the back.

Although judges do adhere to the specific standards of each variety, they're free to rely on their personal opinions as well. They follow a procedure that includes the following checkpoints:

- ✔ **Swimming style:** The koi's movements should appear graceful, with the pectoral fins held out. Swimming should be a smooth, fluid movement as opposed to a twisting motion.

- ✔ **Fins:** Any damage? If your koi's fins were damaged during transport, tell the judge so it won't count against the fish.

✔ **Barbels:** Any missing?

✔ **Body shape:** Plump, Rubenesque females are more attractive than slender males; body should be bilaterally symmetric.

✔ **Colors:** Deep, vibrant colors with distinct edges are preferable to colors that overlap; balanced or pleasing patterns score high, and a unique pattern on the head is a real plus.

The judges generally make their decisions on a consensus basis. One person is usually designated as a head judge to resolve impasses. The details of the actual decision-making process vary widely from show to show and among the various judges. Individual judges may give greater or lesser weight to certain factors, and the effect of this is not at all clear cut. In fact, judging may be quite confusing to the newcomer. But with experience, you can start to make sense of certain (but not all!) aspects of the judging process.

Judges are willing to explain why they selected one koi over another or which factors they found pleasing in a particular koi. Be sure to check the protocol (written and unwritten) concerning these procedures. They differ from show to show, but they're always rooted in the formality and politeness of the hobby's Japanese origins.

Competing without actually showing up

Your koi can compete in shows and you never have to leave your home. How is this possible? You let the breeder show your fish for you before you receive the fish. In the world of koi, a breeder can show fish on behalf of the new owner if the new owner hasn't taken possession of the fish.

Consider this scenario: You go to Japan, buy a koi with promise, and leave it with the breeder to mature for a year or so. During that time, the breeder enters your koi in whatever show(s) he — or the two of you — chooses. When he ships the fish to you, it arrives complete with show awards (or so you hope).

But after this prize-winning Ai Bekko crosses your threshold, the rules change. From then on, you do the work. The rules read, "All fish must be the personal and private property of the registrant."

Sometimes the rules state that the show is not open to individuals who derive a significant portion of their income from breeding koi or that the fish owner must attend the show and sign the entry form. You can't get around rules like these. These rules prevent a professional koi-breeder from dragging out his zillion-dollar Sanke and sweeping the awards. After all, the show is by hobbyists for hobbyists. A professional koi-breeder can easily make everyone feel like yesterday's filter wash.

Respect the judges' opinions; they've gone through a winnowing process that requires years of koi-keeping experience, specialized training with testing at the end, and recertification every four years.

For more information on judging, the Associated Koi Clubs of America (AKCA) has a Web site that lets you try your hand at judging: `www.akca.org/judging/judge.htm`.

After the show: Packing up and heading out

After 3 p.m. on Sunday, the competitors and vendors pack up and head home. You can get packing help from a member of the benching team if you don't mind waiting, but most koi-keepers bag up their own fish.

The general format of closing up follows these steps:

1. **Use your koi net to bowl each of your fish and then pour the fish into its own poly bag.**

   Place smaller koi together in one bag, but be careful not to crowd them.

2. **Carry your bags to the member of the benching team who's handling the oxygen.**

   She may be walking around, pulling a wheeled oxygen tank. She'll squash the bag down to remove excess air, top it off with oxygen, then twist and seal the top with a rubber band.

   With oxygen, your koi should be comfortable for 8 to 12 hours.

3. **Place the sealed bags in their cardboard boxes and close the tops.**

In the meantime, the live fish vendors are delivering bagged, oxygenated, and boxed koi that the show participants have purchased. (Because most vendors prefer payment at the time of sale and not at the time of delivery, this delivery process goes smoothly.)

When you're packed and ready to go, follow these guidelines to safely bring your koi home sweet home:

1. **Place the boxes in your car or van crosswise so the bags lie perpendicular to the direction of travel.**

   When you stop or accelerate, your koi simply rock in their bags instead of jamming their noses into the end of the bag.

Don't allow any box to remain in the sun in your car. Shade it with a towel or jacket.

2. **Open the box at home and place the bags in your pond so temperatures can equalize.**

Make certain that none of them are floating in the sun.

3. **Open the bags after 20 minutes, wet your hands, and lift your koi out of the bag for release into the pond.**

Try not to spill any of the bag water into the pond; after two days of being *home* to your koi, the water's probably not clean any more.

Attending a Show Just for Kicks and Giggles

Some shows include free (with your registration) workshops or lectures on Saturday and Sunday. The judging area is usually open for viewing Saturday and Sunday, and more than half the fun of a show comes from walking around and looking at the fish.

As the judges begin walking around and talking to each other about the fish, protocol puts sort of an invisible shield around them. Only show officials may talk to them or interrupt them. After the awards, judges are available for questions.

Vendor booths and the judging area are open to the public for viewing on Saturday and Sunday.

Playing Host: Setting Up Your Own Show

Although shows at a set location are a long-standing tradition among koi associations, other options are possible. Factors such as logistics, finances, or the personal situations of members may necessitate creative thinking. The house-to-house show is an ideal alternative and often brings together koi enthusiasts who aren't able to view each other's fish any other way.

House-to-house shows

In house-to-house shows, the judges and the crowd travel from house to house to see the competing fish in their own habitat. This type of show works well when

✔ Showing off your pond is part of the fun.

✔ It's the dead of winter and everyone has heated indoor ponds (for more on setting up your own indoor pond, see Chapter 10).

However, this show is harder for the judges because they have to remember the strong points of one koi three houses back and the details on the koi's chin from the first house. Most judges use a point system or digital photos to help even out the judging process.

Because of their unique characteristics, these shows are most easily arranged among people who live within a relatively small area (a couple of miles) and who are comfortable in opening up their homes to other folks. Small, local koi associations are an ideal format for organizing house-to-house shows, either by word of mouth or through the organization's newsletter.

Regional shows

You can sum up shows in one word, *committees* — and plenty of them. A club or regional show requires so many finite tasks that everyone can join in at a level that suits him best. A typical list of committees includes

✔ Show site arrangements

✔ Show set up

✔ Publicity

✔ Hospitality

✔ Registration

✔ Show workers

✔ Judge arrangements

✔ Prizes/ribbons

✔ Fish handlers

✔ Site cleanup

When you're trying to figure out how much work a show is, a helpful guideline is

✔ Half of the work is done before the show.

✔ One-fourth of the work is done during the show.

✔ One-fourth of the work is done after the show.

Before you begin recruiting for committee members, the executive committee needs to get a handle on the show parameters and the overall structure of the event. The following sections highlight these parameters as well as the planning and post-event stages. For more about the show itself, the earlier section "Showing Off Your Pride and Joy" gives a good rundown of the activities.

Show parameters

The executive committee has the responsibility for setting show guidelines. Typical points of discussion that you'll need to agree on are as follows:

- **Registration:** Will you limit registration to owners only?

- **Size classes:** Although koi have eight size classes, will you group the sizes?

   Consider limiting the classes to the four smaller sizes, omitting the larger sizes. Your size classes may run like this:

   - 16 to 17 inches (Group 4)
   - Under 16 to 13 inches (Group 3)
   - Under 13 to 10 inches (Group 2)
   - Under 10 inches (Group 1)

- **Varieties:** Which varieties will be judged together?

- **Awards:** Will you use standard categories for trophies?

   Standard categories include

   - Best in Size for each group
   - Grand Champion for Groups 3 and 4
   - Reserve Champion for Groups 3 and 4
   - Baby Champion for Groups 1 and 2

   If long fin koi are permitted, we suggest a separate award for this category. (All koi are equal, but some are more equal than others.)

   Ribbons and certificates are standard for Best in Class and less formal categories.

- **Local vendors:** Will you ask these folks to donate raffle prizes?

   Supplies for the show, including test kits and AmQuel, should be purchased from local vendors to encourage their participation.

The planning stage

When you're setting up a show, realize that you can't find a perfect date or a weekend without a competing event. Do the best you can and expect to hear, "Oh, the weekend before/after (deep sigh) would have been *so* much better!" from a lot of people. It goes with the territory.

Ask your local vendors to help select a site and a hotel. They may know the area better than you do, and they may be able to help with negotiations. Most hotels have never been asked to host a koi show, so you do have the element of uniqueness on your side. If they have a large, grassy area to stage the show and a source of water nearby, you can hold the show there. If the show is to be outdoors, be sure to check into local weather conditions, and plan for canvas domes or tents if necessary.

When you make arrangements with hotel representatives, they'll want to know how many beds you need for how many nights, what sort of meeting spaces you need, and how many meal functions they can serve you.

Hotels love to sell you meals, and that's how they make their money. To keep costs down, use the hotel for the banquet only.

Promoting the event is critical. These are some ideas:

- Link up with as many online lists as you can find.
- Set up a Web site so people can register and pay fees online.
- Send postcards announcing the event to every koi club within 200 miles and ask them to tell all their members.
- Print a great-looking show poster and get members to put them up everywhere — pond stores, laundromats, art supply shops, bait shops — you get the idea.
- Put the poster online and ask koi enthusiasts within a 200-mile radius to print it and take it to their local pond store.
- Call your local paper and ask for a feature article to appear *before* the show.

  Newspapers love to run articles after an event so they can't be accused of endorsing it. You need to ask them to run it before the event. If they balk, maybe they'll write the article about your club and the popularity of koi and then just happen to mention the show as sort of an afterthought.

The post-event stage

Hold an evaluation after the show with people involved in the planning and with interested participants. Although you can have this meeting the evening the show closes, everyone may be too tired to talk. But do plan to have it within a week, while the show is still fresh in everyone's minds. Provide snacks and drinks (the alcohol level is up to you, but we suggest you limit it to nothing more potent than wine).

You want to cover what worked and what didn't and what should be different next year. Don't take anything personally — you want what's on people's minds. Have someone take notes, or you'll never remember.

Plan a future club program around the show ID photos of the competing fish. Use the photos to illustrate the finer points of koi configuration.

Part V
The Part of Tens

The 5th Wave   By Rich Tennant

" Oh, that's nice. They weren't doing anything
with the tetherball."

In this part . . .

You've heard the songs — "50 Ways to Leave Your Lover," "One Is the Loneliest Number," "Three Little Words." We wanted to put "Twenty Koi Tips" to music but just couldn't think of a catchy tune. Instead, we simply offer you two lists of ten tips (not lyrical but still a thing of beauty!). Coming up in this part are easy-to-follow ways to take action should you end up electricity-less or have a sick koi on your hands.

Chapter 17

Ten Things to Do When the Power Goes Out

In This Chapter

▶ Minimize the numbers: That's what friends are for

▶ Maintain water values: Cut the feedings and test the water

▶ Provide short-term solutions: Ammonia and nitrites down, oxygen up

▶ Solve the pump and filter problem: Alternative energy sources

As anyone with electricity in her home knows, the power is bound to go out (when you least expect it, when you're late for work, and when you're drying your hair). For a koi-keeper, a power loss means more than frizz — this small inconvenience can turn into a hairy ordeal if you have a koi pond and want to keep your koi from going belly-side-up.

The great news is that you don't have to feel like a duck in a shooting gallery when your power goes out — you can take certain actions after the power goes off. To help save your koi (we figure you can take care of yourself just fine), your first concerns are

  ✔ Providing oxygen to the fish

  ✔ Keeping water quality from deteriorating to a dangerous level

We hope you never need this info, but at least you'll have some course of action to follow when the lights go out. (You did remember to keep fresh batteries in the flashlight so you can read this, right?)

Lower the Fish Load in Your Pond

If the power goes out, your koi can't check into a hotel and use the Jacuzzi. They're stuck in the pond and they're going to be distressed pretty soon. What to do? Just like the wranglers out West, you head 'em up and move 'em out.

In this case, you're moving koi, not cattle, and they're only going into show tanks that have battery-powered pumps. Be sure that you have enough tanks on hand to handle an emergency. See Chapter 3 for directions on calculating the ideal number of koi per tank so you'll know how many tanks to keep, and be sure to check Chapter 5 for advice on moving koi and adjusting them to new water.

If you don't have show tanks, bag up some of your koi and take them for temporary residency in the ponds of your koi friends who still have power. Trust us, these people will understand. Next year, they may be the ones without power. Be sure to alert your benefactors of any of your fish's health concerns so they can take appropriate quarantine measures.

Stop Feeding Your Fish

Your koi may gather at the pond edge and beg shamelessly, but it's all show. They can go for a week without food and not suffer. When the power goes out, don't feed your koi, even if that little Chagoi hottie makes eye contact and goes "Wa-wa" with her mouth. The last thing you need is your koi dumping ammonia and nitrites into the water — which is exactly what they do when you feed them.

Do a 30-Percent Water Change

The easiest way to provide oxygen to your koi and dilute the ammonia and nitrite levels at the same time is through 30 percent partial water changes. We provide all the details you need to tackle this process in Chapter 9.

Plan on doing these 30 percent changes daily until the power comes back on. You do have lots of dechlor on hand, don't you?

Test Your Water Daily for Ammonia and Nitrites

As depressing as it may seem, you have to be extra vigilant about your pond's water chemistry when your power goes out. Use your test kit daily and record the levels so you can see where they're headed. (To find out how to test your pond's water quality, head back to Chapter 9.) If the ammonia and nitrite levels get to the top edge of the safe area, you need to take further steps to protect the health of your koi. See Chapter 9 for this too.

Add Salt or Zeolite

Ordinary kosher salt, that miracle tonic, can help reduce the nitrite level in your pond. Just add 10 pounds per 1,000 gallons, but be careful that no other medications are in the pond. If you're combining salt with partial water changes, use a salt meter or a test kit to keep the salt level around 1 percent.

If you forego salt, a mesh bag of the mineral zeolite can suck up ammonia all on its own, and you can recharge it overnight by soaking it in a garbage can filled with heavily salted water. Shake out the bag the next morning and it's good to go.

Obviously, you can use salt *or* zeolite in your pond, but never, ever at the same time.

Use an Inverter to Power Your Air Pump

An inverter is a device that changes DC to AC, meaning it can convert power from your car battery into power for one of the devices you use in your pond. Just plug it into your car's cigarette lighter.

The inverter may not be able to provide enough current for your filter pump, but it can power an air pump (see Chapter 6) or a 6-volt bilge pump. You don't use the bilge pump to empty your pond; you use it to aerate the water, directing the pump outflow through your bog pond or across a 2 x 4 piece of plastic corrugate before the water drips back into your pond.

Let ol' Sol Power Your Pond

Solar power can actually be practical (meaning that it's handy when you need it, not that it's cheap). You can buy and install solar-powered aerators. These are designed primarily for ponds in isolated areas (but then again, when your power's off, anyone can feel plenty isolated). You have to provide a housing enclosure for the compressor and batteries and a pole for mounting the solar unit, but who cares? These same solar units can power water pumps.

Solar-powered aerators are made by several manufacturers — most are made for lakes, which is more than what you need. Use your browser to search for a manufacturer of solar aerators for fish ponds, or ask your local utility company for leads on solar panels for pond aeration. Here's one vendor for a pond-sized solar aeration unit (about $400 for one large enough to handle 100 square feet of pond surface; one unit would work for our basic 6-x-9-foot pond): Pennington Equipment Company, 1520 NW 6th St., Springfield, IL 62702; phone 888-261-4726, fax 886-422-0018; Web site www.solaraerator.com.

Mist Your Pond

Add a mist nozzle to your garden hose and place the end over the edge of your pond. Brace the hose in place with a couple of bricks and turn the water on. The water absorbs oxygen from the air as it sprays into your pond. This can be done continuously, along with the other measures mentioned. If you dechlor for your daily 30 percent water changes, you don't need to worry about dechlorinating the water added by the misting.

Use Compressed Air

You can also rent tanks of compressed air to bubble air into your pond. Your local pond store can usually recommend a local source, or search online. (Sorry, you can't get tanks of oxygen except with a physician's prescription, and those small tanks only last four hours. Besides, you may need the oxygen yourself when you figure out what it's going to cost to replace all the food in that doublewide freezer you just bought!)

Use a Portable Battery System to Power Your Filter

You can actually buy an emergency back-up power system for your pond. One model is a 1,500-watt system with an inverter to power two AC outlets. This same unit can power air pumps and air-powered filters. You recharge the unit with your car battery or with a solar charging unit (you provide the car battery; the vendor can supply the solar unit). Use your phone book to find a local vendor to save on shipping costs, but if you can't find one locally, try an Internet search. One we found was Superpond, 422 E. Columbia Dr., Kennewick, WA 99336; phone 509-586-1945.

Chapter 18

Ten Things to Check If Your Koi Seem Sick

* *

In This Chapter

▶ External forces: It's all in the water (values and temps)

▶ Physical symptoms: From chin to fin

▶ Finny behaviors: Swimming and socializing

* *

Koi don't just turn over and die. They show signs — some overt, some not — that something's funky. Keep a close eye on your pond and watch for any of the signs we talk about in this chapter; then take action before you finny friends get really sick. (Try not to be paranoid, though, or you'll defeat the purpose for keeping koi — to sit back, relax, and enjoy them.) Chapter 13 has all the important details on diagnosing and treating a sick fish, but this chapter guides you through the checkpoints for reaching a diagnosis.

The Pond's Water Quality

You'll hear this advice so much that you'll begin muttering it in your sleep: The health of your koi is directly related to the quality of their pond water. When water chemistry values get out of whack, especially the ammonia and nitrite levels, they compromise your koi's immune systems. Practically any nearby bacteria or virus can move in and set up housekeeping. Then you and your koi have compounded problems. Head back to Chapter 9 to find out how to check and fix the water quality if a chemical's out of balance.

The Pond's Water Temperature

Is the pond's water temperature between 75 and 85 degrees F? It should be. Koi are remarkably adaptive fish, but they have a limit to what they can deal with successfully. If the water's too cold, their immune systems can't fight off infection, particularly the opportunistic cool-water bacteria, *Aeromonas* and *Pseudomonas* (see Chapter 13). When water temps near the mid-80s and the normal afternoon pH rise elevates the ammonia level, your koi are subjected to the flesh-curdling effects (fin rot and gill plate swelling) of ammonia. Think of Goldilocks's porridge when it comes to pond temps — not too hot and not too cool. For the how-to on correcting the pond's water temperature, consult Chapter 9.

Your Koi's Scales

Do any of the scales stick out from the body? Those that stand out are called *pine cone* scales, and they indicate a severe internal infection, the kind that makes the body swell up. This isn't a good sign at all, and it calls for all of the following steps:

- ✔ Immediate transfer to a spacious quarantine tub (spacious because your koi's going to be there for a while)
- ✔ Antibiotic feed or injections
- ✔ Careful monitoring

Don't be surprised if this symptom also calls for a one-way trip to the garbage can. After a koi undergoes this sort of internal pressure, recovery is a surprise.

Your Koi's Gills

Does the fish seem to have trouble breathing? Gill plates swell and can't accept enough oxygen when the water's ammonia levels are too high. Your poor koi not only feels awful, he's also oxygen-deprived. Make an immediate 30 percent partial water change and track down the cause of the ammonia problem. Check the color of the gills — are they the color of your own gums? (Good.) Are they pale pink? (Not good.) Do they look spongy, like moist bread? (Oh, not good.) Gill plates that develop white patches and appear to be disintegrating may indicate koi herpes virus. This virus is highly contagious and is usually fatal. See Chapter 13 for more details.

Your Koi's Finny-Fin-Fins

Human eyes may be the window to the soul, but the window to your koi's health is through the thin skin covering their fins:

- ✔ Tattered fins mean the koi has fin rot or has been handled and netted too much.

- ✔ Bleeding fins indicate rough handling, poor water quality, or a pond bottom that's too rough.

- ✔ Swollen spots on the leading edge of a fin may indicate carp pox. (You can't do anything about this virus except increase the water temperature enough to activate the koi's own immune system. Increase water temps only a few degrees a day to enable the koi to adjust.)

Check out Chapter 13 for additional fin remedies.

Your Koi's Underside

As part of a general checkup, bowl your koi and lift it to check its underside, or bag it and examine its underside through the bag. Aeromonas, the cause of hole-in-side disease (see Chapter 13), tends to erupt as an ulcer on the underside of koi, particularly between the pectoral fins. However, the ulcers can show up nearly anywhere. Aeromonas can also bloat the body and cause pine cone disease.

You can usually avoid the problem by keeping the pond temp above 68 degrees. Treatment consists of bringing the koi inside for a month or two of careful water temperature regulation and antibiotic treatment. Alternatively, you can treat the entire pond with salt, potassium permanganate, or a commercially available antibacterial, or you can admit you don't know what's happenin', baby, and call in a koi vet or a more experienced koi-keeper.

Your Koi's Body

Does the koi's body have tiny white spots? This may be Ich (a parasitic disease) or a fungus. Take a scraping and examine it under the microscope to make a diagnosis. (Chapter 13 walks you through this process.)

Pet stores carry several off-the-shelf medications for Ich, or you can use malachite green, salt, or temperature manipulation, as we describe in Chapter 13.

The diagnosis of fungus calls for a different approach because fungus is a secondary infection, one that appears after your koi's protective mucous coating has been damaged. Identify and eliminate the problem (from netting, poor water quality, or inadequate diet) and then treat for the fungus (see Chapter 13 for treatment plans).

Your Koi's Belly-Side Behavior (Are You Being Flashed?)

Do your koi seem to be rubbing their bodies against the sides or bottom of the pond, or are they turning over at the surface of the water? This maneuver is called *flashing,* and it usually indicates a parasitic infestation or an electrical short in the pond.

External parasites on your fish are about as comfortable as head-to-toe poison ivy on you. Do a skin scrape to ID, and then treat for the little varmints.

In case of a possible electrical problem (damaged electrical cord, cracked housing, or the suspicious scent of bad circuitry), unplug, remove, and examine any submerged pumps or filters for a possible short circuit.

Your Koi's Swimming Style

Do your koi swim strong and in a straight line? Koi that have difficulty remaining upright while swimming may

- ✔ Have metabolic bone disease
- ✔ Have been shocked by an electrical current
- ✔ Be in the close-to-terminal stages of disease
- ✔ Have been exposed to toxic substances such as fertilizer or insecticides

These are all bad news. No matter what the exact cause, you need to identify it and deal with it (but turn off the power to your pond before you try to pull up that submerged pump, please!). Chapter 13 can help you with these problems.

Your Koi's Social Savvy

Does a formerly friendly koi seem to avoid contact with other koi and with (gasp!) you? Sick koi often stay away from other koi and may be uninterested in food. A koi that suddenly elects to avoid other koi is the proverbial canary in a coal mine, at least in terms of his health. Keep an eye on him for a couple of days. If he doesn't elect to rejoin the herd, you may want to bowl him to look him over. (Let Chapter 13 be your guide for your observations.)

Index